# THE 74TH (YEOMANRY) DIVISION
## IN SYRIA AND FRANCE

J. Russell & Sons, Southsea.

MAJOR-GENERAL E. S. GIRDWOOD, C.B., C.M.G.

[*Frontispiece*

# THE
# 74th (YEOMANRY) DIVISION
## IN SYRIA AND FRANCE

### BY MAJOR C. H. DUDLEY WARD
### D.S.O., M.C.

WITH A FOREWORD
### BY FIELD-MARSHAL VISCOUNT ALLENBY
### G.C.B., G.C.M.G.

WITH MAPS, PORTRAITS AND OTHER ILLUSTRATIONS

LONDON
JOHN MURRAY, ALBEMARLE STREET, W.
1922

# FOREWORD

The History of the 74th Division is a shining example of patriotism, of devotion to duty, and of self-effacement when the call of duty came.

These Yeomen, trained to mounted warfare, had already gained distinction as mounted troops when they were taken from their horses and formed into a Division on foot.

Few would have wondered, had the bold experiment failed.

The experiment did not fail; it resulted in a grand success.

Those fine Cavalries converted themselves into as fine Infantry, and, now, the 74th Division hold a record

Second to none of the Infantry Divisions who fought in the Great War.

Gratefully, I testify to the valour and endurance of the 74th Division; who, under my Command, took a leading part in the Jerusalem Campaign; and sorry I was when these brave soldiers were called to France in the crisis of 1918.

There, war-worn but not war-weary, they added to their fame; and made a record that the country they so well served will never forget.

Allenby F. M.

London.
3 . X . 21.

# CONTENTS

## PART I
### *EGYPT*
### 1914—1917

## CHAPTER I
### THE CENTRAL POWERS

## CHAPTER II
### THE SINAI DESERT

## CHAPTER III
### THE SYRIAN FRONT

## PART II
### *SYRIA*
### JUNE 1917—APRIL 1918

## CHAPTER IV
### PREPARATIONS FOR THE ADVANCE INTO PALESTINE

# CHAPTER V

## THIRD BATTLE OF GAZA

# CHAPTER VI

## THIRD BATTLE OF GAZA

# CHAPTER VII

## THE AFFAIR AT EL FOKA

# CHAPTER VIII

## THE BATTLE OF NEBY SAMWIL

# CHAPTER IX

## THE DEFENCE OF JERUSALEM

# CHAPTER X

## 1918

# CHAPTER XI

## THE CAPTURE OF JERICHO

# CHAPTER XII

## ACTIONS OF TEL AZUR

# PART III

## *FRANCE*

# CHAPTER XIII

## FRANCE

# CHAPTER XIV

## THE LYS SALIENT, VTH ARMY

# CHAPTER XV

## THE IVTH ARMY FRONT

# CHAPTER XVI

## THE BATTLE OF EPÉHY

# CHAPTER XVII

## THE ADVANCE OF THE VTH ARMY

## APPENDIXES

# LIST OF ILLUSTRATIONS

## MAPS

# PART I

*EGYPT*

1914—1917

# CHAPTER I

## THE CENTRAL POWERS

THE emblem borne by the 74th Division was a broken
spur. No doubt when General Girdwood chose it
he was influenced by a certain bitterness against the
fate which had condemned the fine yeomanry units
from which it was formed to be deprived of their
horses, and to fight as infantrymen in a country
where mounted troops had the most favourable
opportunities for manœuvre, initiative, and " dash "
—conditions which are prayed for and seldom granted
to the mounted soldier. But although these yeomanry regiments may regret that they were not
given a chance of showing their worth as cavalry,
they are rightly and justly proud of their achieve-
ments in the Great War, of which this volume is a
record.

.        .        .        .        .

As a cause of war the assassination of the Archduke
Francis Ferdinand at Serajevo, on the 28th June
1914, is as true and false as the other well-known
historical fact that England went to war in 1739
because the Spaniards cut an ear from a certain Mr.
Jenkins. It was a conspiracy, inspired by France,
which made Mr. Jenkins and his ear famous, and it
was a conspiracy, inspired by Germany, which has

3

made the name of Francis Ferdinand immortal. But
in the one case there had been a growing resentment
against France and Spain, certainly amongst com-
mercial classes, and, despite all the efforts of Walpole,
war was declared amidst a ringing of bells and great
popular rejoicing, whereas in the other the events
which followed the Serajevo assassination were, for
the British Empire, bewildering, appalling, incredible!

One cannot appreciate the account of any military
undertakings in the Great War, no matter where they
may have been, unless the Central Power conspiracy
is borne in mind. Turkey was not an ally won over
to the German cause after the declaration of war, a
kind of afterthought : for years Germany had been
steadily strengthening her hold over Turkey, and a
glance at the map will show the power which would
be acquired through the extension of her influence
to the Indian Ocean. Whether she meant to use
this combination against England or not is beside
the point ; the adhesion of Turkey was necessary in
a move against Russia or the British Empire, or both,
and German aims, on this occasion, were obviously
not directed towards the acquisition of small and
insignificant territories.

The dream of world domination is as old as man-
kind. The amazing plot was revealed, amazing in
the completeness of its preparation and its sudden
exposure, and Britain was forced to act. War was
declared with Germany on the 4th August. There
followed immediately the chase of the warship *Goeben*
to Constantinople, and then a period of development.
War was declared on Turkey on the 5th November
1914—it seemed to spread like a prairie fire.

The position of the Central Powers, in spite of the

defection of Italy, who joined the Entente on the 25th May 1915, was favourable. They lay as a wedge between the sprawling Russian Empire and the Anglo-French combination, and if one considers the war as an attempt of the Central Powers to " hack a way through," as the Germans so often expressed it (presumably to get a " place in the sun "), and the effort of the Entente Powers as a rounding-up of dangerous madmen, it will be seen that India (through Persia) and Egypt were two weak spots for the Entente—especially Egypt, which was under the nominal suzerainty of the Sultan, and was more accessible, not only to active warlike demonstration and adventure, but to the more subtle influence of religion. It must not be thought that the fear of the whole of the African shore of the Mediterranean falling into the hands of the Central Powers was an absurdity ; that which had seemed fantastic suddenly became an actual and menacing threat in the Great War, and when you may read in one newspaper of engagements fought in France, Russia, Austria, Italy, Serbia, Egypt, Tripoli, Darfur, West Africa, East Africa, Mesopotamia, the North Sea, and Ireland, there are potent possibilities of disaster.

The weakness of the Central Powers was the junction with Turkey—it was not complete. Still, neither accomplishment nor prevention could be carried out in a moment, and the British Empire, as regards war preparation, was in no better case than the Turkish Empire.

In a comparatively short space of time the German and Austrian armies were pinned down to trench warfare on the east and west frontiers—that is, to a state of siege. But the situation outside Europe was

2

uncertain, was as a flank in the air, offering tempting
results to both sides.   No one had had the time to
think seriously of the position beyond France and
Russia : the need for men, their training, their equip-
ment, their organisation into units, was the absorbing
occupation of the moment, and although every one
of the enormous Cabinet, which was trying to control
the war, had a policy, he had no firm foundation on
which to build it—many thought the war would be
over in a few months !   The confusion of thought was
indescribable, but that it should have been so is not
so extraordinary and incomprehensible.

.        .        .        .        .

The construction of the Suez Canal has had the
effect of fixing a very definite line of defence across
the desert which lies between Syria and Egypt.
This desert covers the whole of the Sinai Peninsula,
that curious triangle of land which separates Africa
from Asia, and forms a serious obstacle to all movement between Syria and Egypt : it is a difficult
problem for the traveller, a harder one for the
soldier.   Although a natural bulwark between the
two countries, it has been successfully overcome by
many commanders since the days of Alexander.   The
Syrian frontier lies on the eastern side of it.

The great highroad across the Desert follows, very
naturally, the line where most water is to be found,
which is that of the low-lying Mediterranean coast.
We have the journey described by Napoleon, through
General Bertrand :

" The desert which separates Syria from Egypt
extends from Gaza to Salhiya ; it is seventy leagues
[a French league is 4,850 yards].   Caravans march
eighty hours to cross it.   Gaza is one hundred leagues

from Cairo. The desert is divided into three parts : first from Salhiya to Qatia there are sixteen leagues of arid sand ; one finds no shade, no water, and not a vestige of vegetation ; the caravans march for twenty hours. The French troops covered the distance in two days, but three are necessary for the camels, wheeled vehicles, and artillery. Near Qatia are moving sands, very tiring for transport. Qatia is an oasis ; there were two wells of water, rather bitter, but, nevertheless, drinkable ; there were about a thousand palm trees which could provide shade for four or five thousand men. . . .

" The second part extends from the oasis of Qatia to that of el Arish, a matter of twenty-five leagues. Caravans are thirty-two hours on the march ; the French Army took three and a half days for the journey. One passed on this road three wells which marked the stations, but these wells only contained supplies for one or two battalions. . . .

"El Arish is an oasis much more extended and much more productive than that of Qatia. There are six wells which can provide for the needs of an army of from fifteen to twenty thousand men, and several thousand palms which can give it shade. There was a large stone village, containing five to six hundred inhabitants, and a stone fort. . . .

" The third part of this desert extends from el Arish to Gaza, a matter of twenty-nine leagues. Caravans are twenty-three to twenty-four hours on the road. French troops took three days to cross it. Four leagues from el Arish one finds el Kharruha ; four leagues farther the wells of Zowalid ; four leagues from Zowalid the wells of Rafa ; two leagues farther the castle of Khan Yunus ; Syria commences here. From Khan Yunus to Gaza there are seven leagues ; it is no longer the desert ; it is an intermediary state between desert and cultivated country. All along the road one follows the coast at a distance of a league, or half a league. . . . A big army requires, therefore, twelve days to cross the great desert and the isthmus of Suez, counting one day spent at Qatia, and one at el Arish. . . .

" It is a very exhausting and delicate operation to cross the desert in summer. First the heat of the sand; second, the lack of water; third, the lack of shade, are all capable of perishing an army, or of weakening it, or of discouraging it more than it is possible to imagine.

" . . . Of all obstacles which can cover the frontiers of empires a desert, similar to this, is incontestably the greatest." (*Guerre d'Orient: Campagnes d'Egypte et de Syrie*, 1798–99. Memoires pour servire a l'histoire de Napoléon dictés par lui même à Sainte-Hélène, at publiés par le Général Bertrand.)

But the construction of the Suez Canal, and the sweet-water canal, not only reduces the effective size of the Desert but, if the short water communication with India is to be maintained, renders the defence of the Canal imperative.

With the bulwark of the Desert, a small force to defend it, a Turkish partisan as Khedive,[1] and little hope of immediate help from England, the war with Turkey commenced. The Canal was organised for defence in three sections, under Major-General Alex. Wilson, with centres at Suez, Ismailia, and Qantara. The first brush with the enemy was on the 20th November, at the oasis of Bir el Nuss, about eighteen miles from Qantara, on the road to Qatia—an affair with a raiding Arab tribe.

At the same time many tribes in the Sudan assumed

[1] On the 19th December 1914 the British Government declared Khedive Abbas Hilmi deposed, and proclaimed Prince Hussein Kamel Pasha as Sultan of Egypt.

a hostile attitude : the situation was one of grave
anxiety—sparks falling on straw do not always cause
a fire, but are, none the less, all the better for being
extinguished. The most serious of these occurred in
the province of Darfur. The Sultan Ali Dinar ruled
over a population approximate to 1,000,000, and the
basis of his power rested on a slave army of 10,000
armed with firearms : his rule was not very popular
with all his subjects, but he was sufficiently formidable
as an enemy, and a supporter of Turkey. On the
declaration of war Ali Dinar became defiant, and in
April 1915 formally renounced his allegiance to the
Sudan Government, and declared himself in sympathy with the Turks, with whom he was in communication through the Senussi (the anti-British
attitude of the latter was not active until April 1915).
Only those who have lived in the East can realise
how such risings can spread.

As to the Turkish strength, at the outbreak of war
the regular army consisted of thirty-nine divisions,
but they were not up to full establishment : as a
combatant force they were about 150,000. But they
had great resources, and during the war 2,700,000
additional men were raised (Lt.-Colonel C. C. R.
Murphy, Indian Army, in the *Journal of the Royal
United Service Institute*).

At first the situation on the Canal remained quiet.
Reports were received of advance posts of the enemy
at Khan Yunus, el Arish, el Auja, and Kasseima,
about the eastern borders of Sinai.

In the middle of January 1915 the Turks started to
move, and they destroyed one of the illusions of the
Desert, for they came from all directions. Not only
did they advance against the Qantara section and

the Ismailia section, but three columns, of from two to three thousand each (estimated), struck across the centre of the Desert, from the direction of Beersheba, and were located by aeroplane at Bir Mabeuik, Moiya Harab, and Wadi Muksheib, which lie opposite the Great Bitter Lake–Suez section of the front. A large concentration of Turks took place against this southern portion of the Canal, around Gebel Habeita, and on the 3rd February an attempt was made to cross the Canal south of Toussoum ; but only some twenty men succeeded in doing so, and they surrendered the next morning : the crossing was made in light steel pontoons which they had dragged across the Desert. At the same time half-hearted attacks were launched against Ismailia, Ferdan, and Qantara. In all the Turks were estimated to be between twelve and fifteen thousand in number, but it is exceedingly difficult to arrive at an accurate figure from the information at present available. The " Canal Expeditionary Force " was formed at the end of 1914 from part of the 10th Turkish Division, but General Wilson says : " It appears from accounts received from prisoners that the attacking force consisted of the VIIIth, and portions of the IIIrd, IVth, and VIth Turkish Army Corps." It was obviously a determined attempt to storm the Canal defences, and made by a large force.

General Sir J. E. Maxwell, commanding the Force in Egypt, had, in February–March, 30,000 men [1] at

---

[1] The British troops in Egypt before the outbreak of war were : 3rd Dragoon Guards ; XIth Brigade R.H.A., T Battery ; 2nd Bn. Devons ; 1st Bn. Worcesters; 2nd Bn. Northampton Fusiliers ; 2nd Bn. Gordon Highlanders. The 1st Suffolks and a detachment of R.G.A. were stationed at Khartoum under the Governor-General of the Anglo-Egyptian Sudan.

his disposal. General Sir A. Wilson's command was known as " The Indian Expeditionary Force ' E.' "

That uncertainty and absence of information which has been named the " fog of war " has not been dispersed by peace, and will, apparently, last for many years ; but from time to time a volume has been issued to the public containing an account of the adventures, more or less true, of its author, who had, during the period of the war, either occupied a responsible position, or made it his business to meet those who did, and which contains mostly a mass of innuendo, with here and there a small scrap of fact. But from a most illuminating, and discreet, essay by Viscount Esher, we get a faint picture of the state of affairs in the Cabinet which controlled the destiny of the British Empire.

The Kitchener Armies were growing in England, and there was a strong feeling in the Government that the field of Allied strategy should be widened, and these troops used elsewhere than on the French and Belgian Fronts. An expedition to Salonica was strongly supported by Mr. Lloyd George and M. Briand, and there were others who favoured an attempt on Gallipoli. But there was no definite agreement on the strategy which should govern the war as a whole. In view of this, and with an anxious fear of the Balkan States, Lord Kitchener held fast to his armies. And yet, it would seem, he himself had definite views.

" All those who were closest to Lord K., Fitzgerald better than anyone, were well aware that he looked with stern dissatisfaction upon the strategic conception of the war which limited its possibilities to the

Western Front.    But he was too experienced and too
wary not to realise that to attack the enemy in flank
required secrecy and careful preparation over a
considerable period of time.    Left to himself he would
have selected, as all his friends knew, some point in
the Near East, and would have launched an attack
with every man and gun and shell which could have
been begged, borrowed, or stolen from the Western
Front."    (*The Tragedy of Lord Kitchener*, by Viscount
Esher.)

And from the same knowledgeable source we learn
that in January 1915, in answer to a question of his
own on the danger points for Germany, Lord
Kitchener placed a tracing finger on the map and said,
" Here is one—Salonica ;   here is another—the
Dardanelles ;   and here is the last—Alexandretta !
But it would take time ; and no one would have to
know ! "

The decision to force the Dardanelles was made.
Apparently such an undertaking had been the
subject of a former inquiry and study, but the
conclusions arrived at were not read or remembered.
Lord Kitchener refused to give the necessary troops
for a landing in conjunction with the attack of the
Fleet, on the ground that they might be required
elsewhere ; but if the Fleet succeeded he was willing,
and would be able, to find them !

The British and French Fleets attacked the
Dardanelles on the 25th February, with disastrous
result, and then, in spite of all the former hesitation,
all the reasoned objections, Sir Ian Hamilton was
sent in command of an expedition, which landed on
the Gallipoli Peninsula on the 25th April.

The direct result of this enterprise was the reduction

of the British forces in Egypt, and also a concentration of Turkish troops on Gallipoli, which became
the storm-centre ; there were occasional patrol
meetings in the Sinai Desert, and small bodies of
the enemy attempted from time to time to place
mines in the Canal, or damage the railway, and
sometimes succeeded ; but the Egyptian Front
remained quiet.

At the time of the British landing the Turkish Vth
Army at Gallipoli consisted of six infantry divisions
and a cavalry brigade ; at the time of the evacuation
there were sixteen infantry divisions and one cavalry
brigade (138,879).

This glorious but ill-fated attempt will always be
the subject of controversy : its failure permitted the
junction of Turkey and Germany, its success would
have shortened the war. But already the want of
unity of command, which would ensure unity of
effort, was being felt. Salonica had become a political
question in France ; Gallipoli was an unpopular
subject in England. In November 1915 Lord
Kitchener met General Gallieni " and found him as
reluctant as he was himself " to face the evacuation
of Gallipoli and transport the troops to Salonica, and
both felt that the effect on the Mahomedan people
would be a blow to the prestige of the Entente
Powers. " I cannot see light," said Lord Kitchener ;
" it is impossible to forecast the effect in Egypt and
India." And Gallieni was of the opinion that the
effort in Salonica was too late. Lord Kitchener said,
" Your Government seems to have no plans, only
aspirations ! " He might have said the same of the
British Government ! And during the last week of
his life he agreed with an opinion of Sir Maurice

Hankey's that success would have been attained
on the Peninsula during the following summer, but
for Salonica.

During the months of September and October four
brigades of yeomanry — the Highland Mounted
Brigade, the South-Western Mounted Brigade, the
Eastern Mounted Brigade, and the South-Eastern
Mounted Brigade—were sent to Gallipoli (dis-
mounted).   But they did not stay there very long, as
the evacuation was completed on the night 8th/9th
January 1916.

In the redistribution of the Gallipoli forces the four
yeomanry brigades went to Egypt.

# CHAPTER II

## THE SINAI DESERT

IN January 1916 General Sir Archibald Murray, who had been Chief of Staff in France, was sent to Egypt with instructions to take command of " all organised formations then in Egypt, or on their way to Egypt, with the exception of such troops as might be considered necessary for the defence of Egypt and the Nile Valley against attack from the west, or for maintaining order in the Nile Valley and the Nile Delta." His task was, therefore, to protect Egypt from attack from the east, and a rough line, about five miles west of the Canal, was drawn, to limit the area of his command. Unification of command in Egypt was not restored until the 19th March.

Egypt became a kind of central exchange for troops. Every day ships discharged their loads of troops, animals, vehicles, guns, at Alexandria and Port Said, and all units required reorganisation and re-equipment. It was heavy work.

And what was to be done with these troops ?

The evacuation of Gallipoli had released the whole of the Turkish Vth Army. " When I arrived in Egypt," says Sir A. Murray, " the intentions of the enemy as regards the attack on the Suez Canal were by no means certain. Though his new means of communication in Southern Syria and Sinai, commenced with this end in view, were still in a backward state, he undoubtedly had at his disposal the troops, amounting to 250,000 men, or more, necessary for such an attack." At one time there were as many as thirteen divisions in Egypt to meet this threat, but the re-embarkation of troops for service in other theatres commenced in February, and continued until the end of March. There does not seem to have been any definite policy for dealing with Turkey. Well might General Gallieni rave and prophesy that without co-ordination of activities the Entente would lose the war, and point out the danger of junction between Germany and Turkey. " In the East," he said, " the defensive is never the most prudent form of military action." [1] Maybe the British Cabinet had such a complete knowledge of the psychology of the Turk that all risks were nugatory, for they seem to have played into the hands of the Turks, at this period, in a most surprising fashion.

In Mesopotamia the 6th and 12th Indian Divisions, under Generals Townshend and Gorringe, had commenced to march into the centre of the Turkish Empire. General Townshend was now securely shut up in Kut el Amara. Despite the efforts of General Gorringe, and the gallantry of the 3rd, 7th, and 13th Indian Divisions, General Townshend was forced to surrender on the 29th April. From the commencement of the year the operations of the VIth Turkish Army, composed of six divisions, one cavalry brigade, and the Baghdad Group, had been very successful in Mesopotamia.

As against the satisfactory manœuvres of their

---

[1] *The Tragedy of Lord Kitchener*, Esher.

VIth Army the Turks had to place a disaster to their IIIrd Army, of eight divisions, at Erzeroum, where it was defeated by the Russians on the 16th February. But Sir A. Murray's anxiety seems justified, for in May 1916 the Turks reached the maximum of power developed by them in the war, consisting of forty-three divisions, with an aggregate of 650,000 combatants.

In fairness to those who conducted the war it must be remembered that in the multitude of counsels presented to them, and the cross-currents of political influence, chicanery, and jobbery which assailed them, and in which they took part, one fact dominated all theories—the massive armies facing each other in France and Belgium. The call for men and munitions was insistent, and the interest of the nation was with the bulk of its relatives and friends. The battle of Loos in the autumn of 1915 had been disappointing, and had achieved nothing ; Sir Douglas Haig was now preparing for his offensive on the Somme. But in the first months of 1916 the situation in France was not so serious as later in the year : the German attack on Verdun started in February, but it is doubtful if anyone foresaw its extent.

In Egypt men put their trust in Providence and kept watch on the Suez Canal and the Senussi.

Sir A. Murray's chief concern was the defence of the Canal :

" The work on the stationary defences was backward. Difficulties of water supply on the east bank were increased by shortage of piping ; labour troubles had delayed the progress of roads and railways. Guns had still to be emplaced, and no part of the front defence line was actually occupied by troops.

Nevertheless, as there were no signs of an imminent advance on the part of the enemy, the question of the stationary defences caused me no serious anxiety. ¿ . . The organisation of the offensive-defence, which time has proved to be paramount, was, however, a pressing matter hitherto untouched.   Practically nothing had been done towards the organisation of mobile forces. The collection of a large number of riding and transport camels had to be undertaken at once, and a plan of campaign devised.   Moreover time was short, for it was plain that any offensive on a large scale by the enemy must be commenced before the middle of March.   For the force under my command the only possible line of advance was along the northern line from Qantara towards Qatia and el Arish, and the task was at once taken up of examining possibilities of an offensive on this line and solving the problem of maintaining a considerable force at Qatia during the summer months."

The Russian victory in Armenia, at Erzeroum, was helpful, as the estimate of Turkish troops available for an attack on the Canal fell to 60,000.  And patrolling revealed that the northern desert was clear of all enemy force to Hod Um Ugba, on the eastern side of Qatia.

Free from the threat of imminent attack in force, permanent posts were pushed out, week by week, in the direction of Qatia.

    .     .     .     .     .

We have mentioned the arrival of certain Yeomanry units in Egypt between the months of December 1915 and March 1916.   The South-Eastern and Eastern Mounted Brigades, composed of the East Kent, West Kent, Sussex, Norfolk, Suffolk, and Welsh Horse Yeomanry Regiments, landed at Alexandria   in

February (they had been in Gallipoli from 7th October to 31st December), and after a month at Sidi Bishr, were sent to el Kubri, on the Canal Defence Line, north of Suez, where they were employed in digging trenches in the sand. The climate was found to be very hot, and the Brigade Major—for the two brigades were now known as the 3rd Dismounted Brigade—also grumbled at the lack of motor ambulances : " There are none at el Kubri. They would be very useful to run to railhead and the station at el Kubri West. There are hundreds of motor ambulances at Alexandria, doing nothing but drive nurses about ! " But he adds that the health of the brigade was very good !

The other two yeomanry brigades from Gallipoli, the Highland Mounted Brigade and the South-Western Mounted Brigade, composed of the 1st Lovat Scouts, the 2nd Lovat Scouts, the Fife and Forfar, the 1st Royal Devons, the North Devons, and the West Somerset Yeomanry Regiments, were sent to the Western Front, where they became the 2nd Dismounted Brigade.

Trouble on the Western Front had started in August and November 1915 (it had been brewing since the earlier months of the year), when one Sayed Ahmed, the Grand Senussi, had allowed himself to fall under the influence of Nuri Bey, a half-brother of Enver Pasha. His followers were not many, consisting of Mohafizia (Senussi regulars) and Bedouin tribes—in March 1916 Sir A. Murray estimated them at 3,000—but his influence over the Arab population of Egypt was great. A reverse to British arms was to be avoided at all costs, and so a policy of caution was pursued : Sollum Bay, near the Tripoli Frontier, was evacuated, and the Western British Force concentrated at Mersa Matruh.

Across the Desert of Egypt, from south of Sollum Bay to Assiut, on the Nile, is a diagonal line of oases, and followers of Sayed Ahmed appeared at Baharia Oasis and Kharga Oasis, approaching the Nile Valley in the south.  This was the district to which the Highland and South-Western Mounted Brigades were sent.

Two other yeomanry brigades, the South Wales and the Welsh Border Brigades, sailed from Devonport on the 5th March 1916, and from Alexandria were despatched to Miniya, the section on the right of the 2nd Dismounted Brigade ; and they also were amalgamated, and renamed the 4th Dismounted Brigade.  The units were : the Cheshire, the Denbighshire, the Glamorganshire, the Montgomeryshire, the Pembrokeshire, and the Shropshire Yeomanry Regts.

The 2nd Dismounted Brigade patrolled the Kharga front, and the 4th Dismounted Brigade the Baharia front.  The Senussi, however, were more active, when they did anything at all, between Siwa Oasis and Sollum Bay, to the north, so, although the duties in the heat and sand were arduous enough, there was no fighting.

At the end of July, the 3rd Dismounted Brigade was moved from el Kubri to Sollum, Matruh, and Dabaa, along the coast.  There were, however, no events of importance at that time, the diaries merely recording many refugees coming through the lines at Sollum, and that the sentries of the Suffolk Yeomanry were puzzled by bright meteorites, which they reported as rockets.

.          .          .          .          .

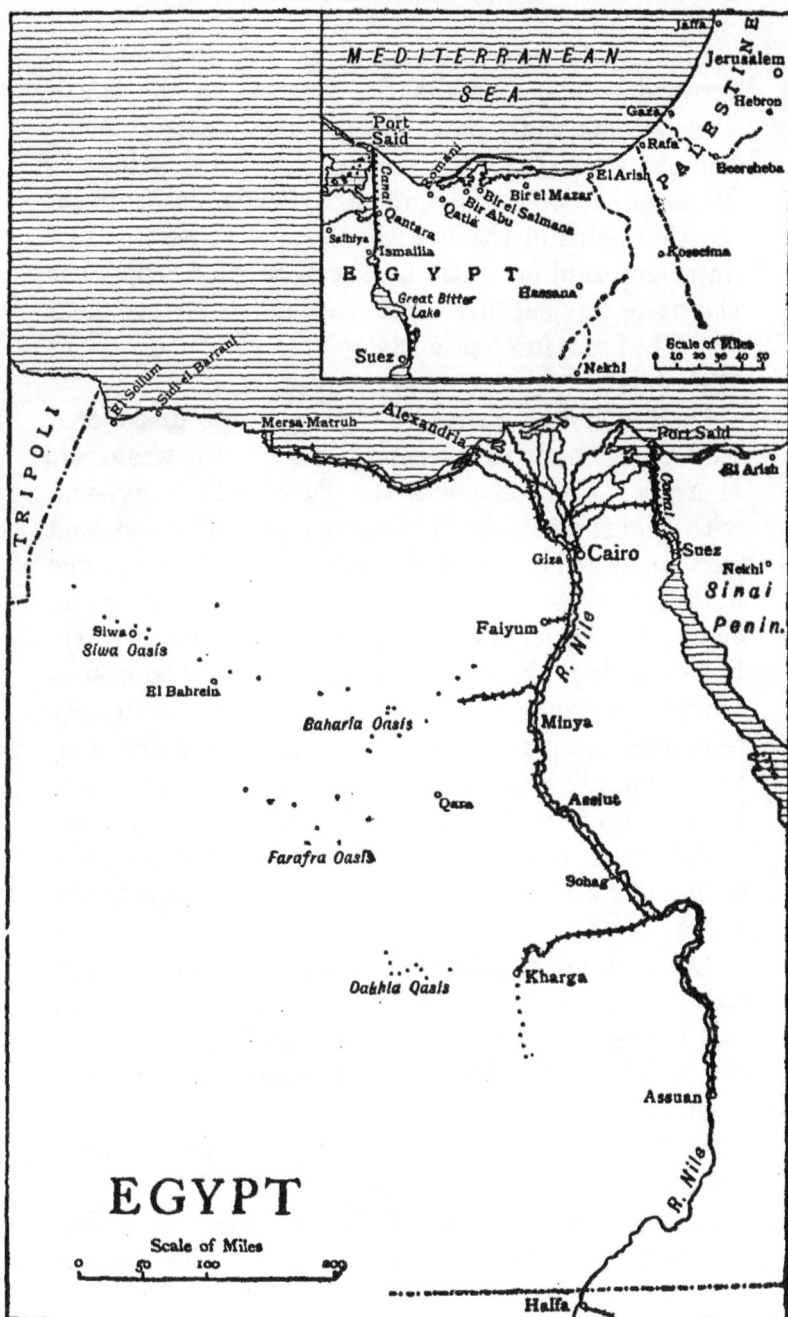

MEDITERRANEAN
SEA

Jaffa
Jerusalem
Hebron
Gaza
Rafa
Beersheba
Port Said
El Arish
PALESTINE
Bir el Mazar
Bir el Salmana
Bir Abu
Qantara
Qatia
Selhiya
Ismailia
Koseoima
EGYPT
Great Bitter
Lake
Hassana
Suez
Nekhl

Scale of Miles
0  10  20  30  40  50

TRIPOLI

El Sollum
Sidi el Barrani
Mersa Matruh
Alexandria
Port Said
El Arish
Canal
Giza
Cairo
Suez
Nekhl
Sinai
Penin.
Faiyum
R. Nile
Siwa
Siwa Oasis
El Bahrein
Baharia Oasis
Minya
Qara
Assiut
Farafra Oasis
Sohag
Dakhla Oasis
Kharga
Assuan
R. Nile
Halfa

EGYPT

Scale of Miles
0     50    100              200

Emery Walker Ltd. sc.

Meanwhile, on the Canal front, the railway crept forward to Qatia, while the Desert, to the south, was systematically patrolled and kept clear of enemy bodies : there was, for instance, a brush with the Turks at the wells of Jifjaffa, fifty-two miles from the starting-point of the British patrol. There was also an enemy raid on Qatia on the 23rd of April, when the oasis was captured, and evacuated on the next day ; but no further activity was shown until the 19th July.

On the above date the Flying Corps discovered that a large body of the enemy was moving west from el Arish : this force was the Turkish 3rd Division, with eight machine gun companies (officered and partly manned by Germans), mountain artillery, some batteries of 4-inch and 6-inch howitzers (manned chiefly by Austrians), and a body of Arab cavalry. For some days the enemy, after advancing to within striking distance of Qatia, and being continually reinforced from the north, manœuvred for position, and eventually attacked from the south-east, towards Romani, on the 4th August. The attack was pressed with vigour, but after a day of hard fighting the enemy exhausted himself and was driven back to the south.

The heat was terrific, but the pursuit was continued relentlessly ; Qatia was found evacuated on the 6th, and the enemy was followed to Bir el Abd and Salmana, where, on the 12th, further advance was stopped.

In this battle of Romani 4,000 prisoners were captured from a total force estimated at 18,000.

As the railway advanced so the sphere of action was extended. On the 17th September there was a

smart little affair against the Turkish camp at Bir el
Mazar, well on the road to el Arish; between the
13th and 17th October there was a reconnaissance
against Gebel Maghara, sixty-five miles east of
Ismailia; on the 17th November patrols reached
Uyret el Zol, within eight miles of el Arish. By the
1st December the railway was east of Mazar.

The work entailed was enormous. By this time
Qantara, which had been a place of a few huts, was
a town, a railway and water terminus, with wharves,
cranes, a railway ferry; and the Desert was dotted
with standing camps, with tanks and reservoirs,
railway stations, sidings, aerodromes, signal stations,
wireless installations, protected by strongly entrenched positions and hundreds of miles of barbed
wire.

The chief difficulty was water. As troops got
farther away from the pipe-line, which was conveying
water from the sweet-water canal, so the difficulty
presented itself with full force. In the beginning of
November it was acute, but was relieved by the pipe-
line reaching Romani on the 17th, and then increased
again until the pipe-line reached Bir el Abd. West of
Bir el Abd there had been local brackish water for
horses, mules, and camels, but to the east there were
few wells, and they were widely separated. At the
end of November Sir A. Murray says:

" Every tactical preparation for the offensive had
been made, naval co-operation planned, and arrangements made for the landing of stores and construction
pipes as soon as el Arish was in my possession. But
the difficulty of water supply, even with my advanced
railhead, was immense. The enemy was so disposed
as to cover all available water in the neighbourhood

of el Arish and Masaid. Between his position and ours and south of his position, no water could be found. . . . If, therefore, he should be able to force us to spend two days in the operation of driving him from his position, it would be necessary to carry forward very large quantities of water on camels for the men and animals of the formations engaged. This entailed the establishment of a very large reserve of water at railhead, and the preparation of elaborate arrangements for the forwarding and distributing of water. . . . The water supply for the striking force was not adequately secured until the 20th December."

When Napoleon invaded Syria the actual headquarter movements of General Regnier's division were : Salhiya 23rd January, Qatia 5th February, wells of Mecoudiah 8th February, and he engaged the Turks at el Arish on the 9th. Kléber's division did part of the journey by sea, and landed on the coast above Qatia. Napoleon says that the army had "three thousand camels and three thousand donkeys" —one thousand camels carried the food of fourteen thousand men and three thousand horses, for fourteen days; and two thousand camels carried water for three days, " in view of the fact that one can refill with water at Qatia and el Arish." The donkeys were allotted to the men at the rate of one donkey to every ten infantrymen.

He was, of course, unopposed until he reached el Arish, but Napoleon notes the difficulties of crossing the Desert in the face of an enemy, and the necessity of establishing large " magazines " at successive stations. As his campaigns marked a great change from the tournaments of the Middle Ages, and even of the days of Marlborough, so the military under-

takings of the Great War establish a further stage in
the profession of arms.

But the Turks allowed Sir A. Murray to occupy el
Arish, and took up a position on the Wadi el Arish.
They were attacked on the 23rd December and
defeated, retiring on Rafa, from which position they
were driven on the 9th January. The engagements
fought by General Kléber in 1799, and by Sir H. G.
Chauvel and Sir Philip Chetwode in December 1916,
have some interesting points of resemblance.

On the 28th February mounted troops entered
Khan Yunus. The main British force was now on
the frontier of Syria.

The advance along the coast, the old highroad
between Egypt and Syria, which has been followed
by so many strange and romantic figures, forced the
enemy to retire from Nekhl, Hossana, and Maghra
—although expeditions were sent out to occupy
Nekhl and Hossana in February, the one from Zogha,
twenty-three miles east of the Great Bitter Lake, the
other from el Arish—and the Sinai Peninsula was
clear. The British and Turkish Armies faced each
other on the Frontier.

.        .        .        .        .

With the new year the three Dismounted Brigades
on the Western Front began to move east. The 2nd
Dismounted Brigade were at Moascar on the 5th
January, el Ferdan on the 15th, Qantara on the 5th
March, and el Arish (by rail) on the 6th. The Lovat
Scouts dropped out of this brigade in August 1916,
and were replaced by the Ayr and the Lanark
Yeomanry Regts.,[1] in January 1917. The brigade
was renamed the 229th Infantry Brigade.

[1] These two regiments had been in Gallipoli with the 52nd Division.

The 3rd Dismounted Brigade went to Sidi Bishr on the 2nd April, and to Deir el Belah on the 9th. It was renamed the 230th Infantry Brigade.

The 4th Dismounted Brigade, moving to Assiut on the 1st January, Zeitoun on the 1st March, Helmia on the 1st April, and Khan Yunus on the 10th, became the 231st Infantry Brigade.

### 74TH DIVISION

Commander: Brevet Col. (Temp. Maj.-Gen.) E. S. Girdwood, C.B., Scottish Rifles.

#### 229TH INFANTRY BRIGADE

Commander: Col. (Temp. Brig.-Gen.) R. Hoare, D.S.O., late 4th Hussars.

16th Bn. Devonshire Regt. (Royal 1st Devon and Royal North Devon Yeomanry Regts.).

12th Bn. Somerset Light Infantry (West Somerset Yeomanry Regt.).

14th Black Watch (Fife and Forfar Yeomanry Regt.).

12th Bn. Royal Scots Fusiliers (Ayr and Lanark Yeomanry Regts.).

4th Machine Gun Company and 229th Light Trench Mortar Battery.

#### 230TH INFANTRY BRIGADE

Commander: Lt.-Col. (Temp. Brig.-Gen.) A. J. McNeill, D.S.O., Lovat Scouts.

10th Bn. Buffs (Royal East Kent and West Kent Yeomanry Regts.).

16th Bn. Royal Sussex (Sussex Yeomanry Regt.).

15th Bn. Suffolk (Suffolk Yeomanry Regt.).

12th Bn. Norfolk (Norfolk Yeomanry Regt.).

209th Machine Gun Company and 230th Light Trench Mortar Battery.

#### 231ST INFANTRY BRIGADE

Commander: Col. (Temp. Brig.-Gen.) E. A. Herbert, Somerset Light Infantry.

10th Bn. King's Shropshire Light Infantry (Shropshire and Cheshire Yeomanry Regts.).

24th Bn. Royal Welsh Fusiliers (Denbighshire Yeomanry Regt.).

25th Bn. Royal Welsh Fusiliers (Montgomeryshire and Welsh Horse Yeomanry Regts.).

24th Bn. Welsh Regiment (Pembroke and Glamorgan Yeomanry Regts.).

210th Machine Gun Company and 231st Light Trench Mortar Battery.

## ROYAL ARTILLERY

Commander: Lt.-Col. (Temp. Brig.-Gen.) L. J. Hext, C.M.G.
117th Brigade R.F.A. (A, B, 366th and D Batteries).
44th Brigade R.F.A. (340th, 382nd, 425th, and D Batteries).
268th Brigade R.F.A.
X74 and Y74 Medium Trench Mortar Batteries.
74th Ammunition Column.

## ROYAL ENGINEERS

Commander: Maj.(Temp.Lt.-Col.) R. P. T. Hawksley, C.M.G., D.S.O.
No. 5 (Royal Monmouth) Field Company.
No. 5 (Royal Anglesea) Field Company.
439th (Cheshire) Field Company.
74th Divisional Signal Company.

## ROYAL ARMY SERVICE CORPS

Commander: Lt.-Col. J. G. Needham.
447th, 448th, 449th, 450th Companies R.A.S.C.

## DIVISIONAL TROOPS

261st Machine Gun Company.
74th Employment Company.
59th Mobile Veterinary Section.
" A " Squadron 2nd County of London (Westminster Dragoons) Yeomanry. (This squadron was moved to Corps Cavalry Regt.,
23/8/17.)

# CHAPTER III

## THE SYRIAN FRONT

The formation of the 74th Division— The First Battle of Gaza—The
Second Battle of Gaza.

THE change from yeomen to infantry was received
with good-humoured philosophy : no one attempted
to explain why it was done, and it was merely referred
to as a decree of " the powers that be " !  The explanation is probably to be found in a peculiarity
which prevails in the army.  Protected as it is with
entanglements of red tape, and breastworks of army
forms of different shapes and colours and numbers,
it has, nevertheless, a most disconcerting habit of
improvisation.  Sir A. Murray was about to attack.
He had the 52nd, 53rd, and 54th Infantry Divisions,
the New Zealand and Australian Mounted Division,
the Imperial Mounted Division, and the Imperial
Camel Corps on the Syrian Front, and he had organised
this force into the Desert Column, under Sir Philip
Chetwode, and the Eastern Force, under Sir Charles
Dobell.  He required more infantry, and was more
or less at loggerheads with the Cabinet over the force
which he considered necessary to effect an advance
beyond el Arish.  It must be admitted that his
position was not an enviable one : the Cabinet
seemed to alter its mind from day to day—first urging
him to an offensive, and then instructing him that the
policy required was purely a defensive one,  Mean-

while the yeomanry units were dismounted, and doing nothing in particular. That the yeomanry should give birth to an infantry division is quite in keeping with the order of things which manages to produce from infantry battalions such progeny as machine gun companies, trench mortar batteries, employment companies, and many other " units " which were not in existence before the war, but were in active being long before they were officially recognised. It is, of course, obvious that if dismounted cavalry are used, their formation constitutes a difficulty when working in conjunction with infantry in such matters as relief of front-line troops.

However, it was a very healthy child that was born in March 1917.

General Girdwood and his staff arrived at el Arish on the 4th March. The order was that divisional troops, apart from R.A.M.C., would not be found pending further instructions.

Headquarters of the 229th Brigade arrived on the 7th, with the 16th Devons ; the 12th Somersets and the 14th Black Watch arrived on the 8th ; the Royal Scots and the No. 4 Machine Gun Company on the 9th.

The journey across the Desert by rail was uneventful, but interesting to eyes used to the waste of the Egyptian Desert : there was scrub and camel grass !

The Brigade then began to march to Kahn Yunus —through el Burj, on the 21st ; Sheikh Zowaiid, on the 24th ; Rafa, on the 25th—and arrived on the 29th. Men who found the sun hot in Egypt discovered that it was hotter on the borders of Syria ; water was scarce ; and the track was over deep, fine sand, which made marching hard, except where wire netting had been laid down.

At Khan Yunus the 231st Brigade assembled : the 10th Shropshires on the 3rd April ; the 24th Royal Welsh Fusiliers and 24th Welsh Regiment on the 4th ; the 25th Welsh Fusiliers and 210th Machine Gun Company on the 5th ; Headquarters on the 6th.

From thence the Division moved to Deir el Belah, where units took over sections of trenches, and where the 230th Brigade assembled : the 15th Suffolks on the 9th April ; the 16th Sussex and 209th Machine Gun Company on the 10th ; the 12th Norfolks on the 12th ; the 10th Buffs on the 13th.

The infantry brigades had now completed their concentration, but other units had joined during this period : the 496th Field Company R.E. on the 26th March ; the 231st Field Ambulance on the 11th April, the 230 Field Ambulance, and a section of the Monmouth R.E. on the 12th ; the Mobile Veterinary Section on the 13th ; the Anglesea Field Company on the 14th.

Before the concentration was complete the Devons and the Black Watch had relieved the 162nd Brigade, 54th Division, in the outpost line at In Seirat, on the 7th April ; and the 231st Brigade took over the outpost line at Khan Yunus on the 11th April. Large working parties were also required for making roads and cutting a crossing over the Wadi Ghuzze. In fact the Division was assembling while the first attack on Gaza was taking place, and was immediately called upon to prepare for the second.

    .     .     .     .     .

When the Turks retired from Khan Yunus, described by General McNeil, 30th Brigade, as " a veritable garden of Eden, with fields, vineyards, and fruit trees," they had taken up a strong position at Weli

Sheikh Nuran, but commenced to evacuate it early in
March. Attempts were made to hold them on this
position, but the distance was too great from the
railhead, at that moment, for any very effective operation. They were found (an estimated strength of two
divisions) to have distributed themselves between
Gaza and Tel el Sheria, with a small garrison at Beersheba, on their left flank.

This sudden withdrawal from carefully prepared
lines altered the whole situation. It seemed very
uncertain whether they would stand on the new position, and Sir A. Murray had to make up his mind as
to the line of attack he would select for his advance
into Palestine. He chose the coast. His reasons for
so doing were that railway construction was easier
along the maritime plain, and was more easily protected; also there was more water along the coastal
zone. He did not like the idea of drawing his line
of communications across the enemy front, which an
attack on Beersheba would have entailed, and decided
that there was no technical advantage to be gained
by linking up the military railway with the Central
Palestine Railway at Tel el Sheria, or Beersheba.

By the middle of the month (March) the railway
had reached Rafa. "There were distinct indications
that the enemy intended to withdraw," says Sir A.
Murray, but "the chief difficulty lay in deciding the
exact moment when it would be wise to abandon the
methodical advance, and to push out to its full radius
of action a considerable force into a country bare of
all supplies and almost devoid of water." He decided
to push forward the Desert Column, consisting of the
Australian and New Zealand Mounted Division, the
Imperial Mounted Division, and the 53rd Division, as

soon as it could be supplied from Rafa.  By the evening of the 25th the Desert Column was concentrated at Deir el Belah ;  the 54th Division was at In Seirat, to the east of Deir el Belah ;  the 52nd Division was at Khan Yunus ;  and the Camel Corps and armoured batteries about Abasan el Kebir :  the advance was to take place early the following morning.

We must now consider the country in front of the British Army.

It is a country of rolling downs, not unlike some parts of England in the spring, and yields, in patches, a goodly crop of barley, with little straw, but, with the sunshine in it, such as brewers like for their bitter ale. Within the British area two curious mounds served a useful purpose, at the time, as landmarks—Tel el Jemmi and Tel el Fara :  apparently they had been used for burial grounds, as bones and coins were found in them.  In Seirat, and what was called Raspbery Hill, afforded a fine view, but the other two places were more easily distinguished against a confusing, monotonous skyline.

Near the sea, where there is water here and there beneath the soil, fig trees and olives flourish, and in some places, such as Khan Yunus, the gardens are divided by enormous cactus hedges, most formidable barriers.  But it is, generally speaking, a dry and treeless land.

In the spring brightly coloured flowers grow in the cultivated fields and on the downland.  Besides the scarlet poppy there is a red and yellow one, with a long seed pod, like that of the English sea poppy. There is also a small white convolvulus, and a large pink one, which grow on the cultivated land.  On the downland there is a beautiful dianthus, with a pink

flower and a long stalk, and a low-growing pink
flower which looks like heath " and isn't."

The soil is a sandy loam, and this brings us to the
torrent beds, the wadis.  Some parts of the country
are very much cut up by these water courses : in the
winter they fill, and a great volume of water ploughs
its way through the light soil, leaving for the summer
a deep ditch, with steep banks and a sandy or stony
bed.

Immediately in front of the army was the Wadi
Ghuzze, a large and important wadi of varying width
—from 30 to 200 yards across, and with precipitous
banks of from 10 to 20 feet high.   There were pools
in this wadi: " Reconnoitred east bank of Wadi G
to Hiseia pools; wonderful to see deep, sea-green
pools of excellent water in such an arid region "
(Brigadier-General McNeil).

On the right bank of the Wadi Ghuzze, which runs
in a north-westerly direction to the sea, one sees first a
wide coastal fringe of sand dunes, and between the
soft, shifting sand and the downlands there is a valley,
along the centre of which runs the old caravan road
to Gaza.   To the east of this valley the country is
much broken up by wadis and dongas, and the broken
tract runs to a point marked by a cliff, Sheikh Abbas,
a few thousand yards south-east of Gaza.   On climbing the cliff a varied view is obtained : to the north-
west, across an open plain, the hill of Ali el Muntar
marks the outskirts of Gaza, and from it, running
parallel to the coast, back to the Wadi Ghuzze, is a
chain of hills ; on the plain, which is devoid of all
cover, Arabs could be seen, at this time of the year,
gathering in their crops, and sometimes grazing cattle ;
in the far distance was the road to Beersheba.

The plain of Gaza is beautiful—says Napoleon—covered with a forest of olive trees, watered by many streams. Colonel Preston, describing Gaza to-day, says that at a little distance, but for two broken minarets, there is little sign of damage owing to the " great quantity of trees which grew all over the town and which had now put on their spring coat of green," but inside it " was a mass of ruins, stark and silent." (*The Desert Mounted Corps.*)

The rough triangle, of which Sheikh Abbas is the apex, is a mass of small wadis running east and west, and joining a main wadi which runs into the Wadi Ghuzze—an admirable country for concealing troops. The Wadi Ghuzze, forming the base of this triangle, is joined at the right-hand corner by the Wadi Sheria, and, a few miles farther inland, by the Wadi es Saba. Following the latter we come to Beersheba, which, as we know, was the left of the Turkish Army, and is sited in the open desert.

The name Beersheba probably means the Well of Seven. To the south of the town is a barren mountainous country, mostly disposed in steep ridges running east and west; to the east is the Parched Land—the Desert. There is one road from Beersheba which leads over wide, rising undulations to Hebron, to the tableland of Judea, and so to Jerusalem—but we must deal with this country later.

There are a few small villages, and the ruins of a great many more. As may be imagined, the country is sparsely populated away from Gaza. But there were always a number of native hawkers hanging round the camps—Brigadier-General McNeil records, " Caught a lot of Bedouins going to water in wadi without passes ; ordered them all to be run in "—and

MEN OF THE 230TH BRIGADE IN A SMALL WADI NEAR EL KUSHAN,
AFTER THE SECOND BATTLE OF GAZA.

TROOPS OF THE 74TH DIVISION IN A BRANCH OF THE WADI GHUZZE.
The country was much intersected by such wadis, and the banks had to be ramped to allow the
passage of artillery, convoys, and troops.

between the British lines and Beersheba there were small tribes of Arabs, more or less hostile.

Major Marsham (The Buffs) gives some interesting details on animal life. Vultures were frequently seen round the wadis, and crested larks were as common as in Egypt. There were a great number of quails in the cornfields in early April, but they soon left : they were observed arriving from across the Mediterranean in an exhausted state, and they would drop immediately into the nearest cover. Swallows were fairly plentiful, as were bee-eaters. " Once I saw five sand-grouse together ; they let me get to within fifty yards, and then flew away a short distance and settled again. A pair of fly-catchers had built their nest close to our Brigade Headquarters (230th), and brought up their young regardless of shell and shrapnel. The cock is a dapper little bird, dressed in black and white. There are also snakes in this part of the country, but I have not heard of any case of snake-bite. On the other hand, a good many men have been bitten by scorpions which, though not serious, is no joke. Tarantulas are also fairly common, but they always run away whenever possible, and only bite when driven into a corner. There are ants in great variety and abundance. Lizards, too, are pretty numerous, and I noticed four or five different species ; they are, of course, quite harmless, though the Arabs say there is one sort which has a poisonous bite."

This was the country in which the army was operating, an intermediate land, between desert and cultivation. Gaza was the gateway from and to the Desert, and the real road to Jerusalem lay along the coast. " To march to Jerusalem without having occupied Jaffa would have been to disregard all the rules of prudence," wrote Napoleon.

.    .    .    .    .

The object of Sir A. Murray's advance was three-fold : to sieze the line of the Wadi Ghuzze and cover the advance of the railway ; to prevent the enemy from retiring without a fight ; to capture Gaza by a *coup de main*, and cut off its garrison.

There was, of course, no continuous line of trenches from Gaza to Beersheba. The enemy was on the far side of the Beersheba Road, and the five miles or so of country between the British and Turkish outpost lines was abandoned to the operations of patrols.

In the early morning of the 26th March, in a thick mist which greatly hampered the movements of troops, the Australian and New Zealand Mounted Division left the neighbourhood of Deir el Belah and crossed the Wadi Ghuzze, closely followed by the Imperial Mounted Division. The Australians and New Zealanders headed for Beit Durdis, about five miles east of Gaza, and the Imperial Mounted Division made for el Mendur, on the Wadi Sheria. The leading division reached Beit Durdis, and then deployed to the sea, closing the exit from Gaza. Meanwhile the 54th Division had crossed the Wadi Ghuzze and occupied the Sheikh Abbas Ridge ; and on the left the 53rd Division advanced with one brigade astride the el Shelufa-Ali Muntar Ridge, and a second from the Mansura Ridge also making for Ali Muntar.

Gaza was surrounded. By nightfall the 53rd Division had taken the commanding Ali Muntar position, and the Australians and New Zealanders were fighting in the streets of Gaza ; but the town had

not fallen, and columns of Turks were approaching
to relieve it from the north, north-east, and south-east.

At this point the waterless condition of the country
made itself felt. Unless Gaza was captured during
the day, mounted troops would have to return to the
Wadi Ghuzze to water their horses. (They went
without water for longer periods at a later date.) The
Australians and New Zealanders were heavily engaged
with the Turks in Gaza, as was the 53rd Division,
occupying the Ali Muntar position, and it seemed
improbable that they would win the town before
night. Between Gaza and the approaching relief
forces of Turks the Imperial Division and the Camel
Corps had spread themselves over a very wide front;
Sir Philip Chetwode decided that he must withdraw
his mounted troops. This was done during the
night. The infantry retired on the el Sire and el
Burjaliye Ridges.

The following day Ali Muntar was again occupied,
but the Turkish reinforcements were in Gaza, and
more were arriving from the north and north-east;
also the Turks had occupied Sheikh Abbas, whence
they directed artillery fire on the rear of our
positions on the Mansura Ridge. The acute salient
formed caused a most uncomfortable state of affairs,
and General Dobell withdrew his infantry to the west
of the Wadi Ghuzze.

The first attack on Gaza was a most disappointing
affair. Some 950 Turks and a few Germans were
captured, together with two Austrian field guns, but
our casualties were about 4,000, and Gaza was
stronger than ever. Turkish casualties were estimated at 8,000, a very doubtful figure under the
circumstances : the main Turkish forces were ob-

4

viously not encountered, and the IVth Turkish Army, responsible for the Syrian Front, only contained, at that moment, three infantry divisions and one cavalry division.

General Dallas, commanding the 53rd Division, reports that he abandoned the positions gained on the 26th with great reluctance. He held a position with his right flank entirely in the air, and could only gain touch with the 54th Division by a withdrawal, but,

" at about one in the morning . . . I learned from my own staff that troops of the 54th Division had appeared in the open plain north of Mansura, having, apparently, closed in on my right for some two miles. . . . Further, at daylight, I learned, for the first time, that the 54th Division, less the detachment which had been placed at my disposal, had been withdrawn during the night from Sheikh Abbas to the line Mansura–Tel el Ahmar–el Burjaliye–el Ahar. Had I known that the 54th were moving to close in on my right, I should have held on to the position gained, possibly with the exception of the hill north-east of the Mosque Hill, and have consolidated the ground gained. I would also have followed my intention of pressing down into the gardens and town, and so of widening and strengthening my position."

The ground gained, however, was devoid of water, and artillery fire made the slow moving camel convoys an impossibility during the daytime.

The defensive line, west of the Wadi Ghuzze, was then divided into sections held by the 54th, 52nd, and 53rd Divisions, and preparation made for a second attack.

.     .     .     .     .

The 74th Division had taken its place in the line early in April, and on the 14th General Girdwood issued his orders for the Second Battle of Gaza.

The enemy strength was estimated at about 20,000 to 25,000 rifles in all, disposed in a chain of detachments along the 16 miles, Sheria–Hareira–el Atawineh–Khirbet el Bir–Gaza, and holding, apparently, a small reserve 12 miles north-east, between Huj and Tel el Hesi. It was believed that there were about 8,500 at Gaza, 4,500 at Khirbet and Kufieh, 2,000 at el Atawineh, and the 16th Turkish Division, about 6,000 rifles, at Hareira–Sheria.

The intention was to advance the right flank of the attacking force so as to seize and occupy the Sheikh Abbas–Mansura Ridge, preparatory to undertaking further operations.

One mounted division would operate against Hareira, the other would protect the right flank and rear of the 54th Division.

The task of the 52nd and 54th Divisions was to attack the Sheikh Abbas–Mansura positions on the first day. On gaining the objective, both divisions would consolidate the position.

The 53rd Division would merely advance to the right bank of the Wadi Ghuzze.

The 74th Division would be in reserve.

The 229th Brigade had taken over the line, held in the right sector by the 162nd Brigade, 54th Division, on the 7th April, and so remained where it was; the 230th Brigade concentrated east of In Seirat; the 231st Brigade assembled close up to the Wadi, ready to counter-attack any enemy movement against the right of the 53rd, or the left of the 52nd Divisions.

As it turned out, there was no opposition, and the
Sheikh Abbas–Mansura positions were occupied with
no trouble of any sort.  The remainder of the day
and the whole of the 18th was then devoted to preparations for the second phase of the battle.

" It became clear," says Sir A. Murray, " that five
divisions and a cavalry division had now appeared on
our front, with an increase of heavy artillery."   In
the interval of time Gaza had been strengthened and
strongly wired ; long lines of trenches along the Gaza–
Beersheba Road, as far as the Atawineh Ridge, had
been constructed, which prevented any enveloping
movement by the cavalry ;  also the Turks had constructed a series of fortifications on the hills of the
el Sire–Ali Muntar Ridge.

The 52nd Division, with the 54th pivoting on its
right, had to attack the Ali Muntar Ridge ;  the 53rd
attacked the positions in the sand dunes, south-west
and west of Gaza.

On the 18th the 230th Brigade, accompanied by one
section of the R.E., one S.A.A. subsection, and two
bearer subsections, crossed the Wadi Ghuzze, and
took up a position behind Sharta, where they remained " hidden in wadis and folds in the ground."

On the 19th the attack opened with a bombardment
at 5.30 a.m.  The guns of the French battleship
*Requin*, and of the British monitors Nos. 21 and 31,
fired on Ali Muntar.  At 7.15 a.m. the infantry of the
53rd Division advanced on the left, amongst the sand
dunes, but the 52nd, in the centre, and the 54th, on
the right with the Imperial Camel Corps, did not
move until 7.30.  Meanwhile, on the extreme right,
a containing attack had been launched at dawn by the
Imperial Mounted Division (dismounted), and the

Australian and New Zealand Division, against the
el Atawineh positions.

It soon became apparent that the Turkish defensive
lines presented a problem of a very different nature to
that of the first attack on Gaza.   The 52nd Division,
in the centre, was held up at Outpost Hill ; the 54th
Division and the Camel Corps, exposed to heavy cross
fire from Ali Muntar and also from the Turkish left,
reached the neighbourhood of Khirbet Sihan ; but
Turkish resistance was strong in all directions.

The 229th and 231st Brigades had moved, with
Divisional Headquarters, across the Wadi Ghuzze to
positions between Tel el Ahmar and the Wadi Nukhabir.   They had started soon after midnight, and
there was some difficulty in settling down, as the
brigades, with transport, had to form up on unknown
ground in darkness, " the difficulty being added to,"
writes Lord Kensington, commander of the 25th
Royal Welsh Fusiliers, " by troops of the 52nd Division being already bivouacked in the same area.
These moved off at about 4.15 a.m., and the units of
the brigade had all gone to ground in the deep wadis
by 5 a.m."   Nevertheless, soon after the attack had
started, they came under shell fire, and Colonel
Shouldham, of the Somersets, was wounded, as were
also sixteen other ranks of the 229th Brigade.

The heat was terrific, and the dust rose in great
clouds, but from the top of Tel el Ahmar occasional
glimpses of the attack could be seen.   Tanks took
part in this battle, and did some useful work, but,
generally speaking, the crews had a bad time, not only
from the heat, which must have been infernal, but
from the enemy artillery, in no way flustered by their
appearance, and deadly in its accuracy ; most of them

were destroyed by shell fire, but one committed
suicide by taking a nose-dive into a wadi. Still,
from Tel el Ahmar the infantry and tanks were seen
fighting on Outpost Hill, the limit of the 52nd Division
advance.

The 230th Brigade soon issued from its concealment
behind Sharta, and moved to Dumbell Hill, where the
15th Suffolks took over a section of the outpost line
on the flank, with the 10th Buffs in support on the
left, and the 12th Norfolks and 16th Sussex on the
right. The Imperial Camel Corps, moving to the
attack across the front of this brigade at 9 a.m., drew
considerable fire which caused a few casualties.

At three o'clock in the afternoon the situation was
not good. The Desert Column was meeting with
some success in carrying out the containing attack on
Atawineh, but the 54th Division had suffered heavy
casualties, and could not advance until the 52nd was
in a position to protect its left flank. The 52nd Division was held up at Outpost Hill. The next hill of the
ridge, Middlesex Hill, and the ground about it, was
seamed with narrow dongas, holes, and fissures,
admirable conditions for the concealment of the
German-manned machine guns, and the brigade on
Outpost Hill was only able to advance on a very
narrow front against an extended broken area, too
wide for any effective concentration of our artillery.

About this time the 74th Division, less one brigade,
was ordered to stand to (which brought on them a
bombing attack from two Turkish aeroplanes), but
General Dobell decided, on receiving information that
our attack had not drawn the Turkish reserves, that
the time had not come for forcing a decision, and the
division did not go into action.

The situation remained unchanged until 6.20 p.m., when Outpost Hill was evacuated. At nightfall the 53rd Division, on the sand dunes, held the Sampson Ridge–Sheikh Aylin line ; the 52nd Division faced Outpost Hill and Ali Muntar ; the 54th Division carried the line round Sheikh Abbas to el Meshrefe ; and mounted troops connected with the Wadi Ghuzze. Casualties had mounted to 7,000.

The bare plain, destitute of all cover, and dominated by Ali Muntar, with the cactus hedges surrounding Gaza, had proved too great a task for the gallant attacking battalions. The machine-gun fire developed by the Turks was stupendous, and the enemy appeared to be unshaken by the preliminary bombardment.

Sir A. Murray's orders were that all ground gained during the day must be held without fail, and the attack on Ali Muntar resumed on the 20th, but

" during the night 19/20th I received a message from General Dobell to say that after careful deliberation and consultation with all divisional commanders, he was strongly of opinion that the resumption of the attack, ordered for the following morning, did not offer sufficient prospect of success to justify the very heavy casualties which such an operation would, in his opinion, involve. He therefore urgently requested my sanction to cancel the instructions previously issued. . . . In view of the strongly expressed opinion of the General Officer Commanding Eastern Force, supported by the General Officer Commanding Desert Column, and the Divisional Commanders, I assented to this proposal (a later attack)."

The line remained, then, as it was—from Sheikh Aylin, on the coast, to Sampson Ridge, in close touch with the enemy ; thence to Sheikh Abbas, the apex of that broken area of country with a network of wadis, which was some two or three thousand yards from the Turks; then back to the Wadi Ghuzze and along its banks to Shellal. The triumphant Turk remained in his original positions.

There was a belief that the enemy would attack on the 20th, and the 74th Division was ordered to concentrate east of the Wadi Nukhabir; but no hostile movement was perceived. In the evening the 231st Brigade was sent to dig a continuous line along the Sharta Ridge to Dumbell Hill. It did not arrive until 8 o'clock, when it was dark, with the result that in the morning the line had to be considerably rectified, and was eventually resited by General Girdwood on the 22nd. The other two brigades carried the line down the length of the Sharta Ridge, across the Wadi Sheria, to Tel el Jemmi.

On the 28th April the 229th Brigade took over the whole line, and the 230th moved to the old Turkish position about Weli Sheikh Nuran, where battalions worked on trenches assisted by the 49th Indian Infantry Brigade. The 231st moved to the east of the Wadi Ghuzze, opposite the mouth of Wadi Sheria, and came under the orders of the G.O.C. Eastern Force.

During these days the men of the 74th Division were afflicted by the khamsin, or sirocco, which they had already experienced in the Egyptian Desert. It is a wind that blows from the parched, sun-scorched desert, either east, south-east, or south. To say that it is hot does not describe it. It brings with it a mist of fine sand, clouding the sun and shortening the horizon. The temperature may be below 60 degrees in the morning when the sirocco starts, and then as the

wind increases, so the thermometer rises through the
seventies, the eighties, the nineties. Men are struck
with a paralysing languor, a raging thirst, and fever ;
vegetation shrivels, scorches, and dies. Sometimes
the wind is very violent ; sometimes the sand clouds
are so thick as to endanger life. Fortunately the
wind does not last, as a rule, more than a couple of
days. Brigadier-General McNeil notes in his diary on
the 19th and 20th :

" Woke to find the khamsin upon us. Not much
wind yet, but getting thick and very hot. . . . Wind
got cooler, but more of it towards evening, and we had
an awful night—mess tent blown down, most people's
' bivvies ' ditto. . . . Woke at intervals during this
terrible night and found myself covered in inches of
sand, but no use moving, so stuck it till dawn, when it
got better. Awful job trying to shave."

He states, too, that motor ambulances at Deir el
Belah were going about in daytime with head-lights,
as in a London fog. On another occasion the Brigadier notes fifty-five heat casualties in the 230th
Brigade, and that camels and mules died of the heat.
There were a good many heat casualties in the division,
and then the end of the month was marked by a
welcome shower of rain.

In the reorganisation which followed immediately
after the second attack on Gaza, Sir Philip Chetwode
took over the command of the Eastern force from Sir
Charles Dobell, and Sir H. G. Chauvell succeeded to
the Desert Column. The front, between Sheikh
Aylin and Tel el Jemmi, was divided into two
sections, and held by a regular system of reliefs.
Further to the right the line was thin, and watched
by mounted troops.

The 74th Division, for the time being, was somewhat scattered.  During the early part of May the 229th Brigade held the line from Dumbell Hill to Tel el Jemmi, and came under the direct command of the 54th Division.  The 231st Brigade, with the 272nd Brigade, R.F.A. attached, was in reserve near Tel el Jemmi, and under the orders of the Eastern Force, but was, later on, also attached to the 54th Division. The 230th Brigade held the Shellal sector, from the left of Hiseia to Tel el Fara.  General Girdwood suggested that this line should be taken east of the Wadi Ghuzze, and to this Sir H. G. Chauvell, who held this area with the Desert Column, assented. The line was, therefore, made on the night of the 16th/17th, and the Anzac Mounted Division was withdrawn.  The 230th Brigade remained there until the 26th May.

The 229th and 231st Brigades had a more lively time.  There was a wide expanse of country between their lines and the enemy positions, giving plenty of scope for patrol work.  The 14th Black Watch and the 12th Royal Scots Fusiliers had several encounters with Turkish patrols, and captured a number of prisoners ;  also many Turks deserted while on patrol and gave themselves up.  The patrolling of the 229th Brigade was done on the Mendur–Dumbell Hill–Sheikh Abbas Front, across which runs the Wadi Sihan at a distance of some 2,000 yards.

The 231st Brigade, after two weeks of fatigues, relieved the 162nd Brigade on the left, occupying trenches which connected with Lees Hill, and having in front of them Ali Muntar and the Beersheba Road. In the daytime large convoys and a continual stream of vehicles and scattered bodies of troops could be

seen on the road, out of range ; but at night the
Turk was seldom met within 1,500 yards of the
British trenches.   On the night of the 20th May a
patrol reached the Cactus Garden, close to Ali Muntar,
while the sirocco was blowing—a very creditable
performance, although when it arrived there nothing
could be seen.   The Turk on this front was not
enterprising—a few prisoners were taken, but patrols
continually found the country absolutely clear, right
up to the Turkish front line.  In fact, the whole front
was very quiet, and nothing of importance occurred
beyond a cavalry raid on the Beersheba–Auja Railway, which was most successful.

On the 26th May General Girdwood assumed command of the right section of the defences from G.O.C.
54th Division.   The 160th Brigade, 53rd Division
(attached), was on the right, the 229th Brigade in the
centre, the 231st on the left.   The 230th moved into
divisional reserve behind Sheikh Abbas on the 1st
June.   During the month this sector was reorganised
into four defended localities, known as Mansura (one
battalion), Apex (two battalions), Dumbell Hill (one
battalion), and Mendur (one battalion).

There was a marked decrease in the number of
Turkish deserters during this month, due to the
ascendency of the 74th Division patrols in the two to
three thousand yards of No Man's Land : desertions
were usually made from working parties, patrols, or
scouts.   As in the preceding month, the greatest
activity was on the 229th Brigade Front.   Two
incidents are noteworthy.

On the 1st June Captain E. J. Holley, with one
officer and twenty men of the 16th Devons, encountered a superior force of Turks about 2,000 yards

from the British lines. A smart engagement, lasting thirty minutes, ensued, in which two men of the patrol were wounded, but four Turks were killed. And on the 8th June Lieutenant R. J. Leversha, with five men from the Somersets, engaged a Turkish patrol of twenty-five, which they found near the Wadi Sihan. Lieutenant Leversha, realising that he was in danger of being surrounded, promptly charged with the bayonet, killing one and wounding two of the enemy, and extricated his patrol from an exceedingly awkward situation.

On the 231st Brigade front much good patrolling was done, but the wily Turk was not easy to find, although he was very active, at a distance, during the day. The 25th Royal Welsh Fusiliers, however, raided the Cactus Garden, with a party of two officers and fifty men. They found about eighty Turks, bayoneted seven, bombed and dispersed the remainder, and returned with two prisoners, and only two slight casualties themselves. The information gained by the 231st Brigade during the month was exceedingly valuable; an interesting item is that the Turks were using a large number of dogs, both as sentries and messengers.

. . . . .

June marks the end of Sir A. Murray's command. He never had a great number of troops under him. At one time, in January 1916, there were thirteen divisions, the result of the evacuation of Gallipoli, but not, one gathers, because of any apprehension on the part of the Government as to the 250,000 Turks said to have been available for an attack on Egypt. If such an attack was ever contemplated by the enemy, all fear of it soon vanished, and there

is little question that the strength of the Turks was
frequently greatly exaggerated ; one must remember
that they, too, were fighting on many fronts. In
January 1917 Sir A. Murray had one mounted and
four infantry divisions ; in March two mounted and
three infantry actually formed, while two others,
although under his command, were scattered, and not
finally assembled until April ; in June he had two
mounted and nine infantry divisions.

In the attacks on Gaza he was well served by his
troops, but in the first attack fortune was distinctly
against him in the shape of the morning mist which
delayed the movement of the cavalry ; the second
has been the subject of much discussion. His comments on each battle bear a resemblance :

" It is perhaps possible," he says of the 26th March,
" that if General Dobell had at this stage pushed
forward his reserve (the 52nd Division) to support the
53rd, the result would have been different, but the
difficulty of supplying water for men and horses would
have been immense and impossible to realise by those
who were not on the spot."

And again on the 19th April :

" It is possible that if the General Officer Commanding Eastern Force had now decided to throw in his reserves, the key of the position might have been taken
with the further loss of between 5,000 and 6,000 men,
but this would have left my small force, already
reduced, with a difficult line of front to hold against
increasing reinforcements of the enemy, who, owing to
the conformation of the terrain, could attack from
several directions."

The two comments, coming in the same despatch,

strike the eye, more especially as the exoneration of Sir Charles Dobell, in both cases, would seem to be based on very solid ground.

The great achievement, during his period of command, was the conquering of the Desert, not so much by force of arms as by mechanical appliances. To cross the Desert was now a matter of a few hours, and the water problem, although it still demanded serious attention, was solved. In fact, the organisation for determined action was now in being.

The pipe line across the Desert was, of course, the basis of the water supply, but local sources were developed. Wells and cisterns were reinforced by canvas tanks. In May the 74th Division drew water from a well 120 feet deep, near Sheikh Nakhrur, which was fitted with an oil engine pump, and was capable of supplying 4,000 gallons per hour. There were also shallow sumps in the wadis, and in the great Wadi Ghuzze a large number of pools spread over a great distance ; this water, however, was a doubtful blessing, as it was mostly foul and hard to control. During the month of June the division sunk three wells in the Wadi Ghuzze which yielded 1,600 gallons per hour. Other old wells were found to be infested with leeches, and cleaned out. The Division also found, on taking over a new administrative area at Um Jerrar, that twelve cisterns, containing 29,894 gallons, had become foul and were breeding mosquitos. But the existence of the army in that bare, desolate land was made possible, and the further advance and conquest of Palestine was based entirely on the work carried out under the directions of Sir A. Murray.

.    .    .    .    .

The sirocco was not the only plague that visited the men of the 74th Division : there were flies. All manner of devices were used to deal with these pests. Fly-traps were made out of biscuit tins and cigarette tins ; breeding-places were sought out and covered with oiled sacking, beneath which, a few weeks later, millions of dead flies were found ; all latrine and refuse pits were sealed with Hessian sacking saturated in crude oil; cook-houses were constructed, and the entrances and roofs covered with Hessian ; in the lines of each platoon sand-bags were placed to receive rubbish ; definite eating-places—a rough table made by cutting a trench in a square—were established, so that scraps of food might be dealt with ; and finally incinerators were kept going everywhere to deal with refuse from all sources. The efforts were rewarded by a great decrease in the number of flies.

There were other animals : scorpions, and spiders of many colours and sizes—and, of course, lice !

One of the most troublesome complaints was septic sores. The slightest scratch, or breaking of the skin, was in danger of becoming septic. The trouble lasted throughout the campaign.

Diphtheria, and scarlet fever, without being prevalent, were present.

Meanwhile, the plagues of Palestine notwithstanding, the Division fought, worked, and played. There was polo, football, and excellent sea bathing.

And the Division increased in size. The Artillery commenced to arrive. The 44th Brigade came from England, and landed at Alexandria on the 2nd June. It was reorganised from three 4-gun batteries, armed with 13-pounders, into two 6-gun batteries, of 18-pounders. It arrived at Deir el Belah on the 6th July.

From the 60th Division came B/301, and D/302
Batteries, which were renamed A/268 and C/268.
The third battery did not join until September; it
was the 266th Battery from the 146th Brigade R.F.A.,
and was renamed B/268.

The 117th Brigade R.F.A., coming from Salonica,
did not reach Deir el Belah until the 9th August.

Artillery brigades were commanded by Lt.-Colonel
F. J. I. Deshon, Colonel C. C. Robertson, and Lt.-
Colonel W. Kinnear respectively.

By this time the Staff was complete.

We give, in the following list, the changes that
occurred from time to time, so as to avoid
breaking into the text to record an alteration in
the Staff.

G.S.O. 1 :
   Maj. (T/Lt.-Col.) P. S. Allan, Gordon Highlanders, 10/3/17 to 7/4/18.
   Maj. (T/Lt.-Col.) A. C. Temperley, D.S.O., Norfolk Regt., 7/4/18 to
      12/11/18.
   Maj. (T/Lt.-Col.) C. N. F. Broad, D.S.O., Royal Artillery, 12/11/18
      to 4/2/18.
G.S.O. 2 :
   Maj. C. R. Roberts West, Essex Regt., 10/3/17 to 30/5/18.
   Maj. M. M. Parry-Jones, M.C., Royal Fusiliers, 25/5/18 to 23/10/18.
   Maj. W. M. Beckwith, D.S.O., Coldstream Guards, 23/10/18 to
      13/11/18.
   Maj. A. E. Saunderson, D.S.O., Oxford and Bucks L.I., 17/11/18
      to 26/3/19.
G.S.O. 3 :
   Lt. (T/Capt.) W. W. Burkett, City of London Yeomanry, 21/3/17
      to 2/12/17.
   Capt. A. Galloway, M.C., Scottish Rifles, 2/12/17 to 10/12/18.
A.A. and Q.M.G. :
   Maj. (T/Lt.-Col.) R. B. Cousens, D.S.O., R.A., 11/3/17 to 31/3/19.
D.A.A. and Q.M.G. (title became D.A.A.G., 23/4/17) :
   Maj. E. J. Butchart, D.S.O., Scottish Horse, 7/3/17 to 10/7/19.
D.A.A.Q.M.G. :
   Capt. (A/Maj.) R. Y. Weir, Lovat Scouts, 12/3/17 to 22/1/19.

A.D.M.S. :

    Lt.-Col. (T/Col.) E. P. Sewell, D.S.O., R.A.M.C., 7/5/17 to 25/1/18.

    Lt.-Col. (T/Col). E. McDonnel, D.S.O., R.A.M.C., 25/1/10 to 24/3/19.

D.A.D.M.S. :

    Capt. W. Mathieson, R.A.M.C., 6/4/17 to -/8/17.

    Capt. (A/Maj.) W. W. McNaught, M.C., R.A.M.C., -/8/17 to 1/3/19.

    Capt. (A/Maj.) L. T. Whelan, R.A.M.C., 1/3/19 to 31/3/10.

### DIVISIONAL ARTILLERY

Commander :

    Lt.-Col. (T/Brig.-Gen.) L. J. Hext, C.M.G., 12/7/17.

Brigade Major :

    Maj. N. A. L. Day, 17/4/17.

Staff Captain :

    T/Capt. J. K. Campbell, 17/4/17.

    T/Capt. K. W. Miles, M.C., D.C.M., 28/2/19.

### DIVISIONAL ENGINEERS

C.R.E. :

    Maj. (T/Lt.-Col.) R. P. T. Hawksley, C.M.G., D.S.O., 25/3/17.

    Maj. (A/Lt.-Col.) W. R. Izat, D.S.O., 25/8/17.

Adjutant :

    T/Lt. (A/Capt.) M. M. Jeakes, M.C., 7/4/17.

### DIVISIONAL MACHINE GUN BATTALION

O.C. :

    T/Capt. (A/Lt.-Col.) B. Barnes, M.C., London Regt., 9/4/18 to 28/12/18.

    Maj. (T/Lt.-Col.) O. M. Norem, D.S.O., Lancashire Fusiliers, 22/1/19 to 28/3/19.

### DIVISIONAL TRAIN

O.C. :

    Lt.-Col. J. G. Needham, R.A.S.C. (T.F.), 10/5/17.

    Maj. (A/Lt.-Col.) W. A. W. Machonochie-Wellwood, R.A.S.C., 11/12/17.

D.A.P.M. :

    T/Capt. E. A. Pratt-Barlow, Royal Irish Regt., 3/4/17 to -/11/17.

    Lt. P. Hurlbutt, M.C., Montgomery Yeomanry, -/11/17 to 24/11/17.

    Capt. F. A. B. Nicholl, Royal Sussex Regt., 24/11/17 to 29/3/19.

D.A.D.V.S. :

    Maj. G. McIntyre, R.A.V.C., 25/3/17 to 16/9/18.

    Capt. (A/Maj.) D. R. Williamson, R.A.V.C., 19/9/18 to 25/3/19.

D.A.D.O.S. :

    Capt. (A/Maj.) V. T. Whelan, R.A.O.D., 23/3/17 to 1/6/19.

5

### 229TH INFANTRY BRIGADE

Commander :

 Col. (T/Brig.-Gen.) R. Hoare, C.M.G., D.S.O., 3/3/17.

 Maj. (T/Brig.-Gen.) F. S. Thackeray, D.S.O., M.C., Highland L.I., 11/9/18.

Brigade Major :

 Maj. Brodie of Brodie, Lovat Scouts, 30/3/19.

 Capt. R. C. Boyle, W. Somerset Yeomanry, 29/5/17.

 Capt. A. J. M. Tuck, M.C., Seaforth Highlanders, 13/4/18.

Staff Captain :

 Capt. Lord Poltimore, Royal N. Devon Hussars, 3/3/17.

 Capt. C. Mackintosh, M.C., 1/4 Royal Scots, 28/5/17.

 Capt. A. H. Grant, M.C., 3rd Lancashire Regt., 11/11/18.

### 230TH INFANTRY BRIGADE

Commander :

 Lt.-Col. (T/Brig.-Gen.) A. J. McNeill, Lovat Scouts, 3/3/17.

 Maj. (T/Brig.-Gen.) H. B. H. Orpen Palmer, D.S.O., Royal Irish Fusiliers, 21/12/17.

 Lt.-Col. (T/Brig.-Gen.) H. J. Bowker, C.M.G., D.S.O., Somerset L.I., 13/2/18.

 Col. (T/Brig.-Gen.) A. A. Kennedy, C.M.G., 1/7/18.

Brigade Major :

 Capt. J. M. R. Yardley, D.S.O., Royal Inniskilling Fusiliers, 3/3/17

 Maj. I. Buxton, Norfolk Yeomanry, 16/6/17.

 Capt. D. Gilroy, 3rd Hussars, 18/1/19.

Staff Captain :

 Capt. J. Agnew, Suffolk Yeomanry, 3/3/17.

 Capt. W. R. Marshall, Lanark Yeomanry, 22/8/17.

 Capt. W. M. Parr, 5th Highland L.I., 7/9/17.

 Capt. P. L. Cockerill, London Regt., 23/9/17.

 Lt. (A/Capt.) A. H. Montgomery, M.C., Ayr Yeomanry, 17/10/18.

### 231ST INFANTRY BRIGADE

Commander :

 Col. (T/Brig.-Gen.) E. A. Herbert, 3/3/17.

 Lt.-Col. (T/Brig.-Gen.) W. J. Bowker, C.M.G., D.S.O., 7/5/17.

 Lt.-Col. (T/Brig.-Gen.) C. E. Heathcote, C.B., C.M.G., D.S.O., Yorkshire L.I., 1/9/17.

Brigade Major :

 Capt. R. E. C. Adams, M.C., E. Surrey Regt., 3/3/17.

Staff Captain :

 Capt. Lord Victor Paget, M.C., 3/3/17.

DREAMS OF HOME

"WHEN GREEK MEETS GREEK".

# PART II
## *SYRIA*
### *June 1917—April 1918*

# CHAPTER IV

## PREPARATIONS FOR THE ADVANCE INTO PALESTINE

The features of Syria—Training—Questions of Supply—Water—
Reconnaissance—Secrecy—Orders.

THE general situation, when Sir E. Allenby assumed command in Egypt, and of the forces in Syria, was complicated. During the year 1916 the chief events, as between the Central Powers and the Entente Powers, had been, first and foremost, the Battle of Verdun, which raged from February to December; then the British and French effort on the Somme, which commenced on the 1st July, and may be said to have ended with the battle on the Ancre on the 13th November. On the Austrian Front the chief effort was Brusiloff's attack, in June; and the Italian attacks on the Isonzo, in August, and in the Carso in November. On the Turkish fronts there were the successful Russian operations at Erzeroum in February and Trebizond in April; the unsuccessful advance of General Townshend, which ended on the 29th April; the capture of Mecca by the Grand Sherif in June; and, finally, Sir A. Murray's advance across the Desert to the frontier of Syria.

On the whole, the year 1916 may be considered as successful for the Entente Powers. There is no doubt that the military power of Germany was severely shaken in France, although it was a grim and terrible year for the British and French armies. And, thanks to the Russians, the Turks had had their hands fairly full.

In the first half of 1917 the situation became involved. In France there was the celebrated withdrawal of the Germans to the Hindenburg Line, combined with the brilliantly executed battles round Arras and Vimy Ridge, in which British troops struck fear in the heart of Ludendorff. In the commencement of June, General Plumer put into action his faultless plans for the capture of Messines Ridge. No less promising was the British campaign in Mesopotamia, where General Maude captured Bagdad, after a series of victories, in March, and politically the Entente Powers had won the great moral support of America's declaration of war on Germany in April.

But Russia, that great mystic, neurotic, baffling Power, had once more proved itself unstable as the winds. Revolution broke out on the 12th March. The Central Powers were jubilant. It was the beginning of the end !

The effect of the Russian tragedy was not felt immediately. The benefit to the Central Powers was a future accretion of strength by the release of troops engaged on their eastern front ; beyond that there was no material gain, as the disorganised state of Russia was as great an obstacle to any outlet, any " hacking a way through," as the armies of the Tsar. But it had an ominous bearing on the future.

The terrific battles in France and Belgium, with their six and seven-figure totals of casualties, will always give the impression that the real trial of strength, or rather the actual field of victory, was there ; but it does not require much imagination to realise that an overwhelming Turkish success in Syria would have altered the whole course of the war, and would have been as great a disaster to the Entente as, in all probability, the loss of Paris. There were infinite possibilities for the Central Powers round the Mediterranean ; a few extra divisions, inspired by an able commander, would have made the danger actual, throttling. The moment, for the Central Powers, would seem to have been in 1916. The reluctance of the British Cabinet to send a couple of divisions to this front was equalled by the mad desire of the Germans to end the whole business by the ferocious battles of Verdun. The opportunity was allowed to slip, by the Central Powers, while the British Cabinet, always seeking, like water, the easiest, though often the most tortuous, outlet, had finally concentrated a considerable force in Mesopotamia and Syria, an act which was brought about by a reverse to British arms rather than forethought.

Ludendorff describes Enver Pasha as a man of great military ability, but without knowledge or professional qualifications—which reminds one somehow of those would-be vocal artists who declare that they have beautiful, natural, untrained voices. At all events, after the capture of Bagdad by General Maude, Enver approached the German General Headquarters and asked them for a German Army Group Headquarters, together with an auxiliary corps to help recapture that city. The German High Command agreed, though " not exactly with enthusiasm," says Ludendorff.

German policy, with regard to the East, seems to have been as vacillating as the British. Ludendorff, after alluding to Austria and Turkey as decaying States, regrets that Germany " neglected to infuse any new life into our perishing allies." In various passages of his book, *My War Memories*, 1914–1918, he points out the difficulties of communications in Syria and Mesopotamia, depending on roads rather than railways, which were in a most deplorable state, and not suited for modern warfare, but admits " the stiffer the Turkish defences in Palestine and Mesopotamia, and the larger the forces absorbed in the English effort to achieve their object, the more our burden in the west would be lightened." He welcomed the XVth Turkish Corps, and other troops, in Galicia after the evacuation of Gallipoli, and praises Enver for his perspicacity in seeing that the war would be settled for Turkey outside that country, and then he complains that he had frequently drawn Enver's attention to the state of the Palestine Front, and requested him to reinforce it and improve the railway communications there. However, having agreed to send material help, the High Command set about collecting the Asiatic Corps, and sent Field-Marshal von Falkenhayn to command a new army the Turks proposed to assemble.

This new army was called the Yildirim, or Lightning Group, and was to consist of the VIth Army, in Mesopotamia, and the VIIth, which was being formed in Constantinople from the troops withdrawn from Galicia, Rumania, and Macedonia.

But, when on the spot, the German Commander saw very clearly that the danger was in Syria, and the Constantinople authorities were persuaded to abandon the idea of recapturing Bagdad, and consider an attack in Syria. The army came into being, and was made up of the VIIth and VIIIth Armies. The IVth Army was given the name of the Syrian and Western Arabian Command, with Headquarters at Damascus, and operated east of the Jordan until January 1918, when it came under the command of the Yildirim Army.

It is curious that Falkenhayn should have been sent to command, for in a document, written in 1915, " to serve as a basis for the report to His Majesty the Kaiser," he expresses himself strongly against any enterprise in the East. He does not see that victories in Mesopotamia or at the Suez Canal can help the Central Powers in the least ! He even goes so far as to say that defeat can do them " no palpable harm " ! and refers contemptuously to the " protagonists of an Alexander march to India or Egypt," for such an undertaking, in his opinion, could have no effect on the course of the war. (*General Headquarters* 1914–1916, *and its Critical Decisions.*)

. . . . .

General Allenby, after consultation with Sir Philip Chetwode, found the situation by no means unfavourable, and formulated his plans by the second week in July.

Enumerating the main features, he says that he found the Turkish Army covering a front of, roughly, thirty miles, from the sea, and along the Gaza–Beersheba Road to Beersheba. Gaza was heavily entrenched and wired ; the remainder of the line was held by strong works at Sihan, Atawineh, Baha, Abu Hareira, and Beersheba. There was a gap of four miles and a half between Hareira and Beersheba, and the other positions were about a mile apart. The British lines lay between the sea and Gamli, a distance of twenty-two miles.

General Allenby decided to attack the left of the Turkish positions.

Beersheba was not an attractive place. East of it

was the most God-forsaken country, and the Dead
Sea.  To the north was Jerusalem, but between that
place and Beersheba were the heights of Hebron, and
the Judean Plateau, an arid, waterless, and mountainous tract of country.  But the defences of Beersheba
were less formidable than elsewhere, and were easier
to approach—and Beersheba had water !  With
Beersheba in his hands, General Allenby would have
an open flank against which to operate, and he was
superior in mounted troops.

His plans, of course, included an advance on
Jerusalem, and it would be as well to consider the
nature of the country between the Wadi Ghuzze and
that city.

The curious geographical features of Syria have
influenced the invading armies of successive centuries
in the same way.  The coast contains no harbours,
and is most unfavourable for a military landing, and
to the east the great Arabian Desert forms an in-
superable obstacle.  It is, therefore, a long, narrow
country.  From the Lebanons, in the north, flows the
Jordan, with a range of hills on either bank.  Putting
on one side the association of this river with Holy
Scripture, it is a most remarkable stream.  The
valley, between the ranges of hills that mark its
course, has been rent so that the river flows, for 160
miles, beneath the level of the sea.  This rent varies
in breadth from 2 to 15 miles, and falls from sea-level
to 1,292 (Dead Sea level) feet below it—actually the
bed of the Dead Sea, which receives the Jordan, lies
1,300 feet deeper still.  The eastern range of hills
have a mean height of 2,000 feet above sea-level ; but
we have little to do with this country.  On the west
of the Jordan the range runs from the Lebanons to

the south of the Sinai Peninsula, a great wall of limestone broken by the plain of Esdraelon.

At this break the hills scatter into separate groups
through Samaria, but the wall rears itself again, in
a solid mass, known as the Table Land of Judea, at a
height of 2,400 feet above the sea, until, south of
Hebron, it tumbles down to the plateau of the Desert.

The descent of this range to the Jordan is precipitous, but, on the western side, although the average
fall to the maritime plain is long, there are important
under features.  It seems as though a second range,
of a different limestone, and less formidable in nature,
had thrust itself up against the Judean mountains ;
these are known as the hills of the Shephalah.  The
width of Syria, seen in section, presents itself, therefore, as a maritime plain, of gentle contours, and with
a strip of sand along the coast—the soil of the plain
is brown, broken by gullies containing a greyish
shingle, puddles of water, and reeds ; then the Shephalah, a country of short, steep hills, a lot of brush-
wood and oak scrub, scrags of limestone, and rough
torrent beds ; then the plateau of Judea, a stony
moorland, with no water, no streams, some rough
scrub, and a few dwarf trees—stones, boulders, rocks,
and glaring sun ; and then comes desolation, hills
like gigantic dust heaps, twisted, contorted, with an
outcrop of jagged rock, and falling in broken chaos
to the Dead Sea, the awful, enervating, fantastic
ditch.

It will be seen that all the important features of
Syria run from the Lebanons to the Sinai peninsula,
and that the obstacles that lay in the way of an
advance to Jerusalem could not be penetrated by
General Allenby, but would have to be traversed in

their entire length! It is this curious geographical
formation which has made of the maritime plain the
invading road to Jerusalem. From the plain, the
best-known passes to the heights of Judea are from
the Vale of Ajalon and the Vale of Surar. Above
all, it must be remembered that for wheeled traffic
it was practically a *roadless* country.

. . . . .

In drawing up his plan of battle, General Allenby's
chief difficulties were water and transport. There
was water at Beersheba, but the quantity and the
time which would be required to develop it were
uncertain; there was a possibility that the Turks
might destroy the wells before retreat from the town,
and, except for Beersheba, no large supply of water
could be found until Sheria and Hareira were captured.

The transport problem was that there were no roads
worthy of the name, and the use of motor transport
was very limited. Also the country was intersected
by steep-banked wadis, which would prevent the
general use of all wheeled transport. And yet, in
order to provide water, food, and ammunition, he
would have to use practically the whole of his
organisation (including 30,000 camels) for one
portion only of the eastern force, operating at fifteen
to twenty miles from railhead. Preparations to overcome these difficulties took several months.

. . . . .

The Division left the line on the night 9th/10th
July, and remained, in reserve to the 52nd Division,
about Dorset House until the first week in August,
when the 54th Division took their place.

From a camp in the sand dunes, west of the railway,

a period of arduous training followed. For regimental
officers it was, no doubt, very trying. It started with
a reorganisation of battalions, based on the development of the modern infantryman's weapons within
the platoon. There was to be a section of bombers,
a Lewis gun section, a sniper section, and a rifleman
section; but, like many other schemes, the Staff
responsible for it failed to realise that you cannot keep
on sending men away to "courses," turning others
into cooks, transport men, sanitary men, batmen, etc.,
and demand guards, men to work on odd jobs for the
Brigadier, for the General, for the Corps Commander,
for the Commander-in-Chief, and still have the number
of men available in a battalion as laid down by the
Army Council. And yet it is scarcely a matter of
mathematics; it is simple arithmetic. However, the
reorganisation was carried out, the regimental officer
exercising the soldier's privilege of "grousing." But
when a division starts training in earnest for a battle,
and the thermometer is about 100 in the shade, one
cannot help sympathising with the men who have to
supervise the details of the multitude of courses each
individual is supposed to go through. The courses
were merely a preliminary to battalion and brigade
training. Outpost schemes, night marching, night
attacks followed, and a certain amount of field firing.

Colonel Powell Edwards, of the Sussex, has an
illuminating note on physical training:

"The writer remembers seeing, in the grizzly light of
dawn, in a back area near the sea, the wretched men
of another brigade doing violent doubling through
sand, hock deep, as a suitable preparation for a
strenuous day in the heat. It was not till quite late
in the war that the British Army as a whole realised

that this question of expenditure of physical energy
in the small hours of the morning was being overdone,
and that there was no real merit in voluntarily (or
involuntarily) undergoing heavy exercise on an empty
stomach."

During the first month of training one brigade was
required for trench digging in the forward areas, and
this duty was undertaken in rotation.  The action of
the 229th Brigade in this locality (amongst the sand
dunes) drew the following letter from the G.O.C.,
54th Division :

"MY DEAR GIRDWOOD,—Although your 229th
Brigade will be working for us for some days longer, I
want to take this earliest opportunity of letting you
know about the exceptionally good work which was
carried out by it last night when it was given the job of
digging the new line, 1,400 yards in length from
Fusilier Ridge to Jones' Post.
"Colonel Garsia was up there during the night,
and has reported to me the following incidents that
came under his personal observation.  Doubtless
other equally good work was done elsewhere.
"The part of the line to be dug by the Fife and
Forfars ran from our trenches on the right to about
half way to Bunkers Hill, a distance of 350 yards.
The line here is from 400 to 500 yards from the Hog's
Back, a ridge in front of the Turk's position, on to
which they have pushed out several snipers, while
machine guns in rear traverse portions of our line.
In the bright moonlight (two days off full) the Turks
were able to observe our people at work.  When
Colonel Gilmour arrived at the head of his men, two
wiring parties had been driven in shortly before, with
the loss of three men killed and some wounded.
"Colonel Garsia was of the opinion that since the
small wiring parties had been forced to come back,

the very much larger digging parties might suffer severe loss, and he told Colonel Gilmour that he would take full responsibility for suspending the work until the moon went down (at about 02.30), when an hour and a half's work could have been carried out. Colonel Gilmour, however, decided to push men out in small groups and try to make a start. The men all went out splendidly, while a machine gun was traversing the ridge from which they started, and by the end of the first relief were well under ground along the whole of this front. The trench then provided cover from machine gun fire, but not from shrapnel, with which the enemy then opened, wounding several of your men. Again Colonel Gilmour insisted on carrying on with the work, realising what is often overlooked by the man on the spot, in such cases, that every cubic foot of earth moved during the first night and before the enemy has had an opportunity of obtaining day observation of the new line, would mean the saving of casualties later on.

" The casualties suffered by the Fife and Forfar were happily small, but I do not think that this fact in any way detracts from the merit of Colonel Gilmour's action, who could not know that this would be the case.

" Further to the left the Ayr and Lanark sector crossed a ridge, the summit of which proved to be the worst part of the line. When the original covering party went out, it was here that the enemy's fire was first drawn, and a brisk fire was opened by snipers from the Hog's Back; soon after two men of the wiring party were killed. The enemy then brought machine gun fire to bear on the two points. With these he kept up continuous bursts of fire which swept low over the crest of this ridge. Just at the time the second relief took place the enemy opened with shrapnel, bursting them accurately over the new line.

6

" Captain Cooper was at this time leading his company towards this point, and several officers of my division remarked on the determined manner in which he advanced, and the tenacity with which his men, carrying bundles of sandbags over heavy sand, struggled to keep up.

" I am extremely sorry to hear that Captain Cooper was killed.  He certainly gave a fine example to his men of leadership.

" I very much regret the casualties suffered by your men, some of which were undoubtedly due to their determination to carry out the task set them until it was shown to be impossible.  In view of the fact that in the course of the night over 3,000 men were engaged (though not all at one time) in consolidating this line in bright moonlight and under enemy observation at short range, I do not think that the total casualties can be regarded as severe, and consequently I feel that the excellent spirit of determination that animated the whole of the 229th Brigade was abundantly justified.

" We can now afford to complete the consolidation deliberately, in the course of which we shall certainly suffer fewer casualties than would have been the case had last night's task been left incomplete.

" I therefore wish to express my gratitude to the 74th Division, and especially to General Hoare and the 229th Brigade, for the work carried out.

" Yours sincerely,

"S. W. HARE, *Major-General,*

" *Commanding* 54th *Division.*"

General Bulfin, commanding XXIst Corps, also wrote an appreciation of the work carried out by all brigades.

.        .        .        .        .

An order had been issued on the 6th June that the Division would be placed on the establishment of a

division with camel transport, which meant that the
majority of wheeled vehicles were returned to
Ordnance. And on the 22nd of that month all motor-
vans and cars were withdrawn. The massing and
organising of the transport was a tremendous undertaking; the notes of Major H. J. Butchart in the
*Q Diary* will give us some idea of what it entailed :

" The two questions which required most careful
consideration were supplies and water. It was
apparent from the start that in both cases supplies
and water would have to be sent forward by convoy.
In this connection it was decided after careful consideration that convoys should not be sent farther
forward than Divisional Supply Dump. The reasons
were : (1) if a convoy were once split up, considerable
delay must occur before it could be collected and
ready to return ; (2) detached groups of camels would
be apt to get lost, especially at night, when supplies
and water would, in all probability, have to be taken
forward ; (3) owing to the distance convoys would
have to march, it was essential that all convoys should
return to the base as quickly as possible to ensure
that future convoys would not be delayed.

" It was further decided that the Divisional Train
should be used as a convoy.

" It followed that units must draw supplies and
water by their 1st Line Transport. It then transpired
that the batteries of the Divisional Artillery had no
transport available for drawing rations. It was
therefore decided to allot five extra camels to each
battery for this purpose. The operations clearly
demonstrated that artillery brigades are quite unable
to move their technical and other stores, or draw
rations, through the lack of sufficient transport.
Owing to the number of liaison officers, and other
ranks, attached to formations, one extra camel was

attached to each Brigade Headquarters and two to
Division Headquarters."

Each 18-pounder battery had, then, 10 camels;
each 4·5 howitzer battery 9 camels; and the 230th
Light Trench Mortar Battery 44 camels.

When going into battle, it was the universal practice
at this period of the war to leave a certain number of
officers and men behind—9 officers and 117 other
ranks from each battalion, 3 officers and 31 other
ranks from each machine gun company, 1 officer and
11 other ranks from each trench mortar battery—and
these details formed the reinforcement camp. The
reinforcement camp was to provide escorts for the
convoys, and we learn, from their orders, that convoys
of 130 and of 1,360 camels were dealt with on Z–1
day, and of 440 and 1,360 on Z day—this for the
74th Division only.

Water, from the day of attack on Beersheba, was
to be provided at the rate of half a gallon a day for
each man, and five gallons for each horse. Drinking
water was distributed by the exchange of empty
fanatis (a copper vessel in which water was carried
by camels—in the singular tense, fantass) for full at
the Divisional Dump.

The watering of horses was a difficult question—how
was it to be done? At first buckets were suggested;
but that would have meant a great deal of time and,
worse still, a great deal of waste, so it was decided that,
while horses were on five gallons a day, they would
only be watered once a day, from canvas troughs :
a man would be put in charge of troughs, and would
check the amount of water consumed by means of
measuring-stick and time.

A WATER CONVOY GOING FORWARD AT THE BATTLE OF BEERSHEBA.
In the middle distance is a small wadi. This picture gives a good impression of the desolate
country. Frequently the heat registered was 110° in the shade.

TROOPS OF THE 74TH DIVISION.
A bivouac camp by the Wadi Saba after the Battle of Beersheba.

A few extra details of water arrangements are not
without interest. Captain E. F. S. Rodd, 12th
Somersets, was appointed Divisional Horse Water
Officer (this meant another of those appalling rows
of letters beloved by the Army), and Lieutenant
R. P. Griffin, 15th Suffolks, Divisional Drinking
Water Officer—D.D.W.O.! There were also Brigade
H.W.O.'s, and D.W.O.'s; artillery H.W.O.'s, and
D.W.O.'s.

The system arranged was that when camels with
full fanatis arrived, the D.D.W.O. would allot to each
Brigade W.O. the number he was entitled to; the
Brigade W.O. would then move his camels to his own
subsection of the water area, and allot to each man of
his personnel the number required for the unit the
man represented.

For horse water, 35 troughs and 12 canvas tanks
were provided for the division. Chits were to be
issued to all units, covering four horses, or multiples of
four, and no horse would be allowed to water unless
a chit was presented (a few single chits were provided
for odd numbers). The number of animals to be
watered was: Artillery Group (including Divisional
Headquarters), 2,669; 229th Brigade Group, 686;
230th Brigade Group, 687; 231st Brigade Group, 709.

Water supplies were to be drawn from Gamli and
Imara.

The strength of the Division on the 27th October
was: 575 officers and 16,006 other ranks.

The usual amusing discussion arose, without which
no battle preparation is complete. Major Butchart
notes:

" The question as to whether shorts S.D., or trou-

sers S.D. should be worn was considered.   A request
for shorts S.D. Salonica pattern was forwarded to
XXth Corps.   This pattern is sufficiently long to
come down below the knee, but can be doubled up
and fixed so that they are the same length as ordinary
shorts when marching.   Neither shorts S.D. nor
Salonica pattern were available.   Drill shorts were,
therefore, retained."

Without enumerating the multitude of requirements
necessary for an advance, it will be appreciated that
food and water alone were a severe task for the
Administrative Branch of the Division.   The country,
the borderland of the Desert, was without roads,
and such tracks as existed were soon cut to pieces
and made impassable for wheeled traffic.   The orders
regulating all traffic were most stringent, and designed
to protect the surface of the so-called roads or tracks.
Elaborate time-tables regulating the movements of
Camel Convoys and Divisional Train were drawn up.
The difficulties were foreseen, and every effort was
made to overcome them.   The reader must remember
that they were multiplied by the number of divisions
taking part in the advance.

.    .    .    .    .

Concurrently with the preparations for the forthcoming battle, the whole of the army was reorganised.
It will be remembered that Sir A. Murray had divided
his force into the Desert Column and the Eastern
Force.   The Eastern Force was now done away with
—the Desert Column, renamed the Desert Mounted
Corps, remained.

Under the new arrangement the army consisted of
the XXth Corps, commanded by Sir Philip Chetwode,
and composed of the 10th, 53rd, 60th, and 74th Divi-

sions; the XXIst Corps, commanded by Sir Edward
Bulfin, and composed of the 52nd, 54th, and 75th
(Territorial and Indian) Divisions; and the Desert
Mounted Corps, commanded by Sir H. G. Chauvel,
and composed of the Yeomanry Mounted Division,
the Australian Mounted Division (the Imperial), and
the Anzac Mounted Division (Australian and New
Zealand). The Imperial Camel Corps remained a
separate unit, in corp reserve with the 7th Mounted
Division.

Against this force were the two Turkish Armies, with
a total of nine infantry and one cavalry divisions.

It was clear to the enemy that the British would
make another attempt in Syria, and apparently they
realised the weakness of the Beersheba flank; but
they believed the attack would be directed along the
maritime plain. This belief gave a false sense of
security to those on the spot, even while they insisted
on the necessity of strengthening the left flank. The
idea of recapturing Bagdad had been quickly dis-
carded, for the Turkish communications with Constantinople from both Syria and Mesopotamia (also
from Hejaz) were concentrated just north of Aleppo
on a single line of railway which would be threatened
by any British success in Syria. Steps were therefore
taken to defeat this possibility, and a date was fixed
in December for a great attack which was to drive the
British back into the Desert.

On the date of General Allenby's attack the organising of the Yildirim Force was nearing completion.
Marshal von Falkenhayn was at Aleppo, on his way
to Jerusalem. General von Kressenstein, commanding the VIIIth Army, was at Huleikat, and Fevzi
Pasha, commanding the VIIth Army, was preparing

to take over command of the left of the line.   The line
of battle ran : 53rd, 3rd, 54th, 26th, 16th, 24th, and
27th divisions in line, and the 19th and 7th behind
Gaza ;  the 20th was on the line of communications
south of Aleppo.

.          .          .          .          .

The British line had remained the same :  strong,
and in close touch with the enemy before Gaza,
bending round the Sheikh Abbas Ridge to the Wadi
Ghuzze, and following the Wadi until it petered out
with cavalry patrols in the neighbourhood of Gamli.
There was, therefore, a wide tract of country between
Beersheba and the British right.

The first move was to get the enemy thoroughly
accustomed to cavalry in this area, and so, once a fort-
night, the cavalry division that was in the line made
a reconnaissance towards Beersheba, marched all
night, and occupied a line of outposts opposite
Beersheba by dawn the next morning.  " Behind
this line of protecting posts the infantry corps and
divisional commanders, and innumerable lesser fry,
disported themselves in motor-cars and on horseback.
The senior corps commander and his staff used to be
irreverently referred to as ' the Royal Party ' " (*The
Desert Mounted Corps*, by R. M. P. Preston).  But
while they disported themselves, they also did
excellent work by surveying and thoroughly ac-
customing themselves to the country and the general
lie of the land.  Most of the commanding officers,
or the seconds in command who were to lead the
battalions in action, went out on these reconnaissance
rides.

Brigadier-General McNeil's diary gives some details
of these manœuvres :

"23rd August. Sent horses to the Yeomanry Division Headquarters at Fara for to-morrow's reconnaissance. Ten car-loads of us started about 4 p.m. and went to the 179th Brigade Headquarters (60th Division) at Fara. Here they put us up most comfortably for the night—twenty-two of us—they settling for breakfast and dinner—awfully good of them.—24th August. Started 8.30 for the east, and did a very valuable reconnaissance which I fear I cannot here describe. Sufficient to say some of us got to within 2,000 yards of the enemy trenches, and if the light had been good we might have seen everything. We were bombed by enemy aircraft—two bombs came unpleasantly near us. No casualties. Got home 5.30 p.m.—12th September. Started 8 a.m. from the trestle bridge over the wadi near Tel el Ajul. Our car was a very old and 'dud' one, and the driver quite incompetent. However, after many stops and delays, we got to el Buggar soon after 11 o'clock. Here we found the usual crowd of motors and horses. Started off about noon with Hext and Heathcote to reconnoitre south of the main wadi and the crossings. Had a most successful day on the whole and the thing has opened up a good deal. The preliminaries should be plain sailing. Got back to the motors about 4.45 p.m., and started home about 5.—18th October. Reconnaissance to el Buggar, as before. Very satisfactory. Sayer took two officers and did a lot of good work. Self and others busy with positions for transport, etc. Had a brand new Ford, and got home about 7.30."

The cavalry found these outings very tiring. They were out for thirty-six hours, during which time it was impossible to water the horses, and the men had to subsist on one full bottle and one refill from the water-carts. The Turks used to bring out light guns and lie in wait, in concealed positions, as though

they expected these reconnaissances, and when whole
brigades of cavalry had to cross wadis, where there
was only one possible crossing, they were swept with
shrapnel.

The heat, too, was very trying.   The country was
a stony desert, and there was no shade.   The sun
frequently registered 110 degrees in the shade (elsewhere), and " the flies were innumerable and persistent."

Colonel Preston says, " It was with a sigh of relief
that the troops saw the last of the motor-cars of the
' Royal Party ' disappear in a cloud of dust to the
north-west."   But he records with glee that the
Turks issued vainglorious boasts of battles won when
the cavalry followed the Royal Party, and these
reports find an echo in Ludendorff's Memories, for he
states that large masses of English cavalry advanced
on Beersheba so as to work round the left flank of
the Gaza Front at the end of August, and on the 2nd
and 18th October, but the " enterprise failed " in
each case.   Brigadier-General McNeil evidently took
part in two " battles " he knows not of.

Orders for the great attack were issued.   The plan
was that the XXth Corps would deliver the main
attack, capture Beersheba, and drive in the enemy's
left flank, while the Desert Mounted Corps would
make a wide enveloping movement on the outer
flank.   The XXIst Corps and the Royal Navy were
to occupy the attention of the enemy at Gaza during
the early stages of the battle, by a continuous bombardment, followed by an attack on Umbrella Hill
and the defences on the left, to the sea.   This attack
was to take place between the attack on Beersheba
and an attack on the Kauwukah System in front of

Tel el Sheria. The idea of the latter phase was to advance in a north-westerly direction, take the Turkish lines in reverse, and occupy the high ground north of Sheria by nightfall so as to get the use of the water supply.

A most interesting table was issued showing the

| DAY | DESERT MT. CORPS. | XX CORPS | XXI CORPS. |
|---|---|---|---|
| Z—15 | Transport allotted available. | Ditto. | Ditto. |
| Z—15 | Poled signal lines to Esani begun. | Poled signal lines to Esani begun. Water development and supply depots at Esani begun. | |
| Z—9 | Organisation of water supplies at Khalasa begun. | | |
| Z—6 | Ditto at Asluj. | | Systematic bombardment of Gaza defences begun. |
| Z—5 | Imara Railway Station completed. Pipe line and decauville alongside. | As Desert Corps. | As above. |
| Z—4 | | | As above. |
| Z—3 | Railway reaches Karm Station. Pipe line and decauville in line with railway. | As Desert Corps. | As above in increasing volume. Naval co-operation. |
| Z—2 | | | As above. Rails laid up to station site on W. Ghuzze. |
| Z—1 | Karm Station completed. | As Desert Corps. | As above. |
| Night Z—1/Z | Approach March. | Approach March. | Heavy bombardment. Naval co-operation. |
| Z | Attack. | Attack. | As above. |

progress demanded in preparation. It is scarcely
necessary to explain that the letter Z represents the
date of battle, and that the minus sign is used to show
the days previous to that date.

Secrecy was all-important. Sir Philip Chetwode
wrote a personal letter to his Divisional Commanders,
in which he says :

" While it is impossible to conceal the movements
of so large a force entirely, we may be able to deceive
the enemy as to the strength which we intend to put
against him.   I would ask you to give your personal
attention to every device by which enemy airmen
may be deceived, such as leaving your present bivouac
areas looking as much occupied as possible by leaving
tents standing and digging holes wherever you have
blanket shelters, not pitching Brigade Field Ambulances or showing their flags, and allowing no new
ground to be used whatever.   I would ask that the
troops of the 60th, 74th, and 53rd Divisions when
east of the Wadi should be kept concealed as much
as possible in wadis, gardens, near buildings, etc., and
that the strictest aeroplane discipline is enforced,
all ranks lying flat when the whistle is blown, and
remaining so till the ' carry on ' is sounded.   It is
particularly important that no motor lights, either
Ford or ambulance, should be shown east of the Wadi
until after Z day, and then as little as possible.

" Yours sincerely,
" PHILIP W. CHETWODE."

The secret was exceedingly well kept.   With the
right of the line in the air it was impossible to prevent
anyone getting round the British lines, or to control
the natives, and there is no doubt that spies did
penetrate the lines.

" It has come to my notice," writes Sir Philip Chet-

wode, on the 30th September, " that one division has
issued preliminary operation orders, containing the
most secret and confidential matters in connection
with the forthcoming operation.   These orders have
been issued broadcast to A.D.V.S., Divisional Train,
A.D.M.S., Corps Cavalry, etc.   I consider that this is
most unnecessary and, indeed, most dangerous, and
I direct that all copies, except those issued to Infantry
Brigade Commanders, and ' Q ' of Divisions, be at
once withdrawn.   There has been so much time to
consider and consult about operations that no orders,
preliminary or otherwise, should be issued until the
last moment.   Nothing in type or writing should be
outside the Divisional Headquarters (G.S. or Q
Offices), or at most Infantry Brigade Headquarters,
and no departmental officer should have anything
written in his possession until the last possible
moment."

Up to the last moment the Turks, and their German
advisers and commanders, believed that the attack
on Beersheba was a feint, with one infantry and one
cavalry division, and Colonel Powell Edwards tells
a curious story in connection with this :

" It was said that an officer of the Intelligence Staff
went out with the cavalry (on reconnaissance) and
took with him a haversack, containing amongst other
things a letter to his wife informing her that the
attack on Beersheba was a feint, and a five-pound note.
This officer got so near the Turkish lines as to have a
very smart run for his life, in the course of which he
cast away his haversack, which was duly bagged by
the Turk.   The letter alone might have looked
suspicious, but the fiver fixed it, and the information
that a feint attack would be made was duly circulated
by the Turkish intelligence."

The 229th, 230th, and Headquarters Groups were at Goz el Taire, about three miles west of Sheikh Nakhrur; the 231st Brigade Group was at Nakhrur; the artillery was at Goz el Taire. On the night 25th/26th of October the Division marched to Abu Sita. The artillery, except the 1st line waggons and A/117 Battery, did not move until three days later.

Every endeavour was made to carry out the Corps Commander's wishes : all tents and temporary shelters were left standing, incinerators were left burning. On arriving at a new camp, if the accommodation was insufficient, it was made to serve.

On the 26th/27th the Division continued the march to Gamli. It was now in the British Front Line area, and the 230th Brigade took over the defences from the 60th Division. Operation orders were issued, covering the preliminary instructions which had been circulated on the 13th of the month, and from which we make the following extracts :

" The XXth Corps, in co-operation with the Desert Mounted Corps, will attack and destroy the enemy's detachment at Beersheba. The Desert Mounted Corps will co-operate on the right of the XXth Corps, and attack the enemy's defences from the south-east to the north-east of Beersheba, and the town itself. The XXth Corps (less one division in reserve) will carry out the main attack.

" The 60th Division will attack the Beersheba works, on the right of the 74th Division, as far as the Khalasa-Beersheba Road, while the 53rd Division, with attached troops, will cover the left flank of the Corps, from a position on the general line between Kh. el Sufi and el Girheir.

" The 74th Division, and attached troops, will attack, capture, and consolidate the enemy main line between H29 (work Z8) and the Wadi Saba. The time for the commencement of the attack on the main line will depend on the progress of the wire cutting by the artillery, and the attack will be ordered to begin by G.O.C. 60th Division, after he is satisfied that the wire is sufficiently cut. . . .

" The following troops attached to the 74th Division will be known as ' Smith's ' Group, under the command of Brigadier-General C. L. Smith, V.C.—the Imperial Camel Brigade (less two companies), two battalions of the 158th Infantry Brigade. The rôle of these troops is to hold the ground from the Wadi Saba . . . to the right of the 53rd Division, to deal with any counter-stroke against the left of the 74th Division, to prevent the transfer of troops to reinforce the enemy, on the front of attack of the 60th and 74th Divisions, by holding the enemy in his trenches north of the Wadi Saba."

The Instructions, after dealing with the approach march, divided the attack into two phases : a preliminary attack on some advance works known as 1070, which were on the 60th Division Front, and the attack on the main line. It also provided for a subsidiary attack north of the Wadi should the enemy still hold on to that position after the capture of the main defences.

The Division remained at Gamli. But on the 25th of October the 158th Infantry Brigade, 53rd Division, with two machine gun companies, the 266th R.F.A. Brigade, and a heavy battery, had taken up an outpost line from Goz el Basal to the north, covering railway construction which was being pushed forward in the direction of Imara. The Brigadier's instructions were that one mounted brigade, commencing with one from the Australian Mounted Division, would

be to the east of the Wadi Ghuzze by day, with strong
patrols thrown out on the line el Buggar, Hills 720,
630, 550.   By night this mounted brigade returned
to its bivouac, after leaving standing patrols at
Khasif, Pt. 510 (Abu Shawish Road), Dammoth.

" It is of the greatest importance that the working
parties on the railway construction should not be
molested by enemy shell fire.   You will, therefore,
be prepared at all times by day to support the mounted
brigade in maintaining the line indicated above, if
necessary with infantry and artillery. . . . In case of
necessity the 53rd Division, at Hiseia and Shellal,
will support any offensive movement it may be
necessary for you to make, and the Desert Mounted
Corps has been asked to do the same."

Orders were then issued for the whole of the 53rd
Division to move east to occupy the el Buggar line
previously held by the mounted brigade.   For this
purpose the 229th Brigade was attached to the 53rd
Division.   The move was to take place on the night
27th/28th.

At 7.40 a.m. on the 27th it was reported that the
enemy was attacking the outpost line between Pts.
630 and 720.   The attack was delivered by a force of
over 3,000 men of all arms, and it is probable that the
enemy intended to occupy the ridge as a permanent
position : it commanded excellent observation over
the country as far as the Wadi Ghuzze, and completely
masked movement, to the west of it, from the Beersheba lines.   The small garrison on Pt. 720 was overwhelmed, after a gallant fight; the squadron of
Middlesex Yeomanry on 630 occupied a cruciform
trench, which had been sited by the Australians, and
held out.   The 53rd Division and the 229th Brigade

moved off at once to support the Yeomanry, but, fearing that the infantry would not be in time, the 3rd Australian Light Horse Brigade was also despatched to the scene. The line was held, and when the infantry arrived, they found that the enemy had retired. The only alteration of plans occasioned by this raid was that the outpost line was occupied by the 53rd Division by daylight instead of at night.

The artillery arrived at Gamli on the 28th ; and on the 29th the whole Division moved forward to covered positions at Khasif. The 229th Brigade returned to General Girdwood's command on the 30th, when two battalions, the Devons and Royal Scots Fusiliers, crossed the Wadi Saba as darkness fell, relieved a Squadron of the Westminster Dragoons, and extended in a line of outposts to cover the crossing of the Division. Positions had to be found in absolute silence, and the movement was exceedingly well carried out. This advance guard was followed by the remaining battalions of the 229th Brigade and two battalions of the 158th Brigade, which extended the covering line ; the 158th Brigade battalions were part of Smith's Group.

The Division then crossed the Wadi and deployed on the battle positions, the 231st Brigade on the right and the 230th Brigade on the left. The artillery crossed at midnight, and was in position by 3.15 a.m. along the Wadi Abushar.

# CHAPTER V

## THIRD BATTLE OF GAZA

### The Capture of Beersheba

GENERAL GIRDWOOD's orders for the battle covered the following points:

" The attack will consist of two phases : 1st Phase, attack on 1070 works ; 2nd Phase, attack on the main line.

" 1st Phase : The attack on the 1070 works will be carried out by the 181st Brigade, 60th Division. The time at which the 1st Phase will commence will be decided by the G.O.C. 60th Division. This operation will commence by registration and wire cutting by the guns of the 60th Division, and by registration and slow bombardment of works Z15 and Z16 by the 268th F.A. Brigade, 74th Division. This operation is calculated to last one hour.

" During this period the 231st and 230th Brigades will co-operate as follows : A screen of infantry, accompanied by machine guns, will be pushed forward and will perform a double rôle—(a) assist in the advance of the 60th Division on the 1070 works ; (b) cover the deployment in depth of the remainder of each brigade.

" The 231st will conform to the advance of the 181st Brigade, and will endeavour to occupy the tributary wadis of Whale Wadi, and will engage by fire the enemy trenches Z16, Z15, and Z7.

" The 230th Brigade will occupy the best available ground along the 960 Ridge. . . .

" Immediately the 1070 System has been captured,

three 18-pounder batteries of the 74th Division will
move forward to within wire-cutting distance of Z7
and Z6. . . . The remainder of the artillery of the
74th Division will engage the enemy trenches Z7, Z6,
Z5, along their entire front.

" While the three 18-pounder batteries are moving
forward, the assaulting infantry, accompanied by
machine guns, will take every opportunity of advancing to the most favourable positions from which to
commence the assault. The time the assault will
commence will be decided by G.O.C. 60th Division.

" The 231st Brigade will conform to the advance
of the 181st Brigade, on its right ; similarly the 230th
Brigade will conform to the advance of the 231st.

" When the main objectives of the Division have
been captured, and should the enemy still hold on to
the trenches north of the Wadi Saba, the G.O.C. 74th
Division will issue orders for an attack to be made
on that system of trenches. This attack will be
carried out by the 230th Brigade, 74th Division,
from the south of the Wadi Saba in a northerly direction, while the 158th Brigade, 53rd Division, which
will come under the command of the G.O.C. 74th
Division, will attack on the north side of the Wadi
Saba, from the direction of el Hathira."

For the attack of the 74th Division the 268th and
44th F.A. Brigades supported the 231st Infantry
Brigade, and the 117th, 266th (attached), and the
Hong Kong Mountain Battery (attached) supported
the 230th Infantry Brigade. But, in the first phase,
the 268th F.A. Brigade assisted the 60th Division.
The allotment of ammunition was about 200 rounds
per gun.

For the last five days a heavy bombardment had
been maintained on Gaza, and during the night

marches of the Division the horizon flickered, as
though with summer lightning.  Now, still listening
to the distant sound, the men of the 74th Division
waited for the dawn and the hour of attack.  But from
Asluj the Anzac Mounted Division, followed by the
Australian Mounted Divisions, rode through the cold
night to envelop the flank of the unconscious Turks.

At 5.55 a.m. the artillery opened.  At 7 o'clock
the dust caused by the bombardment was so intense
that firing had to cease to allow observing officers
to see the targets.  It was then resumed, and at 8.30
the 181st Brigade advanced and captured the 1070
works with little trouble.

The 231st Brigade, with the 24th Royal Welsh
Fusiliers on the right and the 25th on the left, con-
formed, followed by the 230th Brigade, with the Buffs
on the right and the Norfolks on the left.  At once all
battalions came under heavy shrapnel fire, very
accurately placed.  Fortunately the country was
broken by a number of wadis which afforded occasional protection.  Progress was slow, and not too
easy ; the hills were all of different heights, and
seemed to run in all directions, which made it hard to
keep on the correct line of advance ; it was just a
desert of small hills, rocks, and stones, and as the sun
mounted in the sky, so the heat increased.  The 231st
Brigade edged too much to the right, and the gap had
to be filled by support companies of the Buffs.  In
some places the descent into wadis was made down
a narrow cleft in the rocks, which added to the difficulties of keeping direction.

While the 60th Division consolidated the 1070
position, captured by the 181st Brigade, the attacking
battalions of the 74th Division edged forward, and,

BATTLE OF BEERSHEBA. PATIENTS LEAVING THE ADVANCED DRESSING-STATION.

on the other side of the Wadi Saba, Smith's Group watched the flank.

As the infantry drew nearer to their objectives, machine gun fire was directed on them as well as artillery. This was the most trying period of the battle. Troops appearing on the successive crests met a hail of well-directed, low-flying bullets, casualties increased, the advance became slower, and each sky-line more fatal as the distance from enemy machine gunners decreased. Men wriggled forward lying flat on their stomachs. By 10.40 a.m. the 231st Brigade was about 600 yards from the Turkish lines, and the 230th about 1,000 yards.

Relief from the strain was soon forthcoming. Four batteries came forward to wire-cutting distance, and the whole of the artillery commenced to bombard the main Turkish Position. The 209th, 210th, and one section No. 4 Machine Gun Companies worked well forward, and directed a hail of bullets on the Turkish Front. Many good targets presented themselves on both the 75th and 60th Divisional fronts, and on the Smith Group front, which was covered by a section of No. 4 Company so effectively that the enemy was unable to interfere with the advance from these flank positions.

The main Turkish trenches were now seen to be cut in white limestone rock on the far side of a deep gully, with wire, some 70 to 100 yards in front of them. There was a pause in the proceedings, while the artillery battered the enemy wire and trenches. It was terrifically hot—the sun, the bare earth, the stones, everything seemed to throw out an equal heat.

Sir J. S. M. Shea, commanding the 60th Division,

informed General Girdwood that he thought the wire
on his objectives would be cut at noon, and received
the reply that the 74th Division was prepared to move
as soon as the 60th was ready, although, as far as
could be seen, the wire was untouched (troops had
to cut it themselves).

At 12.15 p.m. the artillery increased to rapid fire,
and, under an overhead stream of bullets from the
machine gunners, battalions advanced to the assault
and soon disappeared in a fog of dust.

The positions were carried with little trouble ; here
and there the enemy stood to meet the bayonet, but
the majority fled.   The 24th Welsh Regiment passed
through the captured trenches and took up a
defensive line some 2,000 yards beyond, while the
attacking battalions consolidated the positions they
had won.

General Girdwood was now in considerable doubt
as to whether the trenches north of the Wadi Saba
were still occupied by the enemy.   Reports kept
coming in that they were empty, but finally the
patrols from Smith's Group reported that they had
been fired on, and the 230th Brigade came under long-
range fire from that direction.  The Corps Commander
had stipulated that this system was not to be attacked
without orders from the Corps, but General Girdwood
decided that it was most necessary to do something at
once.   He therefore asked Sir Philip Chetwode for
permission to attack with the 230th Brigade, supported
by the two 158th Brigade battalions with Smith's
Group.   Permission was given, but the 158th Brigade
reported that the two battalions could not be ready
until 8.30 p.m.   General Girdwood decided to attack
without them.

The attack started at 7 o'clock. The Suffolks and Sussex, who were to carry out the assault, failed to get in touch, and the Sussex took the whole system of works by themselves. Very slight resistance was offered by a few snipers, one of whom knifed an officer in the thigh. Three of them were bayoneted, and about a dozen prisoners, all wounded, were taken, and an abandoned battery of four guns discovered.

An outpost line was put out on the Fara–Beersheba Road, which was relieved in the early morning by the 181st Brigade.

Meanwhile the Mounted Troops had been having some trouble in crossing the plain—swept by Turkish fire from Tel el Saba, which was not captured until late in the afternoon—on the far side of Beersheba ; but farther north the 2nd Brigade Australian Light Horse was astride the Hebron Road by 1 p.m. About 6 o'clock in the evening the 4th Australian Light Horse galloped over several lines of trenches and entered the town.

The 27th Turkish Division, defending Beersheba, was an Arab formation, and did not prove itself to be very good.

. . . . .

The strict orders that no papers, letters, or diaries were to be taken into the field were rigidly adhered to, and impressions, written hot on the battle, are impossible to get. Amongst others Brigadier-General McNeil's interesting diary went into store, but when he succumbed to malaria in December, he wrote down an account of what he had observed, from which the following is extracted :

" 30th October.—Marched 6.30 a.m. to our battle

positions. It was most impressive, the columns upon columns of infantry and guns, moving relentlessly forward to their appointed positions, and it was wonderful how silently it was done. All plans worked out exactly, and my brigade was clear of the wadi crossing by midnight, and by 1.30 or 2 a.m. all the artillery was in position. A truly wonderful performance.

" 31st October.—At dawn we pushed out advanced posts with Lewis guns, on to the heights in front, and the attacking battalions deployed ready for the attack. After daylight the enemy did a good bit of shelling, and the Suffolks had about forty casualties while waiting in support. Some of the batteries in the Abushar Wadi got it pretty hot also. . . . Soon a report came to say that 1070 had fallen. It was now getting near our turn, as the attack was designed to be in succession from the right. Our attacking battalions, lying out on the high ridges, were suffering a good deal from shell fire, and about 11.30 General Girdwood called me up on the phone and suggested going straight on, as being the cheapest alternative. I agreed, and the assault was ordered for 12.25 p.m. By 1 o'clock all the objectives were taken and the enemy in full flight towards Beersheba. About 3.30 I rode forward to make a personal reconnaissance. It was difficult to find out if the high ground and trenches north of the Wadi Saba were held in strength or not, and I so informed Division. I next got verbal orders on the phone to attack this position at 6 p.m. Later General Girdwood called up and said it was postponed until 7 p.m., and all artillery programme arranged for that hour, but the 158th Brigade had said they could not be ready to co-operate until 8.30—would I go alone ? It would save altering the artillery programme, etc., etc. I decided to do so, knowing that Jarvis and Sayer, commanding the Suffolks and Sussex respectively, would much sooner do so, especially as a strange brigade attacking the same objective in the dark at right angles to you is a doubtful pleasure. . . . We soon had a report that they had captured and made good all the ground north of the Wadi Saba up to the Beersheba Road. Leaving two battalions on outpost, I sent the Norfolks and Buffs down to the wadi, to where there was some water.

" 1st *November*.—Soon after daylight broke I rode forward to the captured line. Inspected the Turkish trenches and was amazed at their strength—a much stiffer proposition than we had thought from the aeroplane photographs, and the various reconnaissances. The wire was poor, and not completed, but in front of my brigade no gaps had been cut by the artillery fire, which was extraordinary, considering the intense bombardment. After talking to the C.O.'s and Company Commanders, it appeared that our plan of attack, so carefully rehearsed, had worked out to the letter. I had made my intelligence officer make a sand model of the trenches and ground in front of them as well as he could from air photographs, and everyone had studied this and got the ground and plan of attack well into their heads. . . . For a long time beforehand I had practised the night march and attack after dawn over ground carefully chosen for its resemblance to that at Beersheba. The Norfolks' change of direction, and flank attack, on the last enemy work, Z5, came off like a set piece field day. . . . I sent in several names for immediate reward, and was given four military medals (the ribbons) to present the very next day.

" 3rd *November*.—Early start, and we marched north some five or six miles, and that night we found a sector of the outpost line, relieving a battalion of the 229th Brigade. Very hot, and a khamsin brewing.

" 4th *November*.—Khamsin in full swing—very bad

—all ranks on half gallon of water—orders from Division wisely forbidding washing or shaving. . . . Good deal of shelling on the Beersheba Road—troops moving up drawing the fire."

.    .    .    .    .

The second movement of Sir E. Allenby's plan of battle, designed to draw the Turkish reserves towards Gaza, now took place. We know that up to the last moment of the attack on Beersheba the Turks and their German advisers believed that Gaza was the British objective, and so it was, but not by a frontal attack ; Sir E. Allenby, however, wished them to continue in their belief that his main force would be launched in that direction. He accordingly attacked the coastal defences of Gaza on the morning of the 2nd November.

No date had been fixed for this operation, but a bombardment was started on the 27th October, in which two 60-pounder batteries, five and a half 6-inch howitzer batteries, one 8-inch howitzer battery, the artillery of the 52nd, 54th, and 75th Divisions, H.M.S. *Grafton*, the monitors Nos. 15, 29, 31, and 32, the destroyers *Staunch* and *Comet*, and the river gunboats *Ladybird* and *Amphis* took part.

The ground over which the attack took place consists of sand dunes, rising in places to 150 feet. This sand is very deep and heavy. All the objectives were taken, from Umbrella Hill (2,000 yards south-west of the town) to Sheikh Hasan (2,500 yards north-west of the town). The whole of the Gaza positions were now threatened, and the success could be exploited on the first sign of any withdrawal on the part of the enemy.

# CHAPTER VI

## THIRD BATTLE OF GAZA

### The Capture of the Sheria Position

IMMEDIATELY after the capture of Beersheba the 53rd Division had moved to the north of the town, and was soon in touch with the Turk. Apparently the presence of this division in that area convinced the Turks that more than a feint was intended, and they immediately collected portions of four divisions to oppose the Welshmen. The 53rd became involved in some very heavy fighting, and remained on the right flank of the Corps throughout the subsequent actions.

The original intention had been that the 53rd should make a frontal attack on the Kauwukah System, while the 74th and 60th took the whole of the fortified area in flank and reverse. The plan had to be modified. The 60th was ordered to attack the Kauwukah System, and the 74th had the original task of two divisions.

The water supply at Beersheba was disappointing, time was necessary for its development, and ammunition had to be accumulated; with this necessary and arduous work to be accomplished, there came a sirocco which blew steadily for three days: the thrust on the Turkish flank could not be delivered until the 6th November.

The 10th Division had come up on the left and occupied the Abu Irgeig line, and on the 2nd Novem-

ber the 229th Brigade moved forward and took up a
position between the 10th and 53rd Divisions, on the
high ground north of Kh. al Muweileh.

On the 4th the Division moved forward, the outpost line was held by units from each brigade, and
orders for the attack on Sheria were issued.

The 60th Division slipped in between the 74th
and the 10th, in position for the frontal attack on
Kauwukah ; the Yeomanry Division moved from the
extreme left to come into line, when the attack started,
on the right of the 74th ; the 53rd stood fast on the
right flank.

The intention expressed in General Girdwood's
orders was to capture the Sheria water supply, and
the enemy works south of Sheria, and the attack was
to be pressed with the utmost determination and
rapidity. " The 53rd Division will extend its left so
as to occupy the general line Kuweifeh–Rijn el Dhib.
The Yeomanry Mounted Division will close the gap
between the 53rd and 74th which will be caused when
these two divisions advance. The 60th Division will
attack the works of the Kauwukah System west of
the railway." The objective of the 74th Division
was the railway line, and the 229th Brigade, on the
left, was to direct the attack. The 230th Brigade
was to be echeloned on the right of the 229th ; and
the 231st echeloned on the right rear of the 230th,
with the special rôle of protecting the northern flank
of the division by seizing the high ground south of
the Wadi Sheria, and deny the enemy the opportunity
of counter-attack on the right flank. Advancing on
a bearing of 302, the first objective was the works
V18 to V45. The 231st Brigade, following about 800
yards in rear of the 230th, was to occupy the right of

this line of trenches, refusing its own right, and joining up with the Yeomanry. In the further advance of the 229th Brigade, the 230th and 231st would make good the high ground to the north, and be prepared for any enemy counter-attack against the right flank of the 229th Brigade. Finally, when the 60th Division had captured the Kauwukah Defences, the 229th and 230th Brigades would be prepared to advance against Sheria and seize the high ground to the north of that place to protect the water supply.

Everything depended on the 74th Division. The advance had to be made over very open country, against strongly held positions, which bristled with machine guns.

At 5 a.m. on the 6th November the 229th Brigade passed through the outpost lines, with the 14th Black Watch and one section No. 4 Company Machine Guns on the right, the 12th Somersets, with one section machine guns, on the left, the Royal Scots in support, and the Devons in reserve.

This battle is remarkable for the speed with which battalions advanced. The nearest group of trenches to the 229th Brigade was 4,000 yards from the starting-point, but their line of advance was across the front of trenches that were engaged almost at once by the 230th Brigade on their right.

" The nature of the country over which the advance was made throughout the day," says Brigadier-General Hoare, " is worthy of remark, in view of the fact that in its earlier and more difficult phases, position after position was assaulted by the brigade, which swept along at a great pace, and gave little or no time for artillery preparation. The country is of a gentle undulating character, very open and bare, with a stony surface ; throughout the length of the battlefield the attacking infantry found no cover of any sort between them and each successive enemy position. The Turkish trenches were deep and well concealed, and afforded the defenders ample cover."

The advance of the 229th Brigade was pressed forward with great determination in the face of heavy rifle, machine gun, and artillery fire, much of it taking them in enfilade from the right—until the enemy was attacked by the 230th Brigade, with the 15th Suffolks on the right and the 16th Sussex on the left. The latter two battalions engaged the enemy in works V38, 39, 45, soon after they passed through the out-post lines.

Dealing first with the action of the 230th Brigade, which, as has been explained, was the first to come in contact with the enemy, we find them, after over-running an advanced work, engaged in a fierce fire fight with the section of enemy works at right angles to the Wadi Union. The Suffolks suffered very heavily, all officers of one company were casualties, but they captured the work named V45 and then had to reorganise. The Sussex manoeuvred in field practice style, sections advancing under covering fire, and crept ever closer to the enemy. The Turks did not wait for the bayonet, but gave in : over thirty dead and wounded Turks were found, and seventy prisoners taken.

The taking of these positions and the process of reorganisation took time, and the brigade was now some way behind the 229th. There seems to have been not only a gap, but a certain mixing of units on the left flank. One company of the Sussex followed the 229th Brigade, while some parties of Devons

AN ADVANCED DRESSING-STATION AT THE BATTLE OF SHERIA

attached themselves to the 230th Brigade. Reorganised and steadied, the two battalions now crossed the Wadi Union, support companies extending all the time to the left to try to get touch with the 229th Brigade ; they were also a long way in advance of the 231st Brigade, which had become involved in some very heavy fighting with unexpected works on the extreme flank of the Turkish position. The Sussex obtained touch with their company under Captain G. H. Powell Edwards, who had stuck to the 229th Brigade.

Over the crest of the ridge Captain Powell Edwards observed the smoke of guns, obviously firing at the 229th Brigade. He sent a Lewis Gun section and two rifle sections to a position from which these guns might be engaged. A Sergeant Johnson had, apparently, located the guns, and took command of the whole party ; he led them with great skill, working a Lewis gun himself, and emptying a magazine into the battery. The Turks, surprised, and completely overwhelmed by the fire of this party, surrendered, and three officers with twenty-five other ranks were taken prisoner.

Soon after this exploit the enemy delivered a determined counter-attack on the battalion and drove the company covering the captured guns back into the Wadi Union. Lieutenant Hopkins rallied his platoon, and a platoon of Devons, and retook the high ground at the point of the bayonet. He then found that the enemy had brought up teams of oxen, and were making an attempt to hitch up and withdraw the battery. He promptly charged with his platoon, pistolled the team men himself, and retook the guns. A position was taken up beyond the guns, and further counter-attacks were beaten off with the aid of the artillery, which now came into effective action.

The Suffolks, with their right flank in the air, had also been heavily counter-attacked, but stood their ground until the 231st Brigade, having overcome the resistance on their front, sent up the Welsh Regiment and Shropshires to relieve them.

Meanwhile the Black Watch, on the right, and the Somersets, on the left, had swept forward on the 229th Brigade front at a great speed. They encountered heavy artillery fire, and were raked by machine guns on their right flank, but carried all the enemy advance works, and the Somersets by skilful use of Lewis guns captured a Turkish battery. They were now faced with the main lines, including a strongly fortified area round the Cactus Garden, and the enemy had an uninterrupted field of fire of from 400 to 500 yards. As had been expected, there was considerable opposition at this point, but by 8.30 it was overcome.

The battalions were very much intermixed, and reorganisation was necessary. When the advance was resumed, less opposition was encountered, although artillery fire, from the north of Sheria, was very severe. At about 3.15 p.m. the Brigade delivered a final attack on the railway, simultaneously with the 60th Division attack on the Kauwukah System. In the course of the fight a field battery, in the act of limbering up to escape from the 60th Division, was attacked and captured by the Black Watch.

The 60th Division then reorganised to advance on Sheria.

Orders were issued (about 4.30 p.m.) for the 74th

Division to hold a line astride the Wadi Sheria, facing north-east and in touch with the 60th Division, to the north of Tel Sheria ; this was to be carried out by the 231st Brigade on the right, and the 230th on the left. But before evacuating Sheria Station, the enemy succeeded in setting fire to a large ammunition dump south of the station, which commenced to blow up just before the attack of the 60th Division was about to be launched. The fire raged fiercely and lit up the whole country in the vicinity of the bridge (it was dusk), so that it was impossible to advance until 3.30 a.m. on the 7th. After a stiff fight Tel Sheria was taken about 4.30 a.m., and a line thrown out to the north of the town.

At this time (dawn) the 10th Division stormed and captured the Hareira Redoubt, a work of great natural strength and defended by numerous machine guns.

The Turkish left was now definitely broken. On the right of the XXnd Corps the 53rd Division had repulsed furious counter-attacks with the greatest gallantry, and had contributed materially to the success of the British Army. And the all-important water supply was now in Sir E. Allenby's hands, with a way opened for the cavalry. The Anzac Mounted Division rode through on the right of the 74th Division, and harried the Turks until dark, fighting several sharp actions. The Australian Division sent a dismounted brigade to assist the 60th Division in widening the gap by driving a desperate force of Turks off the high ground over-looking the Wadi Sheria, but it was not accomplished until dusk, when it was too late for the mounted troops to operate that day.

8

But away on the left of the British line Gaza was found by the XXIst Corps to be evacuated on the morning of the 7th.    The Imperial Service Cavalry Brigade immediately rode through, followed by the 52nd Division.    (This cavalry brigade was raised and equipped by some of the ruling Indian Princes, and formed part of Army Troops.)

On the morning of the 8th November the pursuit was taken up in force by the Anzac and Australian Mounted Divisions, and the 60th Division.    The Australians obtained touch before nightfall with the leading cavalry of the XXIst Corps about Beit Hanun, south of the Wadi Hesi.

Giving the Turks no rest on the 9th, the pursuit slowed down on the 10th and 11th, when a scorching sirocco blew from the Arabian Desert.    The enemy made a desperate stand on the 13th, from el Kubeibeh to Beit Jebrin, having been flung back from the coast by the rapid advance of the XXIst Corps.    The battle-field was the Maritime Plain, with Beit Jebrin on the foothills.    The open, rolling country was dotted with villages surrounded by mud walls, with plantations of trees outside the walls.    The line Katrah-Mughar, held by the enemy, in a desperate endeavour to resist the turning movement against his right flank, is on a line of heights.    The position was taken by the 52nd Division, assisted by a dashing charge of mounted troops across the plain from the north.    It resulted in the capture of Junction Station, and the splitting of the enemy's army into two separate parts, which retired north and east (on Jerusalem) respectively.

.        .        .        .        .

The 74th Division did not take part in this advance, but after clearing up the battlefield, in the course of

which 293 enemy dead were buried, marched back
to Irgeig on the 9th, Karm on the 10th, the dust storm
being so bad that battalions did not know where they
were, Shellal on the 17th, and Deir el Belah on the 18th.

The first two battles fought by the Division are
remarkable for the dash shown by the infantry, and
the determined support they received from other
arms. At the Battle of Beersheba the machine
gunners revealed the greatest determination, and
devotion to duty ; and the 229th and 231st Trench
Mortar Batteries were no less dogged and persistent.
The artillery did fine work in this action.

In the Sheria battle the advance was started before
it was light, and in the earlier stages the artillery
could not give support : the maps were bad, the
ground unknown, and, apart from positions that had
been located by aeroplane, the Turks had hastily constructed other trenches. Batteries, however, pushed
forward and gave valuable help to the infantry in the
attempts of the enemy against the right flank of the
Division. The advance by the infantry in the first
stages was only supported by machine gunners, who
worked under distinct disadvantage ; they had only
a few hours for preparation, the country was familiar
in nature, but no reconnaissance had been possible,
and the maps were not contoured. Also the advance
was over five miles, and all the mules had been shot at
the Beersheba battle, so camels had to be utilised for
carrying ammunition (the latter did not prove to be
any disadvantage). But sections hung on to the
infantry, and when the light improved, supported
them with overhead fire most effectively directed. In
both battles the part played by machine gunners was
largely instrumental to the success gained.

The Administrative branch had worked with the
greatest smoothness. On the 2nd November the
229th Brigade moved to the outpost line before
the convoy came up, but, owing to a large number of
horses having been watered at the pools in the Wadi
Saba, sufficient water had been saved for the Brigade
Group to take their supply with them. On two
occasions horse water was not sent up and had to be
found locally, but the convoys with drinking water
always arrived on time. The Battle of Sheria, coming
on top of the sirocco, was very exhausting for the
troops.

Extracts from Brigadier-General McNeil's diary
give us some idea of the difficulties experienced by all
battalions.

"5th November.—Did reconnaissance in morning
and C.O.'s went out to do ditto, according to the plan
of attack to-morrow. But a wire at 3 ordering all
Brigadiers to Headquarters, and plan all changed.
Very hurried verbal orders given, and I rushed back
to get it out to C.O.'s before dark. Poor devils had
no chance of reconnaissance of new ground, but all
swore they understood the rough idea, and off they
went to get things moving, as we calculated it would
take all night getting into position. . . . Finally at
3.30 a.m. all were reported in position, and I then rode
forward to my first battalion Headquarters, under a
cliff at the bend of a wadi, not far from the enemy
advance work called V46, which the outpost battalion
were supposed to rush during the night, so paving
the way for the main attack at dawn. The outposts
(Buffs), however, had no earthly chance of doing so,
as this meant advancing their line after taking it up
some 700 yards, and they had only time to get about
300 to 400 yards on their way before the Suffolks and

Sussex went through them.   However, to my mind,
and I really think I'm right, it was better thus, as the
fall of their advanced work in the very early hours
would have put the whole Turkish line on the alert.
As it was, nothing big in the way of 'strafe' occurred
till dawn—or just before—and then matters went so
quickly that his line was broken before he had rubbed
his eyes or sipped his morning coffee.   There was no
wire in front of the Turkish trenches along the whole
objective of the division, and no wonder they considered it was unnecessary.   They had a wonderful
field of fire, rolling downs of mud-baked clay, without
cover for a rabbit, except here and there a shallow
wadi parallel to the defence, but at long intervals.
There was, however, a good deep main wadi, Wadi
Union, which was my right boundary, and it ran up
parallel to my attack the whole way.   It was of
inestimable value for ammunition supply, evacuation
of wounded, movement of supports and reserves,
etc.   I had to ride up it for the last part of the way
when I galloped forward to my forward battle headquarters, as I found the top was distinctly unhealthy
for any one, even then, especially for a mounted outfit.
According to plan my attacking battalions advanced
over this wadi, where it curled west, behind the enemy
trenches, and occupied the high ground immediately
north of it, and here for the rest of the day, until
pretty well late afternoon, we withstood some furious
counter-attacks.   I then got orders to prolong my
line to the left, and the Norfolks did so, but the map
was absolutely out here, and they went as far forward
as they could, and quite enough to the left; but
Sheria Station and village (so-called) were still in
enemy hands, and no one could advance over the long
incline—1½ miles at least—to the Wadi Sheria until
dusk, when I sent off the Buffs to take up an impossible
outpost line, as it turned out, beyond the Wadi
Sheria.   They were to be sure to get touch with the

60th Division on their left, so I forbade them to go
beyond the wadi until they did get touch.   This they
never did, though Toby Buxton was out literally all
night trying to do so.   The fact was that the 60th
Division never got Sheria that night.   I had myself
reported three columns of Turkish infantry marching
back into it at dusk!   There was one amusing
incident in an otherwise one-horse night—the
Adjutant of the Buffs led the water camels of his
battalion to where their left flank might have been
as ordered, i.e. two miles inside the Turkish lines,
captured one Turk, and came back with convoy
complete !

"*7th November*.—Spent a very cold and disturbed
night on the ridge, and at dawn found a thick fog over
the whole battle zone.   It soon cleared away, and I
rode down to the outpost line which was being
slightly shelled from the north-east.   They had had
a hell of a night wandering about in the dark, but had
taken up very sound positions at dawn, from which
the Turks could be seen trekking away in all directions
—exactly like the Boers in South Africa."

Christians Awake! Salute the Happy Morn!
December 25th 1917 3 Am.

# CHAPTER VII

## THE AFFAIR AT EL FOKA

Enemy Resistance—The roads—The uncertain position—Major Rees'
adventure—The position untenable—Hill 1750—The Devons attack.

IT soon became clear that the hope, at one time
sanguine, of rounding up the Gaza portion of the
Turkish Army would not be fulfilled. It was then a
question of pursuit, and the difficult nature of the
country made itself felt.

On the 10th November the cavalry were thirty-five
miles from railhead. The Turks had blown up all
the bridges and culverts of their railway, and the only
means of supply was by motor-lorries and camels,
along the road from Gaza to Junction Station. All
available transport was, therefore, concentrated on
this line; the XXIst Corps left the 54th Division at
Gaza, and took its transport to help the other two
divisions (52nd and 75th).

The question of water was serious. Already portions
of units of the Australian Division in the Shephalah
had, on one occasion, advanced three days and four
nights without watering their horses (*The Desert
Mounted Corps*, Lt.-Colonel R. E. Preston), and the
Anzac Division, although in the better-watered
coastal area, had been two days without rations for
their horses. Each delay necessary for resting, feed-
ing, and watering the cavalry gave the Turks time to
collect their scattered forces and organise resistance.
They marched stolidly on, destroying all the water-
lifting machinery as they went.

Owing to these conditions of water and transport, the XXth Corps was, therefore, left out of the pursuit. The 60th Division was withdrawn from Huj, and concentrated about Sheria and Hareira, and later marched to Gaza ; while the 74th and 10th Divisions occupied areas north of Deir el Belah. The 53rd Division remained about Kuweilfeh, covering the approaches of Beersheba, from the one road over the Judean Hills through Hebron. On November 18th this division, the XXth Corps cavalry (Westminster Dragoons), the 91st Heavy Battery, and the 11th Light Armoured Motor Battery, came under G.H.Q. orders, and were known as Mott's Detachment.

Between November 19th and 22nd the 60th Division moved up to Junction Station, under the XXIst Corps, and proceeded to Latron the next day. Between the 24th and 27th it relieved the 52nd and 75th Divisions on the front between Soba and Beit Izza.

The Anzac Division had chased the right wing of the Turkish Army until it scrambled to the other side of the River Auja, while the yeomanry had driven the Turkish left wing into the Judean mountains and pursued it through the Vale of Ajalon. In an attempt to cut the Jerusalem-Nablus road, the yeomanry penetrated as far as the village of Beitunia, and the 75th and 52nd Divisions reached Neby Samwil, farther south. But the enemy's resistance had stiffened, some parts of the line were forced back, and it became clear that more deliberate methods of attack were necessary for the capture of Jerusalem.

The broadest defiles which lead into the Judean Mountains are those of Beth Horon, the Wadi Ali, and the Wadi Surar. Of the last two, the present high road to Jerusalem goes through the one and the railway the other. All the defiles are difficult roads to travel, leading frequently up the loose shingle beds of mountain torrents. Water is scarce, and the sun beats down on the limestone until the heat rises in suffocating waves from the ground. But the rainy season was approaching, and black mud lay in the bottom of the ravines, or else they were so many torrents.

The first essential was to improve communications, as the only road suitable for all traffic in the rainy season was the Latron–Jerusalem Road, the high road. A good beginning had been made by the XXIst Corps with the Beit Likia–Biddu track, which was made passable by field artillery, though more work was required before sufficient batteries could be brought up for an attack. A new road was commenced from Latron towards Beit Likia, and from Enab to Kubeibeh, while the existing roads and tracks were greatly improved at the cost of much labour. But traffic became very difficult after a few hours' rain.

The 74th Division started to march north on the 23rd November, when battalions bivouacked east of Gaza and received " tin helmets." Troops were able to visit the Turkish positions at Ali el Muntar, and found that the trenches had not been much injured by the bombardment.

On the 25th the Division marched to Mejdal ; on the 26th to Nahr Sukereir ; on the 27th to the Junction Station ; on the 28th to Latron. The march was uneventful ; but the change from soft sand to hard road played havoc with the feet of the men.

The 10th Division completed the march to Latron between the 27th and 30th.

BIVOUAC IN THE JUDEAN HILLS.

On the 23rd November, just before the XXth Corps took over the line, the Yeomanry Division, holding Foka-Tahta-Suffa, were heavily attacked by the enemy, and the 268th F.A. Brigade, which had just arrived at Latron, was sent up to Hill 1764 to assist in holding the attack. After considerable fighting Foka was given up, and a line was occupied along a wooded ridge between that village and Tahta (Lower Beth Horon).

The 74th Division had some rough fighting before them in a country of terraced hills, of narrow valleys between steep precipitous sided hills, and of ridges like walls. The march from Junction Station to Latron had been up hill all the way, and, although only seven miles, the troops had taken four and a half hours to cover it.

The 231st Brigade arrived at 12.30 p.m., but was on the move again (less artillery) at 7 o'clock, with orders to march to Beit Anan, via the high road to Enab. At the latter place it was found impossible to proceed any farther with the wheeled transport owing to the roughness of the road and the steep gradients. The Brigade proceeded, less transport, along the track to Beit Annan, which was reached about 4.30 a.m. on the 29th. (When studying the map, it is as well to remember that roads marked " Ancient Road " and " Roman Road " were frequently places along which one might go with difficulty in single file. The Romans would never have gained renown as road makers if they had been judged by their work, as it stands to-day, in the Judean Mountains.)

On arrival the Shropshires were ordered to take over the line held by the 8th Mounted Brigade, from

Beit Dukka to Kh. Jufna.  By this time the men
were thoroughly exhausted, having marched twenty-
six miles since the morning along a road rising continually into the mountains, while from Enab to Beit
Anan the road was merely a rough track, covered
with loose boulders, and winding in and out of the
hills.

On the 29th the Brigade was ordered to take over
a line from the Wadi Zait to the left of the 181st
Brigade, 60th Division, south-east of Beit Dukka.
The 25th Royal Welsh Fusiliers, and a section of the
210th Machine Gun Company, were to relieve the 8th
Mounted Brigade from Wadi Zait to Hill 1750 ; the
10th Shropshires and a section of the Machine Gun
Company would prolong the line to Beit Dukka ; and
the 24th Royal Welsh Fusiliers would fill the gap from
Beit Dukka to the left of the 181st Brigade.

The events that followed are somewhat confused,
but of great interest, showing the nature of the
country, designed for ambushes, surprises, and the
manœuvring of small parties, and the tremendous
individual effort that was required.

Apparently Lord Kensington, commanding the
25th Royal Welsh Fusiliers, received a telephone
message from the Brigade Major about 7 o'clock in
the evening, telling him to be prepared to move at
once and take up a line from Hill 1750 to the village
of Beit Ur el Foka, which, it will be remembered, was
relinquished by the yeomanry.  The message stated
further that, failing to occupy the village, the left of
the battalion should rest on the Wadi Zait.  Shortly
after this the Brigade order arrived, with instructions
to relieve the 8th Mounted Brigade on a line from
Wadi Zait to Hill 1750, which did not include el Foka.

The Brigade Major again telephoned supplementary information that there was no one to relieve !

There was brilliant moonlight, but the execution of the order was extremely difficult.  The country was a jumble of steep rocky hills, falling precipitously into deep wadis, and rising over 2,000 feet in some places.  There were no roads, only native tracks running up and down the sides of the mountains.  No reconnaissance was possible, and the only information Lord Kensington could obtain was from two native guides, who knew little of the country beyond the track from Beit Anan, through Beit Dukka, and el Tireh (which was in enemy hands) to el Foka.  The track was said to be a good one, passable for foot soldiers and pack animals, but not camels, and was the only one ever used—it revealed itself as a rocky watercourse.

Colonel Heywood-Lonsdale, commanding the Shropshires, was on the line Dukka–Kh. Jufna, and to him fell the task of pushing his line forward to el Tireh, between Hill 1750 and Dukka.  In consultation with Lord Kensington he ordered Major Glazebrook to advance on the village, with two companies, at 9 o'clock.  By a quarter past ten the village was taken with little opposition, and one company sent forward on to the lower slopes of Sheikh Hassan, about 300 yards north-east of the village.  But it was found that the latter position was under machine gun fire from Hill 1750, still in enemy hands, and from snipers on either flank;  the company therefore moved to the north of the village.

Lord Kensington, knowing that the Shropshires were to occupy el Tireh, and being in complete ignorance of either the enemy or the British dispositions to the left, decided that his only course was to accept the assurance of his guides that there was no other way, and go by the track to el Tireh ; he would then capture Hill 1750 and push on the el Foka.

The road was so appalling that, although the battalion left Beit Anan at 11.15 p.m., Dukka was not reached until 1 a.m. on the 30th. While the heavily loaded men rested, the ground on the southern slopes was reconnoitred with a view to discovering an easier way, but was found to be impossible, as the terraces were too high to be negotiated at night. The battalion continued along the track to el Tireh.

Lord Kensington then sent forward one company to attack Hill 1750, assisted by a company of Shropshires, who occupied a knoll on the right, and two platoons of the Royal Welsh Fusiliers and a machine gun, on a second knoll south-west of the hill. The assault was launched, covered by overhead fire from the machine gun section, and the Hill was captured, ten Turks being killed, two prisoners taken, and two machine guns.

Major Rees was then ordered to push forward on el Foka with five platoons and a machine gun.

At this point Lord Kensington, with the remnant of the battalion, became involved in the bewildering maze provided by the uncertain situation. He followed a track which led him down the Wadi Shebab into enemy lines, where he was caught by machine gun fire and suffered casualties. Retiring, he came in contact with an Australian picket across the junction of the Wadis Selman and Shebab. Here he spent the morning, trying in vain to get touch with the rest of his battalion. There is little doubt that the prearranged position he was to take up with his Head-

# MAJOR REES 115

quarters was in the hands of the enemy, as was the entire line indicated in his orders as being held by British troops. Captain Stable, of the 25th Royal Welsh Fusiliers, had an excellent view from the top of a hill when day broke, and found the surrounding country dotted with groups of " friend and foe " in the most startling and confusing positions.

Meanwhile Major Rees, with a total force of eighty rifles, pushed on, along rough tracks, and up and down wadis in the direction of el Foka. The track brought him out on the Roman Road, in rear of the village, and he saw, in the semi-light of dawn, a considerable force of Turks standing to on the western slope of the hill, near the village, also other posts immediately south of the village, on a ridge which ran between him and the British lines; the latter had fires lighted, and were evidently preparing a morning meal under the shelter of the ridge.

Dawn was breaking, and daylight would reveal him to the enemy in a most disadvantageous position. The only course open to him was to treat the situation with the utmost audacity.

He sent three platoons, under Lieutenant Neale, to the south-east and south of the village, and hurried himself, with two platoons, to the east and north-east, and closed on the village.

When within a hundred yards of the place a Turkish officer, mounted on a grey pony, rode up. He was made to dismount, was put in the ranks of the leading platoon, and his pony led alongside him. It may be mentioned that there was a certain similarity in the colour of the British and Turkish uniform.

Major Rees reached the garden walls on the east side of the village, and called upon the garrison to surrender (through the interpreter). At first it appeared as though they were going to do so ; then they changed their minds, and seemed to consider an attack with the bayonet. Finally they made a pretence of surrendering, and suddenly opened fire with six machine guns. The garden walls and cactus hedges, however, took most of the bullets, and the Welshmen promptly opened rapid fire and kept up a fierce fusillade until the Turks threw up their hands.

An attempt at further resistance was made from the houses, but a few minutes of rapid fire soon caused the whole garrison to surrender.

About 450 prisoners were immediately collected and sent back under escort. On the way towards the British lines this column of prisoners was fired on by the Turks, and, apparently, by the Australians as well ; some 150 escaped, but the small escort managed to join up with the Australians on the Wadi Selman and deliver 308 safely into their hands.

Major Rees now tried to get into communication by flag with the British Line, and despatched runners to get in touch with Battalion Headquarters ; in neither case was he successful.

The enemy soon realised what had happened at el Foka, and commenced to approach from all directions, the ground affording them excellent cover. At 8 a.m. Major Rees was practically surrounded ; fire was being poured in on him from every side, and his force was reduced to thirty men and four officers. Flag signals remained unanswered, and it seemed impossible for assistance to arrive in time to save the small force. He decided to fight his way out due south and try to join up with the British line.

His retirement from el Foka was admirably done.

The Turks appeared on each succeeding ridge, scampered away and hid themselves, and then fired as the little force passed. But he reached el Tireh at 9.45.

Apparently a company of the Welsh Regiment had, about this time, been sent to Lord Kensington (who had gained touch with the Brigade and with Colonel Spence Jones, commanding the Welsh Regiment), and were sent to relieve Australians on the heights commanding each side of the Wadi Shebab. But at Divisional Headquarters the situation was obscure. The original capture of el Foka was not known until 10 o'clock in the morning, nor the loss of it until 5 o'clock in the evening.

After they had recaptured el Foka, the Turks proceeded to work round the flank of Hill 1750, and about 2 p.m. attacked from the north-east and east, rushed the ridge and retained their hold on it. El Tireh village was now rendered untenable, being commanded by hills on the north, north-east, and south of it. Soon after 5 o'clock in the evening Colonel Heywood-Lonsdale (Shropshires) decided to retire across the Wadi Selman. The wounded were collected, and the evacuation was carried out.

As soon as the position was understood at Divisional Headquarters, which, owing to the lack of communication, was very late in the evening, the 229th Brigade was ordered to send a battalion to make good the line from the Wadi Zait to Hill 1750, and the 24th Welsh Regiment was to fill up the gap between Hill 1750 and the left of the Shropshires at Kh. Jufna, and to capture el Tireh at dawn.

In accordance with the order the Black Watch sent one company to the left of the Wadi Shebab, and got in touch with the 52nd Division, and a company and

9

a half advanced on the right of Shebab until, about 2 a.m., on the 1st December, it was thought that they had reached Hill 1750.

During this night one section of A/44th Battery and one section of B/44th took up gun positions near Beit Anan, and the Welsh Regiment, after being delayed by difficulties of country, attacked el Tireh.

This battalion had been in support behind Hill 2172, where the Roman Road, a stony track four feet wide, ran over the skyline, and was ordered to attack early in the morning. The battalion started to move overnight, going by way of the Roman Road, and a track which was indicated on the map as leading into the Wadi Marua. This track has a gradient of about one in three, and was frequently blocked by huge boulders over which men and mules, with ammunition, had to scramble as best they could. In the wadi the only method of advance was in single file; the boulders encountered here were enormous blocks on the loose shingle bed, and the banks were like a wall. It was so dark that the junction with the Wadi Selman was missed, but fortunately the error was at once discovered. The going was better along this wadi, and the battalion climbed up the steep ridge on the left and was ready to attack just before daylight. The position occupied was on a ridge running parallel to Sheikh Hasan and el Tireh, with a deep cleft in between, a branch of the Wadi Shebab.

As the light was fairly good, the enemy in possession of Sheikh Hasan saw the attacking companies and opened fire; machine gun and rifle fire also came from hill 1750: but the attack was launched under cover of Lewis gun fire. Companies had to descend into the wadi and climb the opposite hill, over a succession

of terraces, built for crops and olives trees, with walls
from six to ten feet high.   The crest of the hill was
reached with little opposition from the front, but the
enfilade fire from Hill 1750 held up the advance, and
the Turks then commenced to shell the assaulting
troops.

The mistake of the Black Watch had been discovered by Colonel Younger, when he went to view
the position at dawn, and he directed a company to
advance on a twin peak, which he made out to be his
objective.   Part of this hill was captured, but still it
was not Hill 1750.   The error can be easily understood when it is realised that the maps were the
original Palestine Exploration Fund Maps (from a
survey made by Lord Kitchener when a young man),
on a scale of one mile to the inch, and were not
contoured, but hachured, so that a collection of peaks
appeared as a ridge.   In the contoured map, which
we give, there is not, apparently, any hill of that
height.

Under the circumstances the Welsh Regiment
could not hold el Tireh and was ordered back to the
original line of deployment, which overlooked the
village, with their right in touch with the Shropshires
on the Ancient Road, at Ain Jufna.

The 229th Brigade rearranged its line with the
Black Watch on the left, opposite el Foka, and the
Somersets on the right ; two companies of Devons
were withdrawn from the left to prepare for an attack
on this village.   At the same time more of the
Divisional Artillery, A and C/268, and C/117 came into
action near Beit Likia.

At 1 o'clock in the morning on the 3rd December
the Devons attacked el Foka, advancing from the

head of the Wadi Zait.   After scrambling up terraces
of varying height, the battalion reached the village
about 3 a.m., and was immediately engaged in fierce
bombing and bayonet fighting.   The Royal Scots
Fusiliers, and troops of the 10th Division, sent up
carrying parties with S.A.A. and bombs, which were
used as fast as they arrived.   With daylight the
Turks, holding commanding positions on three sides,
poured in a devastating volume of machine gun fire.
By this time the actual position and condition of el
Foka was beginning to be understood, and appreciated.
There was not sufficient room on the top of the hill
for a battalion, and no digging was possible, owing to
the rocky nature of the ground.   Across the Wadi
Imeish, at a distance of about 1,500 yards, was the
Zeitun Ridge, several hundred feet higher than Foka,
and to the north-west was Kh. Kereina, as high as
Foka and about 2,000 yards away.   Both these
places were occupied by the Turks.   The worst
feature, however, was an unnamed hill, separated
from Foka by a deep ravine, but only about 500 yards
away, and from which the enemy was able to fire into
the backs of the Devons.   Under cover of machine
gun and rifle fire from these hills the Turks attacked
again and again, swarming up the steep face of the
Wadi Imeish, which protected them completely from
the fire of the 74th Divisional Artillery.

Casualties mounted up, but the Devons held on.
After seven hours' fighting they were forced to withdraw, and this was done, under cover of artillery fire.

The next night and day passed quietly, and on the
4th/5th the 229th and 231st Brigades were relieved
by the 10th Division, and went back to bivouac by
Beit Likia and Beit Anan.

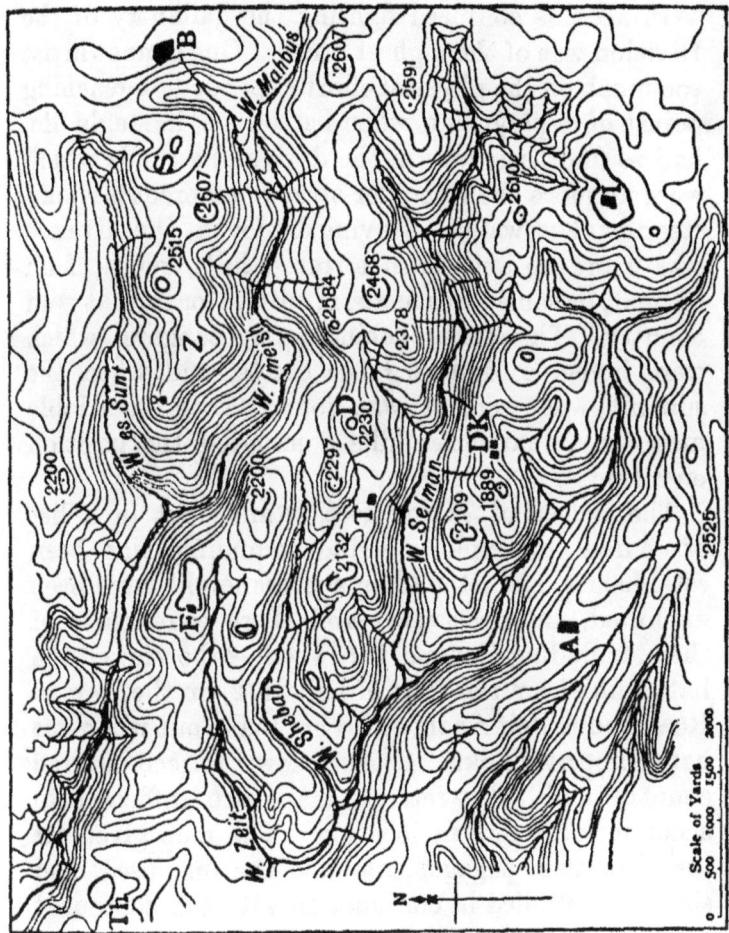

THE FOKA-TIREH FRONT

Emery Walker Ltd. sc.

Scale of Yards
0   500   1000   1500   2000

N

Th = Beit Ur et Tahta
F = Beit Ur el Foka
Z = Zeitun Ridge
T = el Tireh
D = Kh. Dreihemeh
DK = Beit Dukka
A = Beit Anan
I = Beit Izza
B = Beitania
S = Shafa

NOTE.—This map shows no Pt. 1750. The reading from the small sea map places it between Pts. 2182 and 2297. The latter, however, seems to be position meant.

In all this confused fighting the gallantry of the
Division was of the highest order. One cannot insist
too much on the physical effort expended on reaching
points of deployment, when battalions, in single file,
had to find their way in the dark along roads which
were no more than boulder-strewn watercourses and
steep-banked wadis. Having deployed, the advance
was made up and down terraced hills, relics of an
ancient, or sometimes modern, cultivator in that wild
country. The Turks behind stone sangars, which
were invisible, defended the crests, and when the
summit was won, it was found, with invariable
monotony, that other hills dominated the position
on all sides.

The action of Major Rees stands out in a list
of courageous exploits. Had communication been
established, his astounding success might have been
exploited, but observers—and there were many of
them, including General Girdwood—who viewed the
battle line from the crest of Hill 2172, on the Roman
Road above Beit Anan, could not make out what was
happening at el Foka. The unknown, unreconnoitred
country and the wretched maps are sufficient to
account for errors in location. The map given for
the Jerusalem engagements was the one used, and
should be studied in conjunction with the contoured
map.

# CHAPTER VIII

## THE BATTLE OF NEBY SAMWIL

Enemy dispositions—The plan of Battle—Climatic conditions—The attack—Mott's force—The surrender of Jerusalem.

ON November the 29th the Corps Commander met the G.O.C.'s 52nd, 74th, and Yeomanry Mounted Divisions at Yalo, and discussed the situation. The difficulties of forcing a way through to the Jerusalem–Nablus Road and cutting off Jerusalem were very great, not only because of the ruggedness of the hills, but mainly because of the total absence of suitable roads and the shortage of water. Sir Philip Chetwode decided that he would abandon the plan adopted by the XXIst Corps and would attack Jerusalem from the west and south-west.

Owing to the fierce fighting which had been taking place, divisions in the line had become somewhat mixed, and the relief by the XXth Corps was not complete until the 2nd December. The Corps front was then held by the Australian Mounted Division on the left, the 10th Division (which had relieved the 52nd), the 74th, the 60th. The enemy made repeated attacks along the entire front during this period.

As a result of his reconnaissances the Corps Commander decided that it was unnecessary to undertake any more offensive operations on his northern front before setting his plan against Jerusalem in operation. In a conference at Enab, on the 3rd December, he outlined his proposals, which were to attack with

123

the 60th and 74th Divisions in an easterly direction from Ain Karim-Beit Surik, and, skirting the western limits of Jerusalem, dispose these divisions astride the Jerusalem–Nablus Road.   The 53rd Division, which had reverted to the command of the XXth Corps, would advance from Hebron to protect the right flank of the attack, and threaten the city from the south.   The date of the attack was to be dependent on the state of the weather and the time necessary for the accumulation of ammunition, which the state of the roads made difficult.

The preliminary movements of troops, to get into position for the attack on Jerusalem, were made between the 4th and the 7th December.   The 10th Division, having relieved the 74th on the night 4th/5th, extended its line to cover Beit Dukka ; and the enemy having retired on the left, Kh. Hellabi and Suffa were occupied.

The strength and dispositions of the enemy were estimated at the time to be :  East of Bethlehem the 7th Cavalry Regiment, 500 sabres ; covering Bethlehem, and  extending  to  the  Jerusalem–Junction Station Railway, the 27th Division, 1,200 rifles; to the Latron–Jerusalem Road, with strong points at Ain Karim and Deir Yesin, the 53rd Division, 2,000 rifles ;  to Neby Samwil, the 26th Division, 1,800 rifles ; to Beit Ur et Foka, the 19th Division, with 2/61st and 158th Regiments attached, 4,000 rifles ; to Suffa, the 24th Division, 1,600 rifles; thence to the extreme left of the XXth Corps the 3rd Cavalry Division, 1,500 sabres ; and in reserve, about Bireh, the 54th Division, 2,700 rifles.

This was the VIIth Turkish Army, as given by Colonel Murphy, with the addition of the 27th

TURKISH POSITIONS WEST OF JERUSALEM.

124]

Division. He does not mention the 27th Division as having taken part in the defence of Jerusalem, and it will be remembered that this division defended Beersheba and was severely punished. The Desert Corps captured 1,300 prisoners from Beersheba, and the XXth Corps just over 400. The nominal strength of a Turkish division was 8,000, but they do not seem to have been up to strength at any period of the war. There is no doubt that elements of the division were present, and the estimate shows that it was considered the weakest of all the enemy divisions. This was clearly recognised, as the following extracts from the notes of the conference show :

" The enemy are holding a line covering the Hebron–Jerusalem Road, with works in the neighbourhood of Ras Esh Sherifeh, behind which are trenches near el Khudr, and round Bethlehem from about Kh. Esh Shughrah, on the south-east, across the road to Kh. Kebah, and thence northward. . . .

" North of the railway the enemy have a series of trenches and redoubts, from just west of Malhah to Neby Samwil.

" Facing the XXth Corps are believed to be anything from 500 to a maximum of 1,200 on the Hebron Road, and a maximum of 15,000 from the right of the 60th Division to the left of the 10th Division at Suffa, including the reserves.

" The enemy defences are not deep, and once through them the troops have only difficulties of terrain to contend with. . . . (The rearrangement of the front) will give to the attack two complete brigades of the 53rd, the whole of the 60th, and it is hoped two brigades of the 74th Division.

" It is obvious that the form the attack will take will depend a good deal on the action of the enemy on the advance of the 53rd Division towards Jerusa-

lem.  The two brigades of this division reach a point
to-night from which they are two ten-mile marches
from the position north of Bethlehem, which they
will have to reach to co-operate with the remainder
of the Corps.

"Should the enemy decide to strengthen his
defences in front of the 53rd Division by pushing
troops south of Jerusalem, the attack will take the
form of the 60th and 74th Divisions driving straight
in on the Jerusalem–Nablus Road, the 60th Division
throwing out a flank to the south-east, the objective
of the move being the prevention of the escape of the
enemy opposing the 53rd Division, either by the
Nablus or the Jericho Roads.

"Should, however (as is more probable), the enemy
recognise the danger of such a movement, and withdraw from in front of the 53rd Division, the attack
will take the form of a direct advance on the part of
the 53rd Division on Jerusalem, and a wheel by the
60th and 74th Divisions, pivoting on the Beit Izza
and Neby Samwil defences, designed to drive the
enemy northwards, and with the following objectives :
(a) a position covering the Jericho Road to be
occupied by a portion of the 53rd Division ; (b) the
60th and 74th Divisions to seize the general line
Shafat–Newby Samwil, or, if possible, the point
2670–Kh. Ras el Tawil–Neby Samwil.

"In order to inflict a severe blow on the enemy
before he has time to arrange to meet the attack, it
seems obvious that the advance of the 53rd Division
must be as rapid as possible, once it moves from its
present position, and the G.O.C. 53rd Division must
endeavour to ensure, by careful reconnaissance of
routes, that his brigades are on the general line Surbahir–Sherafat by the early morning of Z day.

"Should the enemy retire from before the 53rd
Division, or only oppose that division lightly, the
general attack will take, roughly, the following form :

"*1st Phase.*—The capture as soon as possible after dawn by the 60th Division of the enemy works from the railway to the main Enab Road, and by the 74th Division of the works covering Beit Iksa, as far north as the Wadi el Abbeideh. After this advance it will be necessary to advance more guns of the 60th Division.

"*2nd Phase.*—The advance of the 53rd and 60th Divisions to the general line Jerusalem–Lifta. It is recognised that difficulties of terrain may prevent the 53rd Division from advancing from Sherafat northwards, and that they may have to work up the main road nearer to Jerusalem before they can gain close touch with the 60th Division.

"*3rd Phase.*—The advance of the 60th and 74th Divisions to the general line of the track running out of the main road one mile north of Jerusalem. . . . During this 3rd Phase the left brigade of the 53rd Division, if there is any room, will assist the right of the 60th Division. Otherwise the brigade will drop into reserve. . . . The right brigade of the 53rd will endeavour to place itself in a position covering the Jericho Road, and the east and north-east of Jerusalem.

"*4th Phase.*—The further advance of the 60th Division to a line astride the Jerusalem–Nablus Road about Shafat, and if possible to Point 2670 Ras el Tawil. During this phase the 74th Division will improve its position by throwing its right into Beit Hannina."

The instructions to the 53rd Division contained the following provisions :

" Should the resistance of the enemy be so great that you are unable to reach this line in time to co-operate with the 60th Division, the G.O.C. 60th Division will be instructed to detach troops to advance east, from about Ain Karim, towards the Hebron Road to prevent the escape of the enemy on your front, either by the Jerusalem–Nablus Road or by the Jerusalem–Jericho Road.

" In the more likely case that you are able to break the enemy's resistance south of the line Surbahir–Sherafat, you will advance on December the 8th from the line Surbahir–Sherafat in two groups.

" The right group will move at dawn towards Jerusalem, and pass thence south of the town to seize a position to command the Jerusalem–Jericho Road and to protect the XXth Corps from attack from the east and north-east of Jerusalem.

" The left group will advance between the Hebron–Jerusalem Road and the general line Sherafat–Malhah, to co-operate with and protect the right flank of the 60th Division. . . .

" As soon as you are able to pass troops round the southern and south-eastern outskirts of Jerusalem, you will push forward a portion of the Corps Cavalry Regiment to discover whether there are any forward bodies of the enemy on the Jerusalem–Jericho Road within a distance of six miles from Jerusalem. . . .

" The city of Jerusalem will not be entered, and all movements by troops and vehicles will be restricted to roads passing outside the city."

The artillery arrangements for the attack were that, in addition to the divisional artillery brigades, the 96th Heavy Artillery Group, consisting of three 6-inch batteries, one 60-pounder battery, and one section 60-pounder battery, the Hong-Kong and Singapore Mountain Battery (attached 74th Division), the 10th and B/9 Mountain Batteries (attached 60th Division), and the 91st Heavy Battery of 60-pounders (attached 53rd Division) should support the assaulting battalions.

.    .    .    .    .

Generally speaking, the climatic conditions of Syria may be summarised as a dry season and a rainy season. In the dry season, a period of drought when all vegetation shrivels and the earth is bare, there are occasional mists, and the nights are very cold. In October the rains commence, and by December they are severe. Wind, cold, rain, hail, and snow come sweeping across the hills of Judea, where snow has been known to the depth of two feet. After February gentle showers fall and the whole country is green, even wide portions of the Desert, until the sun once more burns up the country. The difficulties which faced the British Army operating in these precipitous hills can be imagined. On the lines of communication across the plain things were almost as bad. Large areas were completely under water, and the wadis were filled to the banks with black mud. In several places the railway was washed away, and hundreds of camels lay down and died : there were occasions when neither animal nor mechanical transport could move.

.  .  .  .  .  .

Preparations were pushed on for the attack. On the 5th/6th December the 231st Brigade relieved the 60th Division in the Beit Izza–Neby Samwil defences. This salient, a commanding hill, was the pivot of the attack. On the top of it is a Mosque, which was held by us, but the enemy was only 15 to 20 yards away from it.

On the night 6th/7th the 230th Brigade relieved other troops of the 60th Division on the Beit Surik sector, one battalion of the brigade finding the outposts while the rest bivouacked in rear. The 229th Brigade, which was to attack on the right, had left the Devons and Black Watch in reserve to the 10th

Division, so only the Somersets and the Scots Fusiliers bivouacked on the right of the 230th Brigade.

The attack was to open at 5.15 a.m. on the 8th December. The night was very dark, and the rain came down in torrents. At 3 a.m. the assaulting troops, cold and wet to the skin, commenced to move from their bivouac areas, and marched to the line of deployment. The approach had to be done in single file, and the 230th Brigade did not arrive until 5.35 a.m.

Both Brigades found considerable difficulty in negotiating the descent into the Wadi Bowai and the ascent on the far side to the enemy trenches. The ground falls rapidly about a thousand feet on either side of the Wadi, and the hill-sides are terraced with outcrops of rock. Progress was very slow, although only slight rifle fire was met during the climb up to the Turkish line.

The Scots Fusiliers, with the Somersets in support, reached the crest of the ridge, and seem to have taken the Turks by surprise, for they rushed the position with only a total loss of 12, and captured 60 prisoners.

On the left the 230th Brigade, with the Buffs on the right and the Norfolks on the left, took about thirty-five minutes to climb the hill from the wadi bed. On reaching the summit the assaulting troops found that the Turks had abandoned their trenches, and were lined up behind walls and rocks just over the crest. The broken country, strewn with boulders, was admirably suited for this form of defence, a continual retreat to other rocks and walls in rear, and the two gallant battalions worked their way slowly forward over a mile and a quarter of country and reached the village of Beit Iksa at 11.30 a.m.

THE DEEP RAVINE WHICH FACED THE DIVISION AFTER THE CAPTURE OF BEIT IKSA.
The attack was from the right of the sketch to the left, i.e. to cut the roads north of Jerusalem. The Turks were below
the ridge in the foreground.

At Beit Iksa they were held up by an increasing volume of fire from the left, and of shrapnel from the south-east. A company of Suffolks was sent up to reinforce the left, and an attempt was made to continue the advance to the el Burj position. But a most formidable wadi, the size of which was in no way indicated on the maps, lay between the Iksa spur and el Burj and to advance down steep terraces, with drops of about ten feet, in the face of the intense machine gun fire from the left was impossible.

This enfilade fire, which held up the advance, was a mystery to the troops. It came from the slopes of Neby Samwil, which they had been told was in the hands of the 231st Brigade. Colonel Grissell, commanding the Suffolks, says :

" How the machine guns which caused this fire came to be where they were has always been a mystery to the writer, and others. They could never be located exactly, so cunningly were they concealed, and were apparently in some houses in part of the village of Neby Samwil itself, which we were led to understand was occupied by the 231st Brigade. Whoever handled those guns must have been brave men, for they could only have been a few yards from some of the 231st Brigade posts. It is possible that they were fired by natives, and colour is added to this supposition by the fact that several wounded natives were found in this neighbourhood on the advance being continued the next day."

Knowing, however, how close the opposing troops were to each other on the summit of Neby Samwil Hill, the mystery rather explains itself. Colonel Powell Edwards notes that the 75th Division, some weeks before, had been held up by exactly the same

fire from Neby Samwil, when they attacked el Jib
from the north of the salient.

The Scots Fusiliers, on the right, had met with
little opposition after the capture of the Turkish
trenches in the early morning, but they had to wait
on the 60th Division.

The 60th were influenced by the condition of affairs
on both flanks. The attacking troops on the left met
with severe opposition, after the first line of defences
had been taken, from some houses on a ridge, which
delayed them until about 4 p.m., when they dislodged
the Turks at the point of the bayonet. The great
difficulty of the G.O.C. was, however, the right flank,
which was exposed and being pressed by the enemy.
It is necessary to follow the movements of the 53rd
Division.

General Mott had not a very enviable task. There
was only one road leading through the mountainous
country; it twisted and turned, sometimes with
several hairpin corners on one hill, so that his force
was strung out to an appalling length. In itself this
would not have mattered much, although a single
road advance is always a troublesome business, but
his anxieties were added to by the fact that the right
flank of his line of march was entirely exposed. He
had to take risks to keep to his time-table, and up to a
point was ahead of time.

In the early morning of the 7th the Division captured the Sherifeh Ridge, and for a moment the whole
country from Bethlehem to Jerusalem could be seen.
Then the rain and clouds descended, and soon after
7 a.m. the limit of vision was about 200 yards: so it
remained for the rest of the day. At once the column
stuck, for the camels could not move on the greasy

surface of the road ; the advance guard, however, pushed on and secured the water at Solomon's Pools, after a sharp fight. The trouble then was that the lower hills were covered with clouds, and it was impossible to ascertain whence enemy fire was being directed or to organise an attack that night. What with the fog and the state of the road, General Mott's force was strung out many miles. Nevertheless, the Corps' message was inexorable : " Plan proceeds as arranged to-morrow, and you will continue advance regardless of weather."

The problem was to ascertain how near the advance troops were to the Bethlehem defences. It seemed certain from previous air reconnaissance that they must be close, but, with the exception of a momentary glimpse in the early morning, the fog and rain denied any view of the country, or of the position of the enemy lines, so that a plan of attack could be arranged for the next morning ; the only information of a certain nature was that the hills on either side of the road were steep and rocky. The 1/4 Cheshires, who were ordered to protect the right flank that night, were found to be quite " ungetatable."

In this predicament the Division waited for dawn, which was the time of attack, an attack in which their co-operation was vital.

When dawn broke on the 8th, although visibility was poor, an intermittent glimpse of Bethlehem and Beit Jala was obtained. Arrangements were made to attack the high ground to the west of Bethlehem, and to urgent messages from Sir Philip Chetwode to push forward, an answer was sent that the attack would develop about noon. The attack, however, did not take place until about 2.30 in the after-

10

noon, and the position was not occupied until
4 p.m.

The advance of the right flank of the 60th Division
came to a standstill.

In the afternoon Sir Philip Chetwode went to the
60th Division Headquarters and discussed the situation.   He was faced with the difficulty of moving
artillery forward over the sodden ground, the fact
that troops were very exhausted after marching and
fighting in the rain since midnight, and that the
53rd Division at Beit Jala was not in a position to
protect the right flank of the 60th.   He, therefore,
ordered all further advance to be postponed until the
next morning.

The troops of the 74th Division, perched on the
machine gun swept terraces which dropped down into
the Wadi before el Burj, were withdrawn, and an
outpost line was extended on the Iksa Ridge.

The first phase of the advance had been carried out
without artillery preparation.   Owing to the bad
state of the roads, and the heavy rain, the 44th F.A.
Brigade, and the Hong-Kong Mountain Battery had
been ordered to stand fast at Enab and Kataneh
respectively.   The A and B/268th and B/117th
Batteries were grouped under Lt.-Colonel C. C.
Robertson just behind the original outpost line;
A and C/117 and C/268 were round Biddu, under
Lt.-Colonel Kinnear : both groups were occupied in
shelling el Burj.   Neither the artillery nor the
machine gun companies were in a position to help the
infantry to any extent.   Lieutenant A. Murdoch,
commanding the 209th Machine Gun Company, notes
in the diary : " 5.15 a.m., not quite light.   Dawn
broke with thick mist hanging over hills, and in wadis

unable to see more than 100 yards.   7.15 a.m., light better.   8.30 a.m., light bad, observation impossible."

But the morning of the 9th dawned on perfect peace.   Partridges could be heard calling, and patrols reported that the enemy had retired north, with the exception of small bodies at el Burj and on the slopes of Neby Samwil.   During the night the 53rd had advanced to the outskirts of Bethlehem, which was occupied at daybreak, and by 8.30 a.m. the leading battalion of that division was only two and a half miles from Jerusalem.

At 8.30 a.m. the Mayor of Jerusalem and the Chief of Police approached the officer commanding 302nd F.A. Brigade, in a village near Kh. Khanis, and offered to surrender the town.   Instructions from the Corps arrived at 11 o'clock that the chief of police was to be held as hostage, and the Mayor, after surrendering the city to G.O.C. 60th Division, was to be sent back, and told that so long as good order and discipline were maintained, no harm would be done to the city.

Meanwhile, at 10.15 the 60th and 74th Divisions had been ordered to advance.   The line moved forward—the Scots Fusiliers on the right and the Somersets on the left of the 299th Brigade (the Black Watch and Devons rejoined on this day), and the Suffolks on the right and Sussex on the left of the 230th Brigade.   No opposition was encountered, a few shots only being fired by snipers, and a line was taken up in the neighbourhood of Tel el Ful, astride the Jerusalem–Nablus Road, to Beit Hannina, and from thence to Neby Samwil.   During the day the line was extended to include the whole of the front held by the 10th Division, but the march to this flank was a fearful affair : the whole country was inundated, camels and mules could not move, and had to be either left, or, in some cases, the mules were practically carried over bad places. The order was not completed until the morning of the 10th. During the night there was a severe frost.

On the 10th the 53rd Division, which had had a stiff fight on the Mount of Olives the previous day, pushed the line out to Ras et Tawil.

During the pause of the next ten days changes were made on the 74th Division front : first the 229th and then the 230th Brigades were relieved by troops of the 60th Division ; the 231st remained in line with its left on Beit Ur et Tahta.

The notable feature of this battle was the advance over precipitous country under the most appalling weather conditions. In order to climb the heights the men left their overcoats behind, and only carried a waterproof sheet ; they were short of water and short of rations. Wet through, cold, hungry, and thirsty, slipping and falling as they scrambled up the greasy walls, they overcame all resistance. But the Turk had once more escaped. Only about 500 unwounded prisoners were taken by the Corps.

.    .    .    .    .

General Allenby made his official entrance into Jerusalem on the 11th December. In this ceremony the 74th Division was represented by a detachment. On the 15th a special order of the day was circulated.

SPECIAL ORDER OF THE DAY

"G.H.Q., E.E.F.,
"*December 15th, 1917.*

" With the capture of Jerusalem another phase of

AEROPLANE PHOTOGRAPH OF JERUSALEM.

The plate was found amongst the mass of documents captured in the raid on German H.Q., Nazareth.

[*War Museum.*

136]

the operations of the Egyptian Expeditionary Force
has been victoriously concluded.

" The Commander-in-Chief desires to thank all
ranks of all the units and services in the Force for the
magnificent work which has been accomplished.

" In forty days many strong Turkish positions have
been captured, and the Force has advanced some
sixty miles on a front of thirty miles.

" The skill, gallantry, and determination of all
ranks have led to this result.

" The approach marches of the Desert Mounted
Corps and the XXth Corps (10th, 53rd, 60th, and 74th
Divisions), followed by the dashing attacks of the
60th and 74th Divisions, and the rapid turning movement of the Desert Mounted Corps, ending in the fine
charge by the 4th Australian Light Horse Brigade,
resulted in the capture of Beersheba, with many
prisoners and guns.

" The stubborn resistance of the 53rd Division,
units of the Desert Mounted Corps, and the Imperial
Camel Brigade in the difficult country north-east of
Beersheba, enabled the preparations of the XXth
Corps to be completed without interference, and
enabled the Commander-in-Chief to carry out his
plan without diverting more than the intended number of troops to protect the right flank, despite the
many and strong attacks of the enemy.

" The attack of the XXth Corps (10th, 60th, and
74th Divisions), prepared with great skill by the Corps
and Divisional Commanders, and carried out with
such dash and courage by the troops, resulted in the
turning of the Turkish left flank, and in an advance
to the depth of nine miles through an entrenched
position defended by strong forces. In this operation
the Desert Mounted Corps, covering the right flank
and threatening the Turkish rear, forced the Turks
to begin a general retreat on their left flank.

" The artillery attack of the XXIst Corps, and of

the ships of the Royal Navy, skilfully arranged and carried out with great accuracy, caused heavy loss to the enemy in the Gaza sector of the defences.   The success of this bombardment was due to the loyal co-operation of the Rear-Admiral S.N.O. Egypt and the Red Sea, and officers of the Royal Navy, the carefully arranged plans of the Rear-Admiral and the G.O.C. XXIst Corps, and the good shooting of the Royal Navy, and of the heavy, siege, and field artillery of the XXIst Corps.

" The two attacks on the strong defences of Gaza, carried out by the 52nd and 54th Divisions, were each completely successful, thanks to the skill with which they were thought out and prepared by the G.O.C. XXIst Corps, the Divisional Commanders, and the Brigade Commanders, and the great gallantry displayed by the troops who carried out those attacks.

" The second attack resulted in the evacuation of Gaza by the enemy and the turning of his right flank. The 52nd and 75th Divisions at once began a pursuit which carried them in three weeks from Gaza to within a few miles of Jerusalem.

" This pursuit, carried out by the Desert Mounted Corps and these two divisions of the XXIst Corps, first over the sand-hills of the coast, then over the plains of Palestine and the foothills, and finally in the rocky mountains of Judea, required from all commanders rapid decisions and powers to adapt their tactics to varying conditions of ground.   The troops were called upon to carry out very long marches in great heat without water, to make attacks on stubborn rearguards without time for reconnaissance, and finally to suffer cold and privations in the mountains.

" In these operations commanders carried out their plans with boldness and determination, and the troops of all arms and services responded with a devotion and gallantry beyond praise.

" The final operations of the XXth Corps, which resulted in the surrender of Jerusalem, were a fitting climax to the efforts of all ranks.  The attack, skilfully prepared by G.O.C. XXth Corps, and carried out with precision, endurance, and gallantry by the troops of the 53rd, 60th, and 74th Divisions, over a country of extreme difficulty, in wet weather, showed great skill in leading, and gallantry and determination of a very high order.

" Throughout the operations the Royal Flying Corps have rendered valuable assistance to all arms, and have obtained complete mastery of the air.  The information obtained from contact and reconnaissance patrols has at all times enabled commanders to keep in close touch with the situation.  In the pursuit they have inflicted severe loss on the enemy, and their artillery co-operation has contributed in no small measure to our victory.

" The organisation in rear of the fighting troops enabled these forces to be supplied throughout.  All supply and ammunition services and engineer services were called upon for great exertions.  The response everywhere showed great devotion and high military spirit.

" The thorough organisation of the Lines of Communications and the energy and skill with which all the services adapted themselves to the varying conditions of the operations, ensured the constant mobility of the fighting troops.

" The Commander-in-Chief appreciates the admirable conduct of all the transport services, and particularly the endurance and loyal service of the Camel Transport Corps.

" The skill and energy by which the signal service was maintained under all conditions reflects the greatest credit on all concerned.

" The medical service was able to adapt itself to all the difficulties of the situation, with the result that the evacuation of the wounded and sick was carried out with the least possible hardship and discomfort.

" The veterinary service worked well throughout ; the wastage in animals was consequently small considering the distances traversed.

" The Ordnance never failed to meet all demands.

" The work of the Egyptian Labour Corps has been of the greatest value in contributing to the rapid advance of the troops and in covering the difficulties of the communications.

" The Commander-in-Chief desires that his thanks and appreciation of their services be conveyed to all officers and men of the Force which he has the honour to command.

" W. DAWNAY,
" *For Major-General,*
" *Chief of the General Staff,*
" *Egyptian Expeditionary Force.*"

TURKISH POSITIONS WEST OF JERUSALEM.

[*War Museum.*

# CHAPTER IX

## THE DEFENCE OF JERUSALEM

MORE room was wanted for the safety of Jerusalem, and orders were issued for the whole Corps to attack on the 27th. On the right the 53rd and 60th Divisions were given an objective north of Bireh and Ram Allah; on the left the attack was to be carried out by three groups, in an easterly direction.

The general situation was that the Turkish Armies were still in two portions, the one which had retired on the maritime plain to the north, across the Auja, consisting of the VIIIth Army, of five divisions, the other the remnants of the VIIth Army, north of Jerusalem; between these two was a roadless, rocky tract of country, with deep valleys, where no operations on a large scale were possible.

On the front of the XXth Corps the Turkish Army occupied a salient, and the scheme of the attack was to squeeze this salient, by a combined movement northwards from Jerusalem and eastwards from Beit ur et Tahta, the centre being lightly held by the 231st Brigade from Beit Izza to el Tireh.

On the left the 10th Division would have to build up a flank from their junction with the Australian Division, while advancing in a general easterly direction. Both the 10th and 74th Divisions would, therefore, have to keep their right well forward.

141

As a preliminary to this general attack by the Corps, the 24th Welsh Regiment carried out an assault on Hill 1910 on the night 26th/27th. On clambering up the hill the battalion was fiercely opposed and hand to hand fighting took place. The Turks were pushed back, but before the Welshmen had time to consolidate, a well-directed counter-attack drove them off the hill.

Half an hour later a second attack was launched, and this time the hill was held. About seventy enemy dead were counted and three machine guns captured. The left of the battalion also advanced and occupied high ground covering the Wadi Imeish.

But while this preliminary engagement was being fought on the left, the Turks had attacked and driven in the outposts of the 60th Division on the right. An interesting situation had arisen. During the advance from Beersheba, amongst other things captured was the Turkish Wireless code, and now a message had been intercepted to the effect that an attack would be launched by the enemy to recapture Jerusalem. The time and details were all known to Sir E. Allenby.

Plans were altered. The right attack, of the 53rd and 60th Divisions, would obviously not take place, but the left attack was to proceed.

The left attack, with its three groups composed of the 229th Brigade on the right, the 31st Brigade in the centre, and the 29th and 30th Brigades on the left, was, in the initial stages, under the G.O.C. 10th Division. The 229th Brigade accordingly left its bivouacs in the Wadi Selman, advanced up the Wadi Zait, over Foka of tragic fame, and down into the Wadi Imeish, where the Scots Fusiliers and Somersets deployed at 7.50 a.m. for the attack along the Zeitun

Ridge, while the Turks were hammering at the 53rd and 60th Divisions.

The western edge of the ridge rises steeply, almost precipitously from the Wadi Imeish, but, ably supported by the 44th, 67th, and 117th F.A. Brigades, the assaulting battalions stormed the heights and captured their first objective, from Sheikh Abu es Zeitun to Kh. er Ras, with about forty prisoners, by 9.20 a.m. The actual time taken to reach the summit was 1 hour and 25 minutes.

The attack had been carried out so swiftly that the centre group had been left behind. Before any further advance could be made it was necessary for the 31st Brigade to clear the ground north of the Wadi Sunt, whence enfilade fire was sweeping the ranks of the 229th Brigade. While waiting under such cover as could be found, patrols were pushed out to the second objective, a rise in the ridge some 2,000 yards away. This was found to be abandoned, and the Somersets went forward and occupied it.

As soon as the 229th Brigade had taken Sheikh Abu es Zeitun, the two left battalions of the 231st Brigade were withdrawn from the line and came under the G.O.C. 10th Division as divisional reserve.

At 10.15 a.m. the attack was taken up by the 24th Royal Welsh Fusiliers, who during the night had concentrated in the Wadi Selman in front of Beit Dukku. One company captured Kh. Dreihemeh, while two assaulted Hill 2450 and succeeded in reaching the crest; neither assaulting force was able, however, to get farther than the summit of the respective hills, and each was enfiladed by the enemy on the reverse slope of the other. The companies on Hill 2450 were counter-attacked again and again,

and forced slightly down the hill.   During the afternoon a second assault was delivered, after an artillery
bombardment, but the cleverly sited Turkish machine
guns on Kh. Dreihemeh swept over the crest of Hill
2450, and the attempt failed.

At 5.45 p.m. the 229th Brigade was ready to
continue the advance, and with the Black Watch on
the left, in place of the Somersets, who were holding
the second objective, passed over the second objective
to the final assault.   The Scots Fusiliers reached their
goal without much trouble at 7 o'clock, by which
time the Black Watch were advancing up the lower
slopes of the hill to the left of Bir es Shafa, the
Devons were picketing the left bank of the Wadi
Sunt, and the Somersets had assembled and were
following in rear of the Black Watch.

The scouts of the Black Watch were within a short
distance of what appeared to be the summit of the
hill when rifle fire was opened on them.   The two
leading waves of the battalion were soon briskly
engaged with the enemy occupying successive tiers
of stone sangars on the terraces of the hill, which was
now found to have a false crest.   The enemy was
in well - prepared positions, and in considerable
numbers, but was ejected from the first crest at once.
A hot engagement was then fought for about an hour,
the enemy charging frequently and sometimes getting
to close quarters.   By 10 p.m. the whole of the hill
was taken.

For the night the outposts of the 229th were in
touch with the 231st Brigade on the slopes of Hill 2450.

Meanwhile the attack of the Turks on the 60th
and 53rd Divisions had failed, and the whole of the
XXth Corps was ordered to advance on the 28th.

THE WADI SUNT IN SPATE.

Early in the morning the 231st and 230th Brigades, the latter having occupied Kh. el Jufier, received orders to co-operate with the 229th Brigade, and the 60th Division on the right. The advance of the 229th in conjunction with the 10th Division was resumed at 1.30 p.m., the first objectives being Beitania, with Hill 2435 on the right, and the high ground on the left.

The Black Watch were on the right, with two separate points to attack, and the Somersets on the left. The three attacks were launched simultaneously with the object of preventing a concentration of fire by the enemy. The men were as cunning as the Turks, and, knowing that the enemy machine guns were trained on the summit of the hills, they went down into the ravine, which lay between them and the village of Beitania, at a terrific speed. Once down in the cleft the Black Watch paused in safety and organised for the assault. It was a stiff climb up, No. 4 Company Machine Guns supporting with overhead fire, for which the conditions were ideal. The village was taken, after some fighting amongst the houses, with seven machine guns and seventy unwounded prisoners.

The Somersets took their first objective with little trouble, and proceeded to capture el Muntar, about a mile to the north of Beitania, and only just missed three guns which the Turks succeeded in removing under cover of favourable ground.

On the right flank, the 230th and 231st had moved forward—the 230th gradually relieving the 231st, who were drawn into reserve south of Beitania. Finally the 230th held a line from the left of the 60th Division, at Rafat, to Hill 2435, where they connected with the 229th Brigade.

Brigadier-General Hoare gives some interesting details in a letter to Colonel Allan :

" I am sorry to have missed the G.O.C. to-day ; I should have much liked to have shown him my battle-field, so that he could appreciate more fully the good work my gallant fellows have put in.

" The attack on the west end of the Zeitun Ridge was comparatively easy, though it was a very stiff climb up, but it all went off without any hitch, though my fellows had to stick out a continuous shelling for many hours while waiting for the right of the 10th Division to get up somewhere near them—the advance being by the left, I felt bound to do this.

" The second objective also presented no great difficulty, but the last objective of that evening, viz. the attack on the Kh. Shafa Hill, was a teaser. I think we got off cheaply because it was done in the dark, but the Turks had three tiers of sangars built, splendid cover, and many machine guns, and it was pretty hot while it lasted.

" We got shelled and sniped while drawing up orders and making preparations for that attack on Beitania.

" After making a personal reconnaissance I wiped out my original plan of first taking Beitania, and then swinging round to the north for P35 central, and made up my mind to go for Beitania, the village beyond it, and P35 central simultaneously. And I was influenced in this decision by the knowledge that (1) my right flank was unprotected, (2) Beitania itself was untenable unless both the ridge beyond it and P35 central were also held. So I drew up the following plan—*vide* rough sketch.

" Jumping off place Kh. Shafa.

" Ayr and Lanark (Scots Fusiliers) on right, Fife and Forfar (Black Watch) on left to go for Beitania, but the right companies to push straight on without stopping at the village and make straight for the ridge.

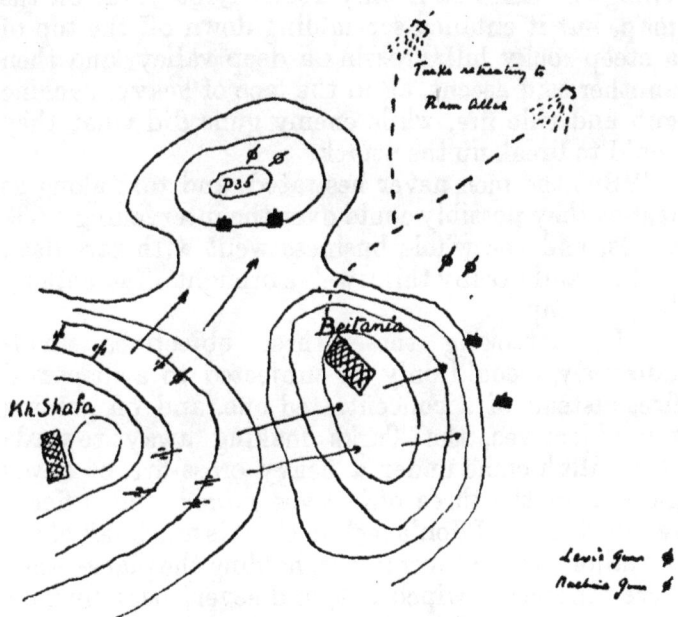

Tanks retreating to
Ram Allah

P36

Beitania

Kh.Shafa

Lewis Gun
Machine Gun

**ROUGH SKETCH OF POSITIONS.**

" As soon as that attack was started, Somersets, with two companies Devons in support, to make for P35 central.

" I kept the K.S.L.I. in reserve behind the Kh. Shafa, and got twelve machine guns into position, giving splendid covering fire to all attacking battalions, and ' turned all the taps on '—they made a proper rattle.

" I must point out that from Kh. Shafa to the village of Beitania is only about 1,000 yards on the map, but it entailed scrambling down off the top of a steep rocky hill, crossing a deep valley, and then another stiff ascent, all in the face of heavy machine gun and rifle fire, while enemy guns did what they could to break up the attack.

" But the men never hesitated, and tore along as fast as they possibly could over the intervening 1,500 yards, and the whole business went with rare dash and go, and I really think we've brought off something like a ' coup.'

" By attacking these three objectives simultaneously I could only be subjected to a dispersed fire, instead of a concentrated one, and on gaining my objectives, the Turks making away towards Ram Allah came under a heavy cross-fire of Lewis guns from the three objectives gained, and suffered severe losses.   I don't reckon there is much left of the battalion, or whatever it was, holding the place—they were practically wiped out, and seven machine guns is no small parcel to pick up in one stunt.

" I am sure that if you want to catch Turks, you must go at them fast, though it's not easy to go fast in this country.

" The nature of the terrain of the operations makes it terribly difficult to find and bring in dead and wounded, as well as to find captured munitions of war, which are hidden among rocks."

BRIG-GEN. R.H.HOARE, D.S.O.
CMDG 229TH BDE.

The next day, the 29th, the advance was resumed by the 230th Brigade, with the Sussex on the right, the Buffs in the centre, and the Suffolks on the left. Ram Allah was occupied without opposition, but further advance was held up owing to the 60th Division meeting with strong resistance at Bireh, which was not overcome until 4.15 p.m.

About 100 wounded Turks were found in Ram Allah. They were in a terrible state, as their wounds had not been dressed for four or five days, and they had had no food since the previous morning. Some British were among them. Most of them were evacuated to casualty clearing stations that night.

During the night the 60th Division continued to advance on Beitun, and the 230th Brigade moved forward in conjunction with them. Colonel Powell Edwards has a spirited account of the proceedings.

" The advance involved a forward move of some 1,500 yards, which, on the left of the 230th Brigade front, involved the crossing of a deep ravine, and, on the right, an advance over very rough boulder-strewn ground. . . . It was as unlike anything previously rehearsed in the way of night advances as could be. It was conducted at a pace as near a run as possible for men who, at every step, were falling over boulders, and had to scramble over a series of stone walls. The ground was covered with enemy snipers, who mostly fired several rounds rapid, and then made off. This scramble continued for some twenty minutes, during which we reached the top of a crest and moved on over a steady downward slope, the going being still very bad. At the bottom of this slope a stony track ran horizontal to our line of march. As we approached it, figures could be seen, dimly against the sky on the next crest, advancing

towards us, and a moment later a storm of machine
gun fire broke out on our front, the crest being
apparently lined with a dozen or more guns along the
battalion front. The 60th Division lay down on
the track, and the machine gun fire, being mostly
high, went over our heads. The impression was
strong that, at the pace we had come, our objective
was now behind us. A patrol sent out to the left
could find no trace of the 10th Buffs, or of A and B
Companies. The opposing line, by the machine gun
flashes, obviously extended well out to the left of our
left flank. . . . Shortly after a message was passed
down the 60th Division front ordering a withdrawal
to the high ground in rear, and this was duly carried
out, that (the high ground) being in fact the objective
of the advance.''

The line el Burj–Kh. et Tireh was occupied. By
daylight nothing of the enemy, beyond a few snipers,
was seen.

During the morning of the 31st December the 230th
Brigade took over the line held by the 229th, which
then went into bivouac in the Latron area. Within
the next few days the whole Division was relieved
and went into Corps reserve.

.          .          .          .          .

The great Turkish attack to recover Jerusalem,
delivered from the north against the 60th Division,
and from the east against the 53rd, was not only
defeated, but resulted in the enemy finding himself
seven miles farther from Jerusalem than when he
started. It had been made by a number of fresh
troops, who had taken no part in the retreat from
Beersheba, and was pressed with great determination
against Tel el Ful in the morning, and with unexpected strength on the whole front in the afternoon.

At night the Turks were back in their original positions, and the next day the 60th Division drove them from Bir Nebala, el Jib, and Kh. Adaseh, and so swept up on the right of the 74th Division.    The final line occupied by the XXth Corps ran from Deir Ibn Obeid, south-east of Jerusalem, to Hismeh and Jeba, to Beitin, and turned west through el Burj, Ras Kerker, to Beir el Kuddis.

.        .        .        .        .

In the whole period of fighting in the Judean Hills the difficulties of the Administrative Branch of the Division cannot be overestimated.    Camels, as is generally known, are delicate animals, and died by hundreds—it was a common sight to see carcases of drowned camels ; but it was also physically impossible for the brutes to move on the muddy roads.    On the 12th December 1,000 donkeys, small white ones from the Nile, were attached to the Division, and 300 were allotted to each brigade, the rest being kept as a depot.    These little beasts were better than the camels, but on Christmas Eve and Christmas Day the weather was too much for them, and they became exhausted from exposure.    Many of them died too.

Under these circumstances it is not to be wondered that there were occasions when troops went short of rations, the wonder is that they were not starved ! Something was always delivered to them.    One finds, amongst the correspondence, a certain amount of good-humoured grumbling over the Christmas dinner of " bully beef and water "—what could be better, one writes, than the canned beef of the Argentine washed down with a sparkling draught of fantassi !— but every man recognised, with gratitude, the efforts of the Q Branch.    This quotation from Colonel

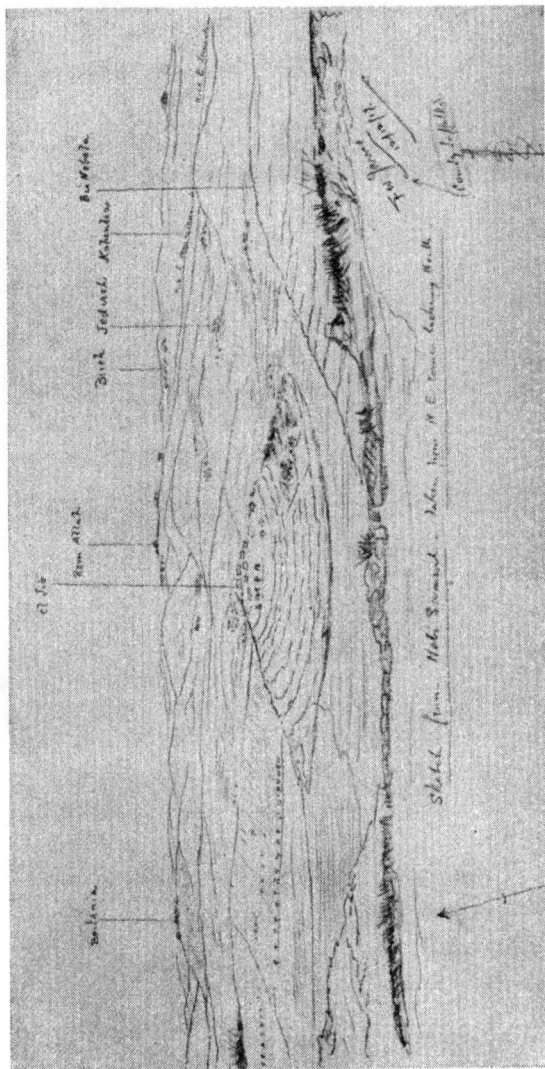

THIS SKETCH FROM THE SALIENT OF NEBY-SAMWIL SHOWS, IN THE DISTANCE, THE COUNTRY ACROSS WHICH THE DIVISION ATTACKED FROM LEFT TO RIGHT.

The 60th Division attacked from the line in the foreground, captured-el Jib and Nebula, and drove through in the direction of Bireh.

189]

Powell Edwards, whose descriptions are extraordinarily vivid, will put the state of affairs before the reader :

" The weather for the period December 21st/26th was vile in the extreme. The beds of the wadis became roaring torrents. Dead and drowned camels were plentifully strewn about. Ration parties had a heartrending time, and the transport, as a whole, had a very harassing and weary existence. Journeys took twice the usual time, the paths were all dangerously slippery, and small white donkeys, which had been rushed up from Egypt to assist camels in this mountainous country, fared very badly in the continuous cold and wet.

" The limit was reached on Christmas Day, when the rain was torrential : bivouac sheets were useless against it, and the thousands of small rivulets which poured off every rock defied any attempts at drainage. Everyone and everything was soaked to the skin, and even the battalion cooks could not manage to produce hot tea. The troops' Christmas dinner consisted of bully beef, wet biscuits, and cold water in abundance.

" It may be said that the work of the battalion cooks throughout this campaign was extremely good. During the campaign in Egypt and lower Palestine there had, at least, been no difficulty in kindling fires, though fuel was sometimes a little short ; but now, in these torrential rains, dry wood was at a premium, and in spite of the great efforts being made down the lines of communication, the quantity of both fuel and rations was diminishing. Yet, however high the wind, and however soaking the rain, hardly ever did any company go without some form of hot food, or drink, on any day when the battalion was not engaged in fighting.

" The battalion cooks, equally with the battalion transport and the administrative service generally, got hardly any tangible reward, in the shape of decorations, for a great deal of hard and devoted service. At the close of these operations commanding officers were specially asked to forward for consideration names of those in administrative service who had done well, but when it is considered that the total allotment for the whole brigade of awards for good administrative work was one officer and two other ranks, it is obvious that a multitude of most deserving cases had to go without recognition of any sort, other than the very real appreciation of their comrades for good work well done, and work which was vital to the continued maintenance of the force in the field.

" It was understood that at this period it was for some time a matter of grave doubt whether the force could be maintained at all in its positions round Jerusalem, and until the end of January rations were short, and seemed shorter still to appetites tuned up by the keen mountain air."

The strain that was thrown on Lt.-Colonel R. B. Cousens and his staff was tremendous, and the conditions were constantly varying. From el Arish onwards the Camel Transport was constantly used, for short periods, by the Army, when divisions had to move in a hurry and it was not possible to take wheels. The order of June did not, as a matter of fact, remain in force for long. The details of the camel transport are :

| | |
|---|---|
| Divisional Headquarters . . . | 22 camels. |
| Headquarters Divisional A.S.C. . . | 3 ,, |
| Machine Gun Company . . . | 49 ,, |
| Headquarters Division Artillery . . | 4 ,, |
| Headquarters Brigade Artillery . . | 7 ,, |
| Each Battery . . . . . | 17 ,, |
| Divisional Ammunition Column . . | 576 ,, |
| Headquarters Divisional R.E. . . | 4 ,, |

AN OLIVE GROVE OF VERY OLD TREES NEAR BEIT MAHSIR.

| | | |
|---|---|---|
| Each Field Company R.E. | . . | 69 camels, |
| Divisional Signal Company | . . | 44 ,, |
| Infantry Brigade Headquarters . | . . | 13 ,, |
| Each Infantry Battalion . | . . | 110 ,, |
| Each Field Ambulance | . . | 233 ,, |
| Mobile Veterinary Section . | . . | 5 ,, |

In the operations which concluded with the capture of Tel el Sheria, the Division was watered and fed entirely by camels. But when the Division returned to roads, the Divisional train was used, although all through the campaign a Camel Transport Company was always attached to the Division and, as previously mentioned, donkeys. During the quick moves and actual battles the Division was placed on what was called a mobile ration :

| | | |
|---|---|---|
| Preserved beef . | . . . . | 12 ounces. |
| Biscuit . | . . . . | 12 ,, |
| Condensed milk | . . . | 1 ,, |
| Jam . | . . . . | 4 ,, |
| Sugar . | . . . . | 3 ,, |
| Tea . | . . . | $\frac{5}{8}$ ,, |
| Cheese (when available) | . . . | 3 ,, |
| Dried fruit . | . . . | 6 ,, |
| Soup squares . | . . . . | 2 ,, |
| Cocoa . | . . . . | 1 ,, |
| Total . | . . . | 2 lbs. 12$\frac{5}{8}$ ,, |

The Indian drivers of the ammunition column received rather less—a total of 2 lbs. 7$\frac{3}{8}$ ozs. The camel drivers received 1 lb. of biscuit, $\frac{1}{2}$ lb. of onions, and $\frac{1}{2}$ lb. of dates.

The weight of the mobile ration was estimated at 4 lbs., the extra weight being made up by packing-cases, etc., and no fuel was carried other than the broken cases provided.

The horse and mule ration was 12 lbs. of oats or barley. No hay was carried, and there was no grazing to be got. They did not last long on this provender, as it made them scour very badly.

The camel ration was 10 lbs. of grain. These beasts required from 15 to 25 gallons of water apiece when they were watered, and they had to be watered every third day.

Altogether the transport required for mobile rations was :

| | | | |
|---|---|---|---|
| 16,000 men (British) . . . . | 64,000 lbs. |
| 200 ,, (Indians) . . . . | 600 ,, |
| 1,000 ,, (Natives) . . . . | 2,000 ,, |
| 5,000 horses . . . . . | 60,000 ,, |
| 2,000 camels . . . . . | 22,000 ,, |
| Total . . . . . | 148,600 ,, |

The load for a Somali camel was 240 lbs., of which there were 620
,, ,, Egyptian ,, 300 ,, ,, ,, 496
,, ,, Indian ,, 350 ,, ,, ,, 425

The Somali camels were not liked, as they refused to move in the dark ; they would, however, work with a full moon.

But the mobile ration was only given in times of stress, otherwise the Division was on the normal ration of fresh meat, bread, and sometimes frozen rabbits. The meat was kept in cold storage at Port Said, and sent up from there to railhead protected by blocks of ice.

The extent of Colonel Cousens' work, when put down in figures, begins to assume correct proportions, but there is no mathematical formula for the weather and lack of roads in Judea.

# CHAPTER X

## 1918

General situation—Plans for the Jordan Valley—Road making.

At the opening of the new year it was felt that the events of the Great War were leading to a crisis. In France the Staff was uneasy, indeed, distressingly anxious. A situation had arisen which pointed clearly to a final trial of strength.

The great British–French attack of the year had been launched on the 31st July from the Ypres salient, and the result, after months of fighting, was an insignificant gain of territory, an appalling list of casualties, and a greatly weakened British Army. It had been a repetition of the battles on the Somme of the previous year, but the offensive, in its incidents, had not been so successful; a bad season had turned a low-lying and naturally water-logged country into one great bog, from which it was impossible for a great army to extricate itself and exploit any success it might have gained in the initial stages of the fight. It was a battle of attrition, in which neither side won an overwhelming advantage, but the British undoubtedly suffered the greater loss.

This was followed by a brilliantly conceived break through the Hindenburg Line at Cambrai, which, nevertheless, achieved nothing.

Our French Allies had suffered from a severe blow in the early part of the year, when their offensive about Rheims had failed, and, to make matters worse, the Italians were severely defeated at Caporetto in October.

In November Russia had fallen into the hands of the Bolshevist maniacs, and had just signed an armistice when Jerusalem was captured.

In Mesopotamia the death of General Maude cast a gloom over his army.

Up to 1918 there seems little doubt that the vital blow might have been received by either side, more probably given by the Central Powers, in any one of the many theatres of war. The internal conditions of the Central Powers now demanded a supreme and final effort, and the Franco–Belgian Front was the nearest and greatest of all battle-fields. No matter how wide the dream vision might have been, it was now too late to think of Egypt or India ; the American Armies were actually in France, undergoing training, and although the German High Command under-rated their numbers, they did realise that time was short, and that they would soon lose superiority of strength on the Western Front.

It is not belittling the achievement of Sir E. Allenby's army to say that the one great object of a commander had not, as yet, been fulfilled. Towns and provinces may still have political meaning in war, but to meet and destroy the enemy's armies is the main consideration. There had been no great capture of men or material; the wily Turk had succeeded in slipping away whenever the circle seemed about to close round him.

In December the 52nd (Lowland) Division had crossed the River Auja, and the whole of the XXIst Corps had advanced along the coast, increasing the

distance between the enemy and Jaffa by from three
to seven miles.  The quay at that place was now
secured from artillery fire and could be used, in
conjunction with the Jaffa–Jerusalem Road, for
supplies.  The XXth Corps had also freed Jerusalem
in the same way, as we know.

The British line, protecting Jerusalem, faced east
on the Jordan side, and then turned at a sharp right
angle to the left, facing north.  Viewed on the map,
it seems peculiarly open to raids, and such an enterprise was quite possible, although difficulties of
country made the line more secure than is apparent.
A more definite obstacle on which to rest the right
flank was the swift-running Jordan, combined with
the control of the Dead Sea.  There were also to the
east of the Jordan friendly Arab forces operating
against the Turks.

That great rent in the surface of the earth, the
Valley of Jordan, is perceived from all the important
heights in Judea.  The peaks, the ranges, the ridges,
suddenly cease, and then, far away in the distance,
the hills of Moab rise in a long line across the horizon.
" The depth, the haggard desert through which the
land sinks into it, the singularity of that gulf and its
prisoned sea, and the high barrier beyond, conspire
to produce on the inhabitants of Judea a moral effect
such as, I suppose, is created by no other frontier in
the world."  (*The Historical Geography of the Holy
Land*, George Adam Smith.)  The hills descend with
steep gradients into the valley, or break off in frowning
cliffs.  There are a number of deep gorges, with such
precipitous banks, that it is impossible, in most cases,
to cross from one side to the other, but there are no
passes.  The road meanders round in the lesser depres-

sions, and along ridges, avoids the cliffs, and drops down the steep incline of an unbroken hill into the valley.

Sir E. Allenby decided to advance across this country with the objects (a) to prevent the enemy from raiding the country to the west of the Dead Sea, (b) to obtain control of the Dead Sea, (c) to secure a point of departure for operations eastward, with a view of interrupting the enemy's line of communication in the Hedjaz, in conjunction with the Arab forces based on Akaba.

The 60th Division had taken over the line from the 52nd, and was facing the Jordan.   On the right flank rose the heights of el Muntar, in the centre of the division the high ground of Ras Umm Deisis and Arak Ibrahim gave the enemy an advantageous position, and on the left Ras el Tawil was an imposing feature.   Behind these hills the ground fell on its first descent towards the Valley of the Jordan, and then rose again at Talaat ed Dumm, the Ascent of Blood, where the stone is streaked with red, and from thence a ridge runs to Jebel Ekteif, in a south-easterly direction, turns east to Neby Musa, and drops into the Jordan Valley about five miles south of Jericho.   But to the left, opposite Jericho, the hills cease abruptly in the cliffs of Jebel Keruntal.   The latter was the objective of the 60th Division, while the Anzac Division would operate on the right flank and enter the Valley near Neby Musa.

But, for the moment, the improvement of communications was most urgent, and the construction of roads was pushed forward.

.          .          .          .          .

During the month of January the Division was in

Corps reserve, and was concentrated in the Latron area, with the exception of the 231st Brigade, which remained at Beitania. All brigades were employed on the all-important task of road-making.

The 229th and 230th worked on the Amwas–Nuba–Sira–Tahta Road.

" We had to make a new road to link up with the Ram Allah Road at Tattenham Corner," writes Major Ogilvie. " It was a most picturesque Wadi, covered with olive trees and, what was more important, with any amount of stones suitable for road-making to hand. On the Latron–Beit Sira Road stones were scarce, and had to be man-handled in limbers, or in baskets often quite a distance, but here there were stones of decent size, and within a few yards of the road. It was a 16-foot road, bottomed with large stones, then two layers of smaller stones, and blinded with gravel. Everyone went at it like a schoolboy on a holiday, and we completed our road two days before scheduled time, on one occasion actually doing 1½ yards of road per man." (*Fife and Forfar Yeomanry.*)

In addition to troops, the native population was also drawn on for labour, and on the main Jaffa–Jerusalem Road men, women, and children were busy carrying stones from the hill-sides to fill up holes ; but this method of road-mending was not too successful, as the heavy lorries soon pounded the patchwork into so much mud.

At this time of year spring flowers commenced to bloom in great profusion, and the men, having made more substantial shelters than was afforded by a bivouac sheet, and built for themselves " houses " of stone, transplanted flowers from the wadis and laid

out " gardens "—in some cases the device of the
" Broken Spur " was traced on the hill-side in limestone.  So comfortable were they, that a downpour
of rain was welcome, for it meant that they could lie
in their " houses " and read, smoke, or play cards !

During the month the Corps Commander called for
reports on training, based on recent experiences.
There was a concensus of opinion that the general
lines of training were correct.  On such matters as
communication there was always great difficulty over
visual signalling.  Flags were impossible to " pick
up," owing to the natural colour of the country—
mostly a grey background, against which neither
white nor blue flags were visible.  The helio had been
successfully used, but in the winter months the fitful
appearance of the sun rendered it useless.  The most
dependable method, when the field telephone did not
work, or could not be used, was the slowest of all—
the runner.

Major C. H. Balston, of the Buffs, gave some
interesting information in his report on the Turkish
rear-guard action :

" It was noticed, almost invariably, that positions
were very lightly held, but that great use was made of
machine guns, skilfully placed, which commanded
approaches, and which were almost always successfully withdrawn.  The country generally favours the
fighting of rear-guard actions, owing to the admirable cover among rocks, difficulty of detection, and
the magnificent observation from hill-tops, from
which hostile rear-guards can always see whether the
position is seriously endangered.  This enables them
to hang on till the last minute.  The procedure which
the enemy seems to adopt in fighting rear-guard actions
is as follows : When the main position is given up, a

general retirement takes place to the next position, with the exception of a few snipers, who occupy the scattered intermediary positions from which they are gradually driven. It has been remarked that the men who are left to cover the retirement are never Germans, seldom Turks, and nearly always Syrians or Armenians."

# CHAPTER XI

## THE CAPTURE OF JERICHO

The 231st Brigade worked on the Biddu–Beitania Road, but on the 16th February it was placed at the disposal of the 60th Division for operations towards the Jordan, and marched to er Ram on the 17th.

The attack contemplated by Sir E. Allenby was launched before dawn on the 19th February, and by 9 a.m. el Muntar, Arak Ibrahim, and Ras el Tawil were captured by the 60th Division, the 210th Machine Gun Company taking part with two sections in action at ed Dawarah. The 231st Brigade, less the Welsh Regiment, which remained at er Ram to find guards for Jerusalem and Bethlehem, was in support to the 181st Brigade at Mukhmas.

The 181st Brigade advanced between the Wadi Kelt and the Wadi Makuk ; the other two brigades of the 60th Division advanced on the line of Talaat ed Dumm and of Neby Musa respectively. On the right the Anzac Division concentrated behind el Muntar to operate against the Turkish left on the 20th.

During the night the two brigades south of the Wadi Kelt deployed in the Wadi Sidr, and attacked Talaat ed Dumm and Jebel Ektief at dawn ; the former was taken at 7.15 a.m., the latter offered a stubborn resistance, and was in such difficult country that only one line of approach was possible : it was not taken until midday. On the right the mounted

WADI KELT.

This picture shows the nature of the country between Jerusalem and the Jordan Valley.

troops, operating through wild, mountainous, desert country, were unable to cross the Wadi Mukelik in the face of the Turkish fire from Neby Musa, but a brigade found a way down into the valley by the Wadi Kumran, and by dusk was at Wadi Jufet Zeben.

Meanwhile the 181st Brigade had been advancing over exceedingly difficult country against much machine gun fire from the ever-retreating Turkish rear-guard, and had reached a point about two miles from the escarpment west of Jericho. In the evening the Shropshires relieved the 21st Londons on the right of the Brigade front, having the 25th Welsh Fusiliers in support. In the early morning patrols reached the escarpment.

This was the small part played by the 231st Brigade in the capture of Jericho, of interest inasmuch as they represented the 74th Division, and that it afforded the Shropshires a view of the unique valley of the Jordan and of Jericho. Mounted troops and armoured cars were seen entering the town, and shortly afterwards the 181st Brigade took over the whole of the outpost line, the Shropshires and Welsh Fusiliers returning to Ras el Tawil.

Some days were spent in road-making in this area, and the Brigade passed into the command of the 53rd Division, relieving two reserve battalions of the 158th Brigade on the 26th, and the outpost line of that brigade on the next night.

12

# CHAPTER XII

## ACTIONS OF TEL AZUR

General Allenby's plans—Preliminary skirmishing—The new operations—The attack opens—Selwad—Yebrud—Burj Bardawil—The Wadi Jib—The objective a bad position—The final line.

THE position was on the left of the Jerusalem–Nablus Road, and the line ran from the high ground south-west of Ain Yebrud to Arnutieh, Surdah, to the high ground south and south-west of Abu Kush. The introduction of the 231st Brigade was in the nature of an advanced unit of the 74th Division, which was to take part, in a few days, in the new operations started by the capture of Jericho, and the clearance of the west bank of the Jordan.

With future undertakings against the Hedjaz Railway and the enemy east of the Jordan in mind, Sir E. Allenby planned to deprive him of the use of important roads leading into the lower Jordan Valley.

" It was essential, in the first place, to cross the Wadi Aujah and secure the high ground on the north bank covering the approaches to the Jordan Valley by the Beisan–Jericho Road (this road runs straight down the Jordan Valley from where the railway from Haifa crosses the Jordan), and secondly, by advancing sufficiently far northwards on either side of the Jerusalem–Nablus Road, to deny to the enemy the use of all tracks and roads leading to the lower Jordan Valley. This accomplished, any troops he might determine to transfer from the west to the east bank of the Jordan would have to make a considerable detour to the north. I therefore ordered the XXth

Corps to secure Kh. el Beiyudat and Abu Tellul, in
the Jordan Valley, north of the Wadi Aujah, and
farther to the west the line Kefr Malik–Kh. Abu
Felah, the high ground south of Sinjil, and the ridge
north of the Wadi el Jib running through Kh. Aliuta–
Jiljilia–Abwein–Arura, thence to Deir es Sudan and
Nebi Saleh."

It will be noticed that General Allenby leaves a wide
gap between Abu Tellul and Kefr Malik : no more
eloquent testimony as to the nature of the country
could be given.   Troops could not manœuvre in this
mass of arid hills, tumbling in wild chaos from the
watershed, about the Jerusalem–Nablus Road, into
the Jordan Valley.   Along the watershed, and to the
west of it, an advance was possible, but ridge after
ridge, separated by deep valleys, confronted the
troops—picturesque no doubt with villages, ruins,
fig groves, and olive trees dotted about on the
terraced slopes, but, as everyone had long since discovered, demanding the greatest physical endurance
and determination of spirit it was possible to extract
from the attacking troops.

The XXIst Corps, by advancing, in conjunction
with the XXth Corps on its right, would improve its
position for a further advance against the Turkish
defensive system which had been constructed from
Jiljulieh through Tabsor to the sea.

The advance must, of necessity, be slow.   The
small-scale, uncontoured maps on which the army
worked could give no indication of the time required
to move from any one given point to another.   Measured by the scale, a few miles would be shown, but
the battalion commander on the spot, viewing his
objective from the crest of a prominent hill, whence

it appeared but a stone's throw away, measuring the depth of the valley below, calculating the height and number of terraces down into the valley and mounting the opposite slope, on the other side of which were other descents and ascents, despaired of even stating an approximate time for covering the distance.

It was raining heavily when the line was taken over on the 27th by the 24th Welsh Regiment on the right, and the 24th Welsh Fusiliers on the left—between the 160th Brigade, 53rd Division, and the 31st Brigade, 10th Division.

The line was carefully patrolled and reconnoitred. It was lightly held by the Turks, with small parties on the tops of hills.   The line was advanced on the 1st March by the Royal Welsh Fusiliers, who occupied the high ground south of Bir es Zeit without opposition.   The next night the Welsh Regiment pushed forward to Ain Yebrud and captured a machine gun ; at the same time the Welsh Fusiliers took Jufna and the commanding hill Kh. Bir es Zeit, overlooking Bir es Zeit.

On the 3rd General Girdwood assumed command of the line and a slight redistribution of forces took place : Kh. Bir es Zeit and the ridge south of the village were handed over to the 10th Division.   At the same time the 229th and 230th Brigades ceased making roads and commenced to march north, the concentration at Balua Lake being complete on the 7th.

Another small advance was made by the Welsh Regiment during the night 6th/7th, to Kh. Kefr Ana, and hills near Yebrud, and by the 24th Royal Welsh Fusiliers to the north-west of Sinia.  Very little opposition was encountered, the steep precipices being the chief difficulty and causing a number of casualties with sprained ankles. The enemy was, however, located in force to the north of these positions.

The Buffs then marched from Balua Lake and took over the line.

In his orders for the attack on the 9th March General Girdwood expresses the hope of the Higher Command. The advance was intended to be so rapid " that the enemy will be driven off the line Turmus Aya–Sinjil–Jiljilia before he has time to recover from the first blow, and it is hoped that this may also result in the capture of the enemy's artillery grouped round Selwad and Attara. The operation will therefore be complete in two days."

The 53rd Division, on the right, had, on the first day, the objective Kh. Abu Felah–Mezrah esh Sherkiyeh. The 10th Division, on the left, attacked in two groups : the right on the objective Attara–Hill 2791, and the left away to Nebi Saleh. The 74th Division, in the centre, would get firmly astride the Nablus Road, with the 231st Brigade, on the right, driving for Mezrah esh Sherkiyeh–Sheikh Saleh–Burj el Lisaneh, and the 230th Brigade, on the left, making for a hill about 1,000 yards due south of Aliuta.

Officers reconnoitred the ground on the 8th, an operation which entailed the expenditure of much physical energy ; horses were out of the question, and the only possible view-point had to be gained by scaling the terraces of a commanding hill, a matter of several hours' stiff climbing.

" The trenches of Burj Bardawil could be seen well enough lying on lower ground to the front. Beyond the mass of Burj Bardawil, commanding

the Nablus Road, and the wells at Ain Sinia, was
evidently a considerable defile which had to be crossed,
and beyond that again the hill known as K12 towered
to the skyline.  To those who scanned the line of
advance, and who had by this time considerable
experience of movement in these mountains, it looked
a very long day's journey to the top of K12, even if
unopposed.  In the foreground, and only some few
hundred yards beyond the outpost line, could be seen
the top of a square building, which was one of the
houses in Yebrud.  The village was reported to
contain at night an advance post of a few Turks, and
immediately behind, or north of it, the map showed
a wadi reported to be steep, and obviously commanded by trenches from Burj Bardawil."   (Colonel
Powell Edwards.)

The strength of the Division at the commencement
of March was 592 officers, and 14,571 other ranks,
giving a fighting strength of 324 officers and 9,597
other ranks.

The 231st Brigade Orders gave the opening attack
on Selwad to the Shropshire Light Infantry, with
the 25th Royal Welsh Fusiliers in support.  From
Selwad the 25th Welsh Fusiliers would move up on
the right against Sheikh Saleh and Mezrah, while the
Shropshires advanced on Burj el Lisaneh ; the 24th
Welsh Regiment would then be in support.

We will follow the action of this brigade.  The
Shropshires commenced their march to the line of
deployment—some trees about 1,500 yards beyond
the outpost line—at about 1.30 a.m. on the 9th.  The
night was very dark, but the position was reached
about 4 o'clock without incident.  They were now
beneath the Selwad defences, which were on the
forward slope of the hill.

Just before the attack commenced a company of
the 25th Royal Welsh Fusiliers was sent to dislodge
some machine guns on the right, which were enfilading the line of advance, and a company of the Welsh
Regiment was detailed, from the reserve, to clear two
hills, also on the right. Both these missions were
successful. With the right flank clear, the Shropshires
then rushed the Selwad trenches, and, after a short
fight, routed the Turks, who left five officers and
twenty-three other ranks in their hands.

The 25th Royal Welsh Fusiliers then deployed on
the right. The 210th Machine Gun Company came
into action, about this time, against Tel Azur, which
had not as yet been captured by the 53rd Division,
and against Burj Bardawil.

The brigade was now faced with the Wadi Nimr
below a steep escarpment. There were only two
paths leading down to the uneven, boulder-strewn
bed of the wadi, and both were under heavy machine
gun fire from Lisaneh and Sheikh Saleh. Neither
the brigade on the right nor the one on the left had
come up in line, and both flanks were exposed. A
temporary halt was necessary, and, while the two
assaulting battalions waited, attacks launched by the
Turks were broken up by the 268th F.A. Brigade and
the 16th Mountain Battery.

Meanwhile on the left of the Division the Buffs had
been holding the outpost line, the rest of the Brigade
being at Balua Lake. The Brigade Orders were for
the Suffolks to open the attack, with the Sussex in
support. After the capture of Bardawil the Sussex
were to move, echeloned in rear to the left of the
Suffolks, and then attack a hill known as K12 in line
with them. The order is not very clear. There is a

paragraph dealing with the Buffs which reads : " The outpost battalion (10th Buffs) will be responsible for the safety of the left flank only of the attacking force during its deployment, and will hold Yebrud until attacking troops have passed," which apparently meant that the Buffs must, at some time or other, capture Yebrud. No doubt there were verbal elaborations, for Colonel Powell Edwards interprets the order as : (1) the 10th Buffs were to drive the Turks out of Yebrud at midnight on the 8th March ; (2) the Brigade was then to move forward through the out-post line, 15th Suffolks leading, 16th Sussex in support, and 12th Norfolks in reserve ; (3) on reaching a point some hundred yards in front of the outpost line and on the east of the Yebrud Wadi, the leading battalion was to deploy ; (4) at the same point the Sussex were to deploy 1,000 yards in rear of the leading battalion and to move up on its left, the two battalions then assaulting the Bardawil trenches from their southerly flank, the assault being covered by the Divisional Artillery ; (5) this objective being secured, the advance was to be continued to K12.

It has, even on paper, the appearance of a compli-cated manœuvre.

The three battalions left Balua Lake at 7.30 p.m. on the 8th March—the officers had been reconnoitring the position all day, and only returned in time to snatch a hasty meal—and a wearisome march fol-lowed. The Nablus Road was a mass of camels, wheeled transport, and artillery, bearing, as it did, the traffic of the whole Corps ; the Brigade had to cross it, and then proceed over broken ground, which necessitated marching in single file to the place of assembly behind the outpost line. The march was a crawling gait, punctuated by long waits while mules were being persuaded to scramble over obstacles, and lasted three hours.

Meanwhile Lord Sackville, commanding the Buffs, had received orders during the day to occupy Yebrud by midnight. Apparently he had sent a patrol out the previous night which reported that the village was held by a few snipers, but when a company tried to rush the place at 8 p.m. on the 8th, it was found to be held by a strong garrison, and it was not taken. The reserve company was ordered up to assist in a fresh attack.

Of the subsequent events Colonel Powell Edwards gives a most graphic account. The time was midnight, and the place of assembly was:

" a deep and cavernous gorge, with a towering cliff facing us. Lying at the bottom of the gorge were some battalions of the 231st Brigade who were to move up ahead of us. About midnight news filtered through that the Buffs had attacked Yebrud with a platoon and failed to take it, the garrison disposing of several machine guns whose presence had not been expected. This news was not unexpected, as, since our arrival, there had been continuous heavy machine gun and rifle fire, and bomb explosions, from our front. Soon after this orders were received that the Buffs would assault Yebrud with two companies, while the rest of the Brigade carried out the pre-arranged movement for the attack on Burj Bardawil at dawn.

" At 1.45 a.m. the battalions of the 231st Brigade moved off, and the battalion (Sussex), following the Suffolks, moved up a long, narrow, and steep track out of the wadi. This again was a single file business, and much interfered with by recalcitrant mules of

battalions in front, which refused to face the slope—
the path had been reconnoitred for some distance by
the officers of the battalion, with the result that our
mules had been placed at the rear of the column, the
Lewis guns and ammunition being man-handled up.

" The night was very dark, and the advance up the
steep and narrow path continued for two hours, or
more. At the top of the slope the battalion should
have continued following the Suffolks to the eastward,
while Headquarters moved slightly northerly, to a
point whence the attack could be directed and visual
signalling maintained with the Brigade. But as
Headquarters approached its destination, men were
seen hurrying across the line of advance. These
proved to be C Company, who said they were in touch
with and following the Suffolks. It was obvious that
something had gone wrong, as dawn was even then
breaking, and in their present position the Suffolks
would have to attack Bardawil frontally instead of
from the flank, and would have to cross the Wadi
Yebrud to get at their objective at all.

" One thing alone was clear, namely, that Yebrud
was not by any means taken, and, in fact, very hot
machine gun and rifle fire was even then proceeding
from it."

The explanation of this confused state of affairs
was that the reserve company of the Buffs, advancing
to attack the village, had taken the one path up the
hill, and had moved just ahead of the Suffolks. The
Suffolks, stumbling after them in the darkness of the
night, had followed blindly, and had missed the point
where they should have turned off to the right.

The attack was now developing on Yebrud, and the
growing light revealed to the Turks the two companies of the Buffs approaching down a forward slope,
through some fig orchards, and in rear of them were

PANORAMIC SKETCH FROM ABBUTIEH [099 M.× 844 JAL.kim SHEET XIV]

the four companies of Suffolks. The advance came
to a standstill. The enemy shelling and machine gun
fire held the Suffolks, so that they could not extricate
themselves to advance on Burj Bardawil, and the
Sussex had to dispose themselves in rear as best they
could.

The Brigade Major (Major Ivor Buxton) exposed
himself fearlessly while trying to straighten out the
tangle. Finally the Buffs, and two companies of the
Sussex, advanced on Yebrud, which was cleared of
the enemy by 8 a.m.

Already there had been considerable delay in
starting. The 231st Brigade was in Selwad, and held
up by the fire from Burj Bardawil, against which
no attack had materialised. But the artillery had
engaged the enemy trenches on Burj Bardawil and
the slopes of Kh. Abd el Muhdy, and maintained an
accurate and heavy bombardment while the Suffolks
and Sussex corrected their position, crossed the Wadi
Yebrud, and advanced on Burj Bardawil, which was
captured by 10.30 a.m.

The Norfolks were then ordered to take the place
of the Suffolks. The line of advance had now to
change towards K12, but the 230th Brigade was not
ready to move until 2.30 p.m. : this was largely due
to the difficult country the Norfolks had to cross from
the position of assembly to the point of deployment.
A start was made, and the two battalions passed Kh.
el Muhdy, to be confronted by the Wadiel Jib.

On the crest overlooking the ravine, troops were
once more checked by machine gun fire from both
flanks. An endless series of terraces led down to the
wadi and to the white streak of the road, and, on the
far side, a formidable terraced hill rose to a great

height, with apparently a cliff half-way up it.   There was no sort of cover down into the wadi except a few olive trees, and the artillery could give no support. It was decided to wait until dusk.

While daylight lasted, most anxious surveys for a possible line of advance were made, and shortly after dusk both the 230th and the 231st Brigades commenced the descent into the main and the branch wadis.   Following the action again from the right, the Shropshires and 25th Welsh Fusiliers deployed in the boulder-strewn bed of the Nimr about 8.30 without too much trouble, and commenced the assault of the precipitous Lisaneh Ridge.

The chief trouble in the arduous ascent was to keep any sort of fighting formation ;  where terraces of an unnegotiable nature were found, and there were many, a congestion of troops took place at the one climable spot, and men were apt to continue the ascent in a bunched up body.   The enemy position was not reached until 3 a.m. on the 10th, and was carried after a sharp hand-to-hand fight.

The remaining hours of darkness were passed in fierce hand-to-hand fighting repelling counter-attacks, three separate and determined efforts being made by the Turks before dawn.

The 230th Brigade, with the Norfolks and Sussex in line, and the Suffolks in support, the whole under the command of Colonel Powell Edwards (senior Commanding Officer), had an even more difficult bit of country in front of them.   While daylight lasted, patrols had not succeeded in finding any obvious track down the mountain-side ; the men would have to slide down the terraces, but it was clearly impossible to take the Lewis gun and ammunition mules.   After a hurried consultation with Captain Fenwick Owen, commanding the Norfolks, Colonel Edwards decided that battalions should try to advance with one company in skirmishing order and the rest in line of platoons in fours, hoping that the platoons would find odd places where they could descend. It was arranged that both battalions should make for the bridge of the Nablus Road over the wadi, which would be assaulted by the Norfolks on the right of the road and the Sussex on the left.

The two battalions started to cross the crest of Kh. Muhdy at 6.30 p.m., and came immediately under heavy machine gun fire, the flashes of the guns showing about half-way up the opposite slope, and on both flanks.

" Very shortly after commencing the descent of the terraces towards the Nablus Road it became obvious that the existing formation was impossible. Frequently not more than one practicable way down a terrace was to be found on the whole battalion front. Platoons had to use this in succession, and the same process being repeated on each terrace, led to a mass of men collecting on each in turn. The Turkish machine guns were apparently sweeping the hill-side more or less at random, but a lucky sweep on a crowded terrace might at any moment cause very heavy casualties. The battalion was, therefore, halted. Company Commanders had their companies in excellent control, and it was the work of a few minutes only to proceed in file or single file, with a small patrol working ahead to find suitable points of descent from one terrace to another." (Colonel Powell Edwards.)

Eventually the battalions made the descent down one track, which the Norfolks had found, in single file.

The bridge on the Nablus was not held by the enemy, and it was exactly midnight when the two battalions moved forward to the assault of the first hill leading to Hill K12 (they had exchanged their positions while crossing the bridge). The climb was very exhausting, and the enemy commenced to throw bombs long before troops were within range. Many of the terraces could only be scaled by the men mounting on each other's shoulders. After some hours they were sufficiently close to suffer casualties from the bombs and to hear the enemy scrambling up the hill in front of them. One officer of the Norfolks, ahead of his men, succeeded in overtaking seven Turks, of whom he shot four and secured the rest as prisoners. At dawn the crest of the ridge was attained, a Turkish officer and a few men were captured, and the main body of the enemy could be seen hurrying up the slopes of K12.

The advance was resumed at 6 a.m., but was again checked by heavy machine gun fire from the front and from a rocky spur running out from K12 on the left flank. The men were very exhausted, and the sun was extremely hot. About this time Colonel Jarvis, 15th Suffolks, arrived from the reinforcement camp and took command. He decided to send for the Buffs before attempting to assault without artillery support. But before the Buffs arrived, a white flag appeared on the spur to the left, and the Sussex advanced to K12 in time to see the last Turkish guns and infantry hurrying down the Nablus Road.

The Buffs arrived in the early hours of the afternoon, and carried the attack forward, stormed Kh. Sahlat from the west, and then captured el Tell.

This last advance was ably supported by the artillery, which had succeeded in closing up.

The 231st Brigade was back on the Lisaneh Ridge, whence the two forward battalions repulsed two counter-attacks during the afternoon. Still in the same battle order they advanced on Sheikh Selim and the high ground level with el Tell just before midnight in heavy rain. There was no opposition other than the natural obstacles of the precipitous country. Touch was obtained with the left flank of the 230th Brigade.

No water or rations had arrived on the 10th for the 230th Brigade, and when supplies came up eventually, ramps had to be cut to enable the mules and donkeys to climb the hill. There was, therefore, a pause until midday on the 11th, when the advance was resumed by the Buffs and the Norfolks. The high ground overlooking Sinjil was taken, and a patrol entered the village and found it unoccupied.

Lord Sackville, commanding the Buffs, and Colonel Barclay, commanding the Norfolks, now found themselves in a difficulty. The position they held fell sharply to the north, and the line indicated as their final objective was overlooked from all sides by commanding hills. It was obviously a most unsuitable line to occupy, and it was extremely doubtful whether they could descend the mountain on that side at all! Orders, however, arrived that the Sussex battalion was to continue the advance at dawn. The night was wet and cold, with a thick mist. Patrols reported that the ground in front was impracticable. Eventually, at 4 a.m. on the 12th, the orders for an advance on the original objective were cancelled.

Meanwhile the 231st Brigade had attempted to

push forward in line with the Buffs and Norfolks during the afternoon of the 11th.   The 160th Brigade, on the right, was a long way in rear, and the 25th Welsh Fusiliers, with the Shropshires on the left, had to advance over a stretch of country devoid of any sort of cover in order to attack Turmus Aya, their objective.   A hot fire was poured into the flank of the Welshmen from Amurieh, and it was clear that further progress was inadvisable until the 53rd Division drew level on the right.   An outpost line was taken up in touch with the 160th Brigade, which swung back to Abu Felah.

Early in the morning of the 12th Sir Philip Chetwode and General Girdwood arrived on the scene to view the line, and the Corps Commander decided to consolidate on the line then held.

The number of prisoners taken in this advance was negligible, the advance itself, measured on the map, was small, the enemy opposing the Division was, in all probability, extremely weak in numbers, and yet it was perhaps the hardest task the Division had been called upon to perform.   It may be said that the hills and ridges traversed were not very high, but they contained all the physical essentials for the strenuous sport of mountaineering ;   under such circumstances a few well-sited machine guns are formidable in effect. To approach the enemy in any kind of battle formation was frequently impossible; to face him, after what one might describe as an exhausting gymnastic achievement, required such determination of spirit as calls for the highest praise.   Where Lewis gun and ammunition mules were unable to climb, their loads were borne on the shoulders of men ;   clothes were torn to shreds ;   boots were cut and worn until only retained

LIEUT.-GENERAL SIR PHILIP CHETWODE, BART., K.C.B., K.C.M.G.

as an indifferent form of protection for the feet by
the ingenuity of the soldier ; food and water were
at times absent. The weather also hampered movement—it was occasionally very foggy.

The country on the extreme right, where the 53rd
Division operated, was, if possible, worse than that
of the 74th. The enemy attached great importance
to Tel Azur, where a strong force had to be overcome.
It was some time before this place was secured, and
counter-attacks were launched repeatedly by the
Turks. The difficulties of country, and the strong
opposition, kept this division slightly in rear, which,
of course, reacted on the advance of the 231st and
230th Brigades.

The artillery was more affected by the nature of
the country than the infantry. It commenced to
move from Latron to the Ram Allah area on the 2nd
March, but, owing to the fact that all units were under
strength in draught animals, and that some 400 had
been sent to rest at Imara (there was a rest camp for
animals as well as men), it could only move in two
sections. C/117 and C/268 had already moved in
February, and were attached to the 53rd Division,
but the first section from Latron arrived at Balua
Lake on the 3rd, and on the 6th A, B, and C/117 and
C/268 were grouped under Colonel Kinnear, and
supported the 231st Brigade in the advance on the
night 6th/7th. The second section, with the 400
horses from Imara, arrived at Balua Lake on the 7th ;
on the same day the 527th Howitzer Battery, from
the 7th (Meerut) Division, and the 16th Mountain
Battery were attached to the 74th Division.

After dusk on the 8th the Divisional Artillery and
attached batteries moved up to positions behind the

13

line—one remembers the state of the roads when the
230th Brigade marched from Balua Lake—and was
disposed in two groups : the right group, supporting
the 231st Brigade, was under Major C. L. Bolton, and
consisted of A, B, and C/268 and the 16th Mountain
Battery ;  the left group, supporting the 230th
Brigade, was commanded by Lt.-Colonel F. G. T.
Deshon, and consisted of the A/44, B/44, B/117, C/117,
and the 527th Battery.  A/117 was also in action
north of Surdah.  The right group took up positions
round Ain Yebrud, with the exception of the Mountain
Battery, which went forward to Yebrud; the left
group was to the east of Jufna.

The first objectives on the right were taken without
artillery support ;  on the left artillery support was
called for, as we know.  During the rest of the
advance the 230th Brigade received little support—
at one time, on the 11th, the 527th Howitzer Battery
started to register with one gun which they had
moved up, but it was defective and so erratic that it
had to cease fire.  The 231st Brigade and the 53rd
Division, however, received most effective support,
the artillery dispersing several counter-attacks.

For the first artillery positions tracks were cleared,
and ramps built by the engineers.  The latter had a
multitude of small but important jobs to do during
the advance, but chiefly the filling up of mine craters
which the enemy had made on the Nablus Road and
the developing of the water supply with the laying
of pipe lines.

Supplies, during the advance, were delivered at
refilling points without much trouble; difficulties
occurred from thence to the front line.  The Divisional
Train was supporting 15,484 British troops, 413

Indians, 1,322 Egyptians, 2,087 horses, 3,380 mules, 1,225 camels, and 840 donkeys (9th March).

During the whole period of the advance the 229th Brigade was occupied in repairing the Nablus Road.

On the 13th/14th the 230th Brigade took over the line held by the 231st, and on the next night the 229th took over the whole front of the 53rd Division, which ran down east of Kafr Malik.   Two days later the Corps Cavalry Regiment (Westminster Dragoons) was placed under the orders of General Girdwood, and carried the line to Kh. en Nejmeh.

The Division remained in this line until the first week in April, and was in no way disturbed by the Turks ; several raids were, however, made against the Turks.

The Norfolks carried out an amusing enterprise on the night 22nd/23rd.   Colonel J. F. Barclay took command of the raid, and marched out from the out-post line at 9.30 p.m., with some enemy works about Abu el Auf as his objective.   His force consisted of two companies and a picked squad of rifle grenadiers. With flank guards of a platoon on either side he advanced a considerable distance, and halted about 200 yards from the selected enemy works.   Here his companies deployed into line, and the rifle grenadiers opened fire.   The Turks evidently thought that the enemy was upon them, and that the grenades were hand bombs, for there was much noise and throwing of bombs on their part, while the Norfolks watched in perfect safety.   In the midst of this Turkish con-fusion the Divisional Artillery opened on the trenches, and, after a few minutes, lifted ; this was the signal for advance, and the Norfolks charged, bayoneted eight Turks, and kept one as a prisoner. They then gathered up all the rifles they could find, and marched back independently. On the return journey they suffered the only casualty—one man was wounded by a stray bullet.

A few hours later, in the early morning of the 23rd, the Royal Scots Fusiliers carried out an even more successful raid, as regards the number of prisoners taken, against the enemy works at Amurieh. This raid was planned by Captain P. M. Campbell, and was carried out by 4 officers and 125 other ranks. The force was divided into two parties : (a) the summit party, which was directed against the ruins of Amurieh on the hill, and (b) the Wadi Amurieh party, which was to go round the north-east of the hill to the Wadi.

An artillery barrage opened at 2.55 a.m., and the advance commenced five minutes later from a hill to the north of Amurieh, which had been previously occupied by a small party of the Black Watch.

While Captain Campbell, with forty-five men, made for the summit of the hill, the wadi party searched the woods on the eastern slopes—at the same time the artillery barrage shifted to the banks of the wadi. As a further means of misleading the enemy, an officer and twelve men of the Black Watch made a rifle-grenade demonstration against another hill to the north.

On reaching the summit of Amurieh, Captain Campbell received a bit of bomb in the leg, and Lieutenant Wylie took command. The garrison was over-powered, some twenty of the enemy were killed, and the raiders returned with seven Turkish officers (including a battalion commander) and thirty-eight

other ranks. The total casualties suffered by the
Scots Fusiliers were five.

On the night of the 27th Captain A. H. Wheeler,
with 3 officers and 100 men of the Somerset Light
Infantry, raided a hill about 2,000 yards east of Abu
Felah. The raiders started under heavy machine
gun fire, but encountered very slight resistance.
About a dozen Turks were killed, and two officers and
seven other ranks captured.

The fighting record of the 74th Division in Palestine
closes with these three raids. On the 3rd April, 1918,
General Girdwood was informed that his division
would be required to embark very soon for France.
The great German offensive had been launched on the
21st March, and every man that could be spared was
being sent to that theatre of war.

Orders embracing a reorganisation of the artillery
and the addition of certain units to the strength of the
Division were received.

On the 14th of the month the Divisional Artillery
was moved to Ludd, and on that date the 268th
R.F.A. Brigade ceased to exist. The other two
brigades became three 6-gun 18-pounder batteries,
and one 6-gun 4·5 howitzer battery each. The 44th
Brigade was then made up of the 340th, 382nd, 425th,
and C/268 Batteries; the 117th Brigade retained
its three old batteries and was joined by the 366th
Battery.

The Machine Gun Companies were organised into a
battalion, with the addition of the 261st Company,
and command was given to Lt.-Colonel B. Barnes,
who had held the position of Divisional Machine Gun
Officer.

From the 60th Division came the 1/12th Loyal North Lancashire Regiment, a pioneer battalion. And the 439th (Cheshire) Field Company joined the Engineers from the 53rd Division.

The personnel of two medium trench mortar batteries also joined the Division.

A few well-known figures disappeared for the time being, amongst them Colonel P. S. Allan, the G.S.O.1, who was given command of the 155th Infantry Brigade. His place was taken by Colonel A. C. Temperley, from the 60th Division.

The Division was concentrated at Ludd by the 14th of April, and the rest of the month was all bustle and movement. It could not be said with truth that the men were smart, so far as clothes were concerned : Colonel Edwards records of his unit that the glissade down the mountain-sides in the last battle left scarcely a seat in the battalion breeches ! So there was much refitting to be done.

Divisional Headquarters opened at Qantara on the 14th, the concentration of the three brigades taking place there two days later. Animals started to embark at Alexandria on the 18th, and were entrained at Marseilles on the 29th for Noyelles-sur-mer. Advanced Headquarters were opened at that place by Major E. J. Butchart, D.A.A.G., on the 30th April.

By the 2nd May the embarkation of 694 officers, 16,758 men, and 2,632 animals was complete. G.S. wagons were left behind.

.    .    .    .    .

It would appear that the victories of General Allenby, in which the 74th Division had taken part, had commenced to attract attention, so much so that the army in Syria was included in the main war

scheme for the year 1918. The position in Europe
was critical. Mr. Lloyd George headed a group who
wished to make a determined effort towards the
crushing of one of Germany's allies and promote the
" side show " into a major operation.

It was during the winter months of 1917–18 that
the long-drawn-out and tortuous intrigues which had
acted as a drag on the willing spirit and valour of
British troops approached a crisis. The truth is not
yet revealed, but one ponders over the comings and
goings of the busy Colonel Repington, as related by
himself, over the prosecution of the *Morning Post* and
that ex-soldier journalist for publishing vital secret
decisions of the War Council, which was instituted by
the Government, over the charges of Mr. Peter Wright
in his book *At the Supreme War Council*. The
testimony of more or less irresponsible persons
certainly leads one to conclude that politicians were
not always responsible for the startling intrigues which
are indicated.

The interpretation of the word " patriot " is sometimes misleading. To use it shows either a lack of
good taste or a desire to be facetious.

Apparently it was decided to crush the Turks by a
serious offensive in 1918, and the efforts of Generals
Allenby and Maude had, by that time, placed the
Entente in a favourable position to do so. Frequently, while studying the Great War, the irritating
reflection comes surging to the mind that the real
difficulty was to decide on a policy, draw up a
definite plan. Numbers were on the side of the
Entente. On the French and Belgian Front the
superiority in men and material was with the Entente during the last three years of the war, and

the same applies to Syria. But one knows that there was vacillation in the latter theatre of war until the advent of Sir E. Allenby.

That the Turks had not been already definitely crushed was due to peculiarities of country and methods of fighting. The psychology of the Turk had puzzled many people, including the German generalissimo Hindenburg. Retreat meant nothing to the Turkish mind. Individually they were stout fighters, but for the love of fighting and, probably, the prospect of loot, for they do not seem to have cared much what happened to Syria or, indeed, to have known what the war was about.

The hills of Judea abounded with caves, and the Turkish soldier's idea was to occupy one of these caves with a machine-gun. It was wellnigh impossible to locate them, and many are the stories told by men and officers of the 74th Division of the sudden appearance of hostile parties in the most unexpected places, between our posts, even behind our posts— for one cannot call it a line—as though they had sprung from the earth, as indeed they had. From the selected cave near the summit of a hill a dominating view over the surrounding country was obtained which insured them against being enveloped. At the last moment even large bodies of Turks would dissolve, scatter amongst the rocks and wadis in rear, and disappear ; they seldom retreated in any military formation. At times they would display the greatest heroism and ferocity in attack and defence—they were uncertain. One required, therefore, superiority in numbers to drive them into a corner and force a decision. In all the battles in which the 74th Division took an active part the Turks had been outgeneralled, but, favoured by the wide and difficult country, they had escaped the full consequences of defeat.

Attack in this country, however, was a matter of the season of year, and, at that moment, more particularly a matter of reinforcement and reorganisation.

The last advance in which the 74th Division had participated had cleared part of the Jordan Valley to permit the raids to the east of the river to be carried out. Before the Division left the line, during the night 21st/22nd, the 60th Division, the Anzac Mounted Division, the Imperial Camel Brigade, a Mountain Artillery Brigade, the Light Armoured Car Brigade, and a heavy battery started to cross the Jordan at Makhadet Hajlah. On the 23rd a bridge-head was established at Ghoraniyeh, and most of the force gained the eastern bank.

The operation was much hampered throughout by rain, but the railway was sufficiently injured to cause a serious interruption in the communications with Hedjaz; it was not done, however, without considerable fighting. By 2nd April the whole force had returned to the west bank of the river.

On the 30th April the 60th Division (less one Brigade), the Desert Mounted Corps (less the 1st Mounted Division), and the Imperial Service Cavalry and Infantry Brigades, carried out a second raid and met Turkish forces at Shunet Nimrin, which were ably handled and forced a withdrawal.

No great results were obtained from either raid, except that they contributed to the deception of the enemy as to the next point of Sir E. Allenby's attack. Nothing much could be undertaken in the summer, but activity of a minor nature was maintained in the Jordan Valley. What this meant to the infantry and mounted troops concerned may be surmised when we find that on several occasions the thermometer registered 130 degrees in the shade !

The summer was spent in reorganisation. The 52nd Division had also left Palestine, preceding the 74th Division by a few days, and, in addition, nine yeomanry regiments, twenty-four battalions of infantry, five and a half siege batteries, and five machine gun companies left for France. The loss of these troops was gradually made good by Indian divisions.

At the beginning of September Sir E. Allenby had two cavalry divisions, two mounted divisions, seven infantry divisions, an Indian infantry brigade, four unallotted battalions, and a French detachment equivalent to a brigade—a total of 12,000 sabres, 57,000 rifles, and 540 guns. He estimated that the Turks numbered, with the IVth, VIIth, VIIIth Armies, 3,000 sabres, 23,000 rifles, and 340 guns.

General Liman von Sanders, who had assumed command on the 1st March, says that divisions numbered only 1,300 rifles, but the number of prisoners actually captured in the battle that followed throws more than doubt on this statement.

The big attack started on 19th September. The Lahore, the Meerut, the 54th, 75th, and 60th Divisions, the French detachment, the 5th Australian Light Horse Brigade, and extra artillery had been concentrated under Sir E. Bulfin on the coast, and in rear was the Desert Mounted Corps, less the Anzac Division—all this had been done without rousing the suspicions of the Turks, who believed that an attack was about to be launched east of the Jordan.

The methods employed to deceive the Turks in this

fashion were admirable, and include the erection of rows upon rows of dummy horses, and the marching of unfortunate men along the same roads, day after day, to the same destination, only to be brought back at night by lorries. People were turned out of houses in Jerusalem, and departmental names painted on the doors, so as to spread the belief that General Headquarters was about to move there. Even considerable works, such as Decauville railways and bridges, were undertaken to further the belief (*The Desert Corps*, R. M. P. Preston).

On the 19th the Anzac Mounted Division, and certain Arab forces, made a strong demonstration on the Jordan, which completely deceived the enemy, who thought that the main attack, which they anticipated, was being launched there ; but on the coast the XXIst Corps attacked and swept the enemy back from the sea, pressed him inland, and opened a way for the cavalry.

The great limestone ridge which runs from the Lebanons down the full length of Syria is, as we know, broken by the Plain of Esdraelon. Along the south-western side of the plain a chain of hills shoots out from the southern portion of the main range towards the sea, ending on the coast with Mount Carmel. The cavalry passed between these hills, emerged on the plain, and raced for the mountain passes on the far side.

The Turkish VIIth and VIIIth Armies were hotly engaged throughout the entire length of their front, from the Jordan to where the gallant 60th Division on the extreme flank turned from the sea and commenced to roll up the enemy line. While the enemy infantry were being held, aeroplane squadrons

attacked communication centres and destroyed all
telephone cables, the cavalry pressed on to pre-
arranged positions, confusion and bewilderment grew
in the enemy ranks, at his headquarters, from front
to rear, from flank to flank.

On the far side of the plain, at the foot of the range
which leads to the Lebanons, lies the town of Nazareth.
Here the German Commander-in-Chief, Liman von
Sanders, waited for news which could not reach him.
Hurrying across the plain, covering fifty miles in
twenty-two hours, the 13th Cavalry Brigade suddenly
appeared and entered the town.  What happened to
the German Commander-in-Chief is not quite clear.
He seems to suggest that he was at the French
Orphan Asylum, outside the town, directing a highly
successful defence which drove off the impudent
cavalry brigade.  At all events he escaped capture
by a hair's breadth.

But the Turkish infantry were now in a desperate
situation, and commenced to retire through the hills
and debauch on to the plain.  It was in vain.  Aeroplanes attacked them in the mountain passes, destroying their transport, blocking the roads, spreading
terror and confusion.  The transport was abandoned,
and loose bodies of Turks streamed across the plain,
still harried from the air, only to fall into the hands
of the mounted troops who were already guarding the
far side of the plain and the exits to the mountains.

The number of prisoners became embarrassing.
The whole of the VIIth and VIIIth Armies were, to
all intents and purposes, captured, but there was no
rest, no respite.  The destruction of the IVth Army,
to the east of the Jordan, followed.  On the 1st
October the Desert Mounted Corps and the Arab

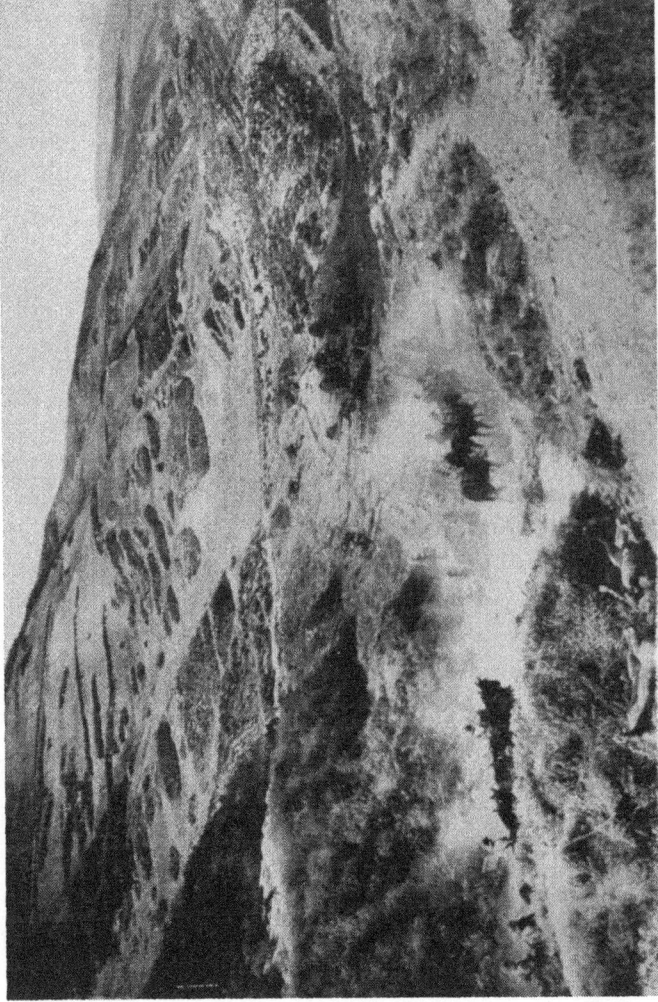

TYPICAL COUNTRY NORTH OF JERUSALEM.

Army entered Damascus.  On the 26th October the 5th Cavalry Division was twenty miles to the west of Aleppo, and waiting the arrival of the Australian Division from Damascus to advance on Alexandretta ; but before the latter division could reach them, the Turks threw up the sponge and an armistice was declared.

In his despatch Sir E. Allenby gives the total number of prisoners captured between the 19th September and the 26th October as 75,000, including close on 4,000 Germans and Austrians, and some 360 guns.  He also gives the interesting fact that the 5th Cavalry Division covered 500 miles between the opening of the battle and the date of the Armistice.

In a general review of the campaign, Sir E. Allenby expresses the following ideas :

" The campaigns in Sinai, Palestine, and Syria formed an important part of the general allied effort against the Central Powers. . . .

" The forces employed in this theatre may be regarded in the nature of a detachment from the main forces on the Western Front, but engaged in the same battle, changing its rôle and action according to the sway of events in the main theatre and the other minor theatres.

" In the first instance the object of this detachment was the protection of the Suez Canal, a vital link in the communications of the Allies.  By the summer of 1917, when I assumed command of the Egyptian Expeditionary Force, Lt.-General Sir A. Murray's brilliant campaign in Sinai had removed the danger to Egypt, and had forced the enemy back across his own frontiers.

" The original purpose of the detachment had been accomplished.  But events elsewhere had given a fresh importance and another rôle to the operations

in this theatre. The collapse of Russia had given
a new lease of life to the Central Powers' weakest
member, and had freed the main Turkish forces for
action elsewhere. It was believed that they would
be used in an offensive, planned and organised by the
Germans, for the recapture of Bagdad. It was,
therefore, important to keep up the pressure on
Turkey, and to anticipate the threatened attack on
Bagdad by striking hard elsewhere.

" The operations which commenced with the
Gaza–Beersheba battle, and led to the capture of
Jerusalem and the freeing of all Southern Palestine,
were therefore planned.

" These operations had far-reaching results. The
danger to Mesopotamia was removed, and it became
possible to reduce the forces in that theatre. Instead
of drawing fresh strength from the reserve of Turkish
troops released by Russia's collapse, the Central
Alliance found themselves compelled to send further
support to their Eastern ally, while a fresh impetus
was given to the Arab struggle for freedom.

" The moral results were even greater. Germany,
hard put to it to hold her own in the close-locked
struggle in the West, saw a great blow struck at her
Eastern ambitions, while the capture of Jerusalem
stirred the imagination of the Christian world.

" . . . The course of the campaigns in this theatre
followed closely the course of events in the main
Western theatre.

" Thus the first period, the defence of the Canal,
corresponded to the first check of the enemy's onrush
in France and Belgium ; the period of the advance
through the Sinai Desert, to the general development
of the allied strength and the building up of a secure
battle line along the whole front ; the 1917 advance,
to the period of increased allied pressure which exhausted the enemy's reserves ; while the last advance
coincided with the final allied counter-offensive.

" The operations in this theatre have thus been part of a studied whole, and not an isolated campaign."

.          .          .          .          .

A few interesting facts about the Turks may be gleaned from an account by Captain S. R. E. Snow (of the Devons), who was wounded and captured at Foka, of his adventures.

He says that within a few minutes of his arrival at the Turkish Divisional Headquarters, near Ram Allah, he was taken to the Turkish Chief of Staff, and examined by a German Intelligence Officer. This individual had an extremely arrogant manner, and, finding he could get nothing from Captain Snow, left the room. A few minutes later Colonel von Bohm, commanding the 53rd Turkish Division, came into the room, and issued orders to his Turkish Staff in the same arrogant and insolent tone as that of his Intelligence Officer. He then departed. The Turkish Chief of Staff seems to have been roused, for he rose from his chair and bolted the door. Secure from further intrusion, he turned to Captain Snow, and asked : " When are you going to capture Jerusalem ? " " Within a week," was the reply. The Turkish Chief of Staff smiled : " That will be good," said he ; " Jerusalem wants you badly. There is no food in the town. As for us, we are controlled by those pigs," indicating the Prussian General, who had just left, " and can do nothing but hope for your advance."

Captain Snow was taken to the hospital at Nablus, where he was attended by a Syrian doctor from Jaffa. While there he was visited by Marshal von Falkenhayn, who asked a few questions, in bad English, and seemed well disposed ; he sent some oranges to Captain Snow and a few other British officers the next day.

After the capture of Jerusalem, Captain Snow was moved hurriedly to Damascus, and when his wound had healed, in February, he was put in charge of a Syrian soldier and despatched on the way to Constantinople. At Aleppo he made friends with a Turkish major, who had fought in the Balkan wars and had been nursed in a British hospital attached to the Turkish Army and :

" we amused ourselves watching the German Generals driving in the streets ; they were covered with decorations, always including the inevitable Iron Cross. It was most entertaining to watch the punctilious salutes and low bows which they gave in response to the salutes of the dirty, unshaven Turkish officers, for whom they felt nothing but contempt. I also had a short talk with an Armenian officer, who did not pretend any love for the Turks, but said that it was impossible not to admire the efficiency of the Germans."

At the terminus of the broad-gauge railway, at the foot of the Taurus range, Captain Snow had a curious conversation with some British prisoners who were working on the unfinished portion of the line.

" I spoke to a Corporal Cheseman of the 1/8th Hampshire Regiment, who had been captured at Kut-el-Amara. He was able to give me particulars of all the Turkish guns, aeroplanes, and reinforcements which had gone down recently to the Palestine and Mesopotamian fronts, the prisoners being engaged in transhipping them from the Decauville to the broad-gauge lines. These prisoners told me openly that no gun or aeroplane ever reached the Turkish Front with all its spare parts, as they took care to throw them away during the transhipment process."

At Constantinople Captain Snow was put in a cell in the criminal prison with a Turkish major who had been sentenced to two years' imprisonment for embezzling military funds. Finally, after several further moves, he settled down in a small town in Anatolia, where there was a prisoners of war camp. Wherever he went he found that the Germans were generally disliked. The Turks were slack, dirty, casual ; expressed no dislike for the British ; were open to bribery. So far as they were concerned, the war was carried on with indolence.

.   .   .   .   .   .

Under the circumstances governing the departure of the 74th Division, there could be no official leave-taking, but the following letters were sent to General Girdwood.

" XXTH CORPS, JERUSALEM,
" *3rd April*, 1918.

" MY DEAR GIRDWOOD,—
" The whole of the XXth Corps, and myself in particular, suffer an irreparable loss by the transfer of your gallant Division to another theatre.
" No man has been better served than I have by them, or could wish to command finer troops. Every task set the 74th has been carried through with uniform gallantry and success, and no division in Palestine has a finer record.
" We shall watch your deeds and follow your fortunes, wherever you may find yourselves, with the most intense interest and sympathy, knowing beforehand that whatever you set your hands to you will carry through with the same gallantry and devotion that you have displayed since you were first formed into a division.
" On my own behalf and that of the whole Corps
14

I wish you and your gallant Division God Speed and Good Fortune.

" Yours sincerely,
" PHILIP CHETWODE.

" Will you communicate this letter to your troops on board ship ? "

" GENERAL HEADQUARTERS,
" EGYPTIAN EXPEDITIONARY FORCE,
" *9th April*, 1918.

" MY DEAR GIRDWOOD,—

" I cannot let you and your Division go without writing to tell you how sorry I am to lose you.

" As you will understand, it is not advisable to issue a farewell order, but I want you to know that I am proud to have had you and the 74th Division under my command. Your work has been splendid, and I am sure that, wherever you may go, you will acquit yourselves equally well and win further distinction.

" You have my warm congratulations and thanks, and my hearty good wishes.

" Yours sincerely,
" EDMUND H. H. ALLENBY."

These were not mere expressions of polite farewell.

*J. Russell, Baker Street*

FIELD-MARSHAL VISCOUNT ALLENBY, G.C.B., G.C.M.G.

# PART III
## *FRANCE*

# CHAPTER XIII

## FRANCE

Arrival of the Division—Contrast of countries—German offensives—
Foch's counter-stroke—Allied offensive.

IN his despatch covering the German offensive of the
21st March 1918, Sir Douglas Haig says that at least
64 divisions were launched, a number which exceeded
the total forces composing the entire British Army in
France. The three German Armies engaged were the
IInd, XVIIth, and XVIIIth. It seems that at that
date they were composed of 32, 38, and 44 divisions
respectively, and that the IInd Army attacked
between Gouzeaucourt and Vermand with 17 divisions,
the XVIIth Army between Monchy and Cambrai
with 24, and the XVIIIth Army between St. Quentin
and La Fere with 27 divisions. (*Die Schlachten und
Gefechte des Groszen Kreiges.*) There is no reason to
doubt the latter figures.

Helped by a thick morning fog, this mass of troops
broke through the Vth Army, and the right of the
IIIrd—there is not much point in arguing how far
the IIIrd Army was influenced by any action of the
Vth; there was a deep penetration of both army
fronts on the first day. Sir Douglas Haig compares
the strength of the two British Armies by the extent
of front held by a division. General Gough's Vth
Army held from the village of Barisis, south of the
Oise, to Gouzeaucourt, and was composed of the
IIIrd, XVIIIth, XIXth, and VIIth Corps, disposing
of fourteen infantry divisions and three cavalry divi-

sions, of which three infantry and three cavalry
divisions were in reserve.  Taking the number of
divisions in line, the Commander-in-Chief gets the
result of one division to 6,750 yards.  General Byng's
IIIrd Army held from north of Gouzeaucourt to south
of Gavrelle, and was composed of the IVth, Vth, VIth,
XVIIth Corps, disposing of fifteen infantry divisions,
of which eight were in the line.  The average length
of line held by a division was therefore 4,700 yards.

As a result of the German effort the British right
had been pushed back some thirty miles, and the
enemy was within striking distance of Amiens.  After
the 5th April there was a lull in the battle.

On the 9th April the German effort shifted to the
Lys front, between the La Basée Canal and Bois
Grenier.  The 1st and IInd Armies were involved in
the battle that followed, and another great salient
was created which necessitated a withdrawal on the
Ypres front.  This battle lasted through the month
of April.

The situation then was that the enemy had penetrated to such a depth on the Somme and Lys fronts
as to interfere effectively with important lateral lines
of railway at Amiens, Bethune, and Hazebrouck, and
also threaten the railway centre at St. Pol.  The
maintenance of communications in Northern France
was, therefore, a matter of the gravest concern.

In the midst of the confusion of great battles and
ever-shifting lines, a momentous decision had been
arrived at : General Foch was appointed to a post
which was at first defined by the term *co-ordinateur
supérieur* on the Western Front.  He analysed the
position on the 30th March, and laid stress on the
unity of the French and British Armies, and on the

defence of Amiens, so as to retain the free use of the Abbeville–Amiens–Paris Railway. His intention was to attack with the French Ist and the British Vth Armies, but the German Lys offensive altered his plans. On the 2nd May he became Generalissimo of the allied armies, including Italy.

.    .    .    .    .

The 74th Division, less artillery, arrived at Marseilles on the 7th May, and the first train left in the evening for Noyelles.

" The contrast from the East was indeed marked and delightful, and the long train journey passed quickly in our joy at seeing once more green fields and green trees, villages and farms, long fair hair and fair complexions. We could hardly have had more beautiful scenery than we had during the first day through the south of France. We kept to the branch lines, to the west of the main Rhone Valley Line, and wound in and out all day at the foot of steep hills crowned with old castles and picturesque villages, which looked so peaceful that it was hard to realise that there was a war on. The second day saw us skirting Paris by Juvisy, and gave us a good view of Versailles and the numerous airships at St. Cyr. The last day our route lay chiefly through water meadows, and by 9.30 we had reached our detraining station, Noyelles, whence, after a hot breakfast, we marched ten miles to our destination, St. Firmin, near the mouth of the Somme." (*Fife and Forfar.*)

The Welsh Regiment found it :

" strange and uncanny to be in a large town again after being so long in a wild and sparsely inhabited country as Palestine. We spent the next day in visiting the best hotels and ordering the best procurable meals. . . . The country looked very beautiful, with its fields and woodlands—such an absolute contrast to the terrible country we had just left and had spent so many dreary months in."

The concentration of the Division was complete on the 18th. Lectures were given to these " green " troops from Palestine on bayonet fighting—any one platoon of the 74th Division had probably made more use of the bayonet than any battalion in France— and on gas ; the latter was, indeed, a new experience. Most of the masks given out in Palestine were found to be defective, and all the containers were obsolete.

On the 21st a move was made to Roellecourt, and on the 25th to le Cauroy, in the Doullens area.

The Division remained here until the 26th June, carrying out tactical exercises in advance guard and attack, in defence and counter-attack, and in training in co-operation with tanks and contact aeroplanes. Billets were good, fine weather prevailed, the French peasants, mostly women, worked in the fields, and traded in many food luxuries. Above all, there was actually " leave " !

But three gallant battalions were to march from the Division for good. In the month of February, before the German offensive, brigades in France had been cut down to three battalions, and the Division was ordered, on the 20th June, to conform. The Norfolks, the Royal Scots Fusiliers, and the 24th Royal Welsh Fusiliers departed the next day to join the 31st Division, a division to which the three battalions taken from the Guards Division had been sent as the 4th Guards Brigade early in the year, and which had gained immortal renown in holding the German attack at Merville. They were a great loss. It must be remembered that when the Division arrived in France it was still composed, in the bulk of it, of the original yeomen, so that there was some meaning in alluding to the departing battalions as old and tried friends.

While the Division was training in the back area round le Cauroy, other developments were taking place in the front line. The Germans made another attack, in a fresh place, on the 27th May. This was an unexpected assault on the Chemins des Dames, a part of the French line which had been considered quiet, and to which the 8th, 21st, 25th, and 50th British Divisions had been sent, constituting the IXth Corps. All these divisions had taken part in the Somme and Lys fighting, and were being filled up with young drafts.

The German attack was launched against the French VIth Army, and involved the whole of the British IXth Corps, which, at that moment, had the 21st, 8th, and 50th Divisions in the line : the French VIth Army comprised only eight divisions. Four thousand guns and thirty-four divisions were brought into action against the total of eleven Allied divisions, and the Germans swept through to the Aisne. This amazing advance was said to have surprised the German Headquarters as much as anyone. By the evening of the 30th May the enemy had reached the Marne.

One does not gather from Ludendorff's book what he really thought of the situation at this time. The Austrian Army attacked in Italy on the 15th June and was repulsed. He says that this unsuccessful attack was extremely painful to him, but that in Palestine local attacks by the British had failed, and that he had hopes of the Bulgarian Army doing something! He was, apparently, slightly disturbed by the number of American divisions he had discovered in France, but thought that these new troops would not fight so well as the old British and French; that they might release British and French troops on quiet sectors was the thought that disturbed him most. But he claims that in the middle of June General Foch had spent his reserves, and that no more could be asked of the French Army. He admits that the British must have made some progress in reconstruction, but makes the discounting reflection that there was no reason why their armies should have recovered more quickly than the army groups of the Crown Prince Rupprecht of Bavaria. As for the Belgian Army, he declared that desertion was continual, and that it was clear the Belgians were becoming more friendly towards the Germans.

Ludendorff decided to attack on both sides of Rheims. With what object? Because, he says, that was the weak point. If that was the sole reason, it was most unfortunate that he should have selected a date so close to the one chosen by General Foch for a counter-offensive against the western flank of the salient. The German preparations were seen, their plans discovered, and Foch merely decided to use his offensive as a counter-attack. He collected British, Americans, Italians, as well as his own troops, and over 400 tanks, which were hidden in the Forest of Villers-Cotterets. On the front which the Germans were to attack he withdrew the infantry, except a few machine gun nests, filled the dugouts with gas, and sowed the ground with bombs.

The Germans met only massed artillery, and were slaughtered in thousands.

And then, on the 18th July, Foch attacked. The enemy was hurled back, fighting desperately, leaving 30,000 prisoners, 900 guns, and 6,000 machine guns in the hands of the Allies.

Having straightened out this salient, Marshal Foch turned his attention to freeing the railways. Ludendorff claims that the attack was held on the 22nd, but all this part of his book is insincere : this battle was the turning-point ; the initiative was with the Allies.

# CHAPTER XIV

## THE LYS SALIENT, VᵀH ARMY

The growth of artillery—The new line—Raids—The enemy retires—
Foch's orders—Enemy opposition.

On the 26th June the 74th Division moved to
Norent Fontes, where it was at four hours' notice for
the purpose of reinforcing either the XIth or XIIIth
Corps, and at twenty-four hours' notice for G.H.Q.
reserve. Work on rear defences was carried out for
both Corps, and training continued until the 10th
July, when, in accordance with XIth Corps orders,
the Division started to relieve the 61st Division in the
line. On the 14th General Girdwood took command
of the right sector of the Corps front.

The line occupied by the Division was between the
la Bassee Canal and the River Lys, with the left resting
on the small village of Corbie. The town of Merville,
in enemy hands, was some 3,000 yards away.

In this flat country, through which the Lys mean-
dered in a sluggish fashion, there had never been anything in the nature of a trench. Attempts had been
made to dig them, and in a very dry season it was
possible to occupy them, in some parts, for a limited
period; but, generally speaking, there was water a
foot or two below the surface. The system of defences
was therefore a line of breastworks, and they had
always been of a somewhat patchy nature. The
Division found that the front line was a series of posts
in the midst of growing crops and shell-holes.

To appreciate the difference in the fighting in

France and Palestine one has only to consider the
relative size of the two great arms of the service in
France. We know that in Palestine the chief weapon
was, for the enemy, the machine gun, and machine
guns were also multiplied beyond computation in
France, but there had been no massing of artillery
in Palestine. The Turks had never had a super-
abundance of ammunition for their Austrian-served
guns. In France the struggle had been in the main
for artillery superiority. When the first great set
battle took place in 1916, the Somme offensive, the
artillery personnel was about half the strength of
attacking infantry battalions, and nearly 13,000 tons
of ammunition was fired on the first day. The proportion of artillery personnel grew steadily, and the
amount of ammunition expended nearly doubled at
Arras and Messines in the early part of 1917. At
Ypres, on the 31st July 1917, artillery was 80 per cent.
as compared to infantry, and 23,000 tons of ammunition was expended in the day. On the 20th and 21st
September 42,000 tons of ammunition was expended,
and on the 4th October the proportion of artillery
personnel amounted to 85 per cent. of the infantry.

At certain periods we had a definite superiority in
artillery over the enemy, but in 1918, during the first
part of the year, the Germans had gained the ascen-
dancy, although it was wrested from them towards
the end of their offensive. Harassing fire, a sudden
crash of many batteries trained on one small area,
a hurricane of fire for ten minutes or a quarter of an
hour, constituted a quiet and uneventful night. Firing
by day was not so intense, but at night shells passed
overhead in an unending succession, and occasionally
round the observer.

The men of the 74th Division were not unduly apprehensive; they had had sufficient experience for the novelty of fighting method to be short-lived. And they soon became used to the conditions of " trench " warfare while holding their breastworks.

But, in view of the new conditions, General Girdwood called a conference at his headquarters on the 15th July to discuss reliefs, policy of work, distribution of troops, drainage, reinforcements—in fact, quite an imposing agenda. It was decided that Brigade reliefs should be arranged so that each brigade would be twenty-four days in the line and twelve in reserve. Amongst items of work to be undertaken was the cutting of crops in two belts on either side of the wire, to make a continuous breastwork along the support line and so facilitate communication, the construction of shelters for infantry and artillery, and plans for raids were to be prepared.

The 229th and 231st Brigades took over the line, and proceeded to patrol actively and get acquainted with the lie of the land. On the 17th we find a Sergeant Varley of the 25th Royal Welsh Fusiliers entering the German trench, or breastwork, and while the sentry had his back turned, quietly picking up his machine gun, which the sergeant succeeded in bringing back safely. An unpleasant and uncanny surprise for the sentry.

And the next day Lieutenant Jowett made a daylight raid with ten men, and brought back five prisoners of the 392nd Infantry Regiment. There were no casualties.

The Sussex then took a turn at raiding. Lieutenant B. J. T. Webber, with twenty men, and artillery support, entered the enemy lines, killed two and brought back three prisoners of the 102nd Reserve Infantry Regiment. Two men were wounded in the course of this enterprise.

On the 27th Lieutenant R. G. Shackles, of the Shropshires, had an exciting experience. He raided the enemy with two N.C.O.'s and eleven men. This small force he divided into flanking and support parties, while he, with three men and one N.C.O., went forward. While going along a ditch in No Man's Land, the assaulting party of five saw a man running down the German line giving warning of their approach : the Germans stood to arms. Lieutenant Shackles made a dash for the line and got in with his men. The Germans were thrown into confusion, and hurled bombs wildly, wounding some of their own men. The assaulting party fired, killed two men and wounded one, and the remaining Germans in the post surrendered. Four prisoners of the 392nd Infantry Regiment were quickly bundled out of the post and through the corn, and, in spite of a tornado of fire, all returned safely.

Apparently reprisals for this raid were attempted on the 29th, when about forty Germans left their line and advanced on the Shropshires. They reckoned without the battalion scouts, who were lying out in No Man's Land. It was scarcely light, about 5 a.m., and the scouts allowed the party to come within fifteen yards before firing. Four men were killed, and no doubt more were hit, as the whole party disappeared rapidly.

The line remained quiet until the 4th August, when the first faint signs of Marshal Foch's counter-offensive were observed. On that date the 74th Division had on its right the 4th Division, which was the left of the XIIIth Corps, and on its left the 5th Division, being the left of the XIth Corps.   The 229th Brigade was in the right sector, and the 230th was taking over the left, the St. Floris sector.

While the relief was in progress, the 4th Division reported that the enemy trenches on their right had been found unoccupied.

A patrol hurried out from the 74th Division front, but found the enemy in his usual strength and positions.   On the night of the 5th/6th, however, a company of the Devons entered the German line, killed one sentry and captured another with a machine gun ; and a patrol of the Black Watch did the same, capturing three prisoners ; later, in daylight, the last-named battalion occupied a stretch of the enemy line, during which operation one German was killed and one taken prisoner.   Touch was established with the brigade on the right.

But there was no sign of the enemy retiring on the left ; indeed, the Buffs, after several attempts, reported that they were unable to advance except by general attack, owing to the enemy machine gun fire.

In spite of the experience of the 230th Brigade, it was evident that the enemy was vacating his line, and orders were issued for an advance to the ruins of the village of Calonne, on the Lys.   Patrols on the left sector found the line occupied all day, but, during the early part of the night, the Buffs and Sussex established themselves in the enemy's front line.

The next day the Division reached the line of the Turbeaute, a small brook, and of the old Lys, as distinct from the canal of that name—an advance of some 3,000 yards.   Opposition was mostly in the form of machine gun fire, although a force, estimated at

100, attacked the right flank of the Buffs during the afternoon, which occasioned a slight check.

A warning order was issued to brigades that, according to the statements of prisoners, the enemy would continue to hold his present line, which should be tested by patrols. This was done, but no change occurred in the line for the next few days.

On the 10th August His Majesty the King passed through the Divisional area during the afternoon, General Girdwood meeting him at Bourecq.

Meanwhile down south the enemy had experienced what Ludendorff has called their black day. Marshal Foch had issued the following order for the August offensive :

" The British IVth Army and the French Ist Army will advance on the 8th, under the command of Field-Marshal Sir D. Haig, the former north and the latter south of the Amiens–Roye Road. The offensive, covered by the Somme, will be pushed as far as possible towards Roye. The French IIIrd Army will attack the left flank of the Montdidier Salient on the 10th inst. The French Xth Army in the Oise Valley (on left bank) will continue to advance eastwards."

The Germans had been compelled, after the battle which started on the 18th July, to break up no less than ten divisions and to revert, at the beginning of August, to the defensive. The General Staff considered, apparently, that the Entente attacks might be renewed on that same front, the Vesle, or between the Aisne and the Oise, or perhaps the less possible alternative of attacks between the Oise and the Somme, at Albert, and on the Lys. But Ludendorff tells us he assumed that these " operations would

15

only take the form of isolated local attacks, for the
enemy was also tired, on the whole not less so than
ourselves." The withdrawal on the Lys, which the
74th Division was engaged in following up, was a
result of decisions following on the battle of the 18th
July.

The truth of Marshal Foch's strategy is not yet
revealed to us. Some people thought at the time that
he had reserves, apart from the American divisions, a
belief which was fostered by the casual meeting of
French battalions which, so their officers declared,
had not been engaged in any fighting during the year.
It would be in accordance with Napoleonic principles,
the great Master, of whom the Marshal is a disciple.
Be that as it may, the attack ordered by the Marshal
was a second blow to the enemy from which he never
recovered. The British IVth Army advanced six
miles and captured 13,000 prisoners and 400 guns ;
the French Ist Army, advancing on the north and
south of Montdidier, encircled the town ; General
Dubeney flung his XXXIst Corps in the direction of
Roye, and the Marshal, master of the situation,
ordered General Byng's IIIrd Army to advance " with
violence," to be followed by an attack still farther to
the left by the Ist Army. The French Xth Army
advanced on the right and captured 11,000 prisoners.
The whole of this stupendous movement was started
in the month of August.

Meanwhile the voluntary retirement of the enemy
continued on the Lys. Fires were observed behind
his lines on the 18th August, and by the 20th the
Division was in possession of the village of Epinette,
just west of Lestrem. This seemed to be the line
selected for a stand by the Germans, for on the 22nd

the 231st Brigade was ordered to co-operate with an advance by the 61st Brigade on its left, and met with fierce and carefully prepared opposition. The Shropshires, with patrols out in advance, started to move forward, and the enemy, concealed behind some houses, allowed the battalion to advance to a pre-arranged spot, when a strong barrage of field guns and machine guns was put down on the line of the patrols and worked back to the supporting companies. Thrown into momentary confusion, the Shropshires were then counter-attacked and forced back to their starting-point. Their casualties were three officers and forty-one other ranks.

No further advance was made on this front until the Division was relieved, on the 26th, by the 59th Division.

On the 29th August battalions commenced to entrain for the Somme, and Headquarters opened at Beaucourt Château. By this time no less than 128,000 prisoners, 2,069 guns, and 13,783 machine guns had been captured from the Germans in the great battle that was raging.

# CHAPTER XV

## THE IVᴛʜ ARMY FRONT

The situation—Buchavesnes—Moislains—The action—The advance—
The Germans' stand. ;

Oɴ the 31st August the Division was ordered into
the line, and was taken by bus from the neighbourhood of Heilly to Maricourt. The 229th Brigade
then relieved the first line troops of the 58th Division
about three miles to the north of Peronne.

The situation on this front is described most vividly
by Sir Douglas Haig in his despatch :

" By the night of the 30th August the line of the
IVth and the IIIrd Armies north of the Somme ran
from Clery-sur-Somme past the western edge of
Marrieres Wood to Combles, Lesboeufs, Bancourt,
Fremicourt, and Vraucourt, and thence to the western
outskirts of Ecoust, Bullecourt, and Hendecourt,
Any further advance would threaten the enemy's
line south of Peronne along the east bank of the
Somme, to which our progress north of the river had
forced him to retreat.

" This latter movement had been commenced on
the 26th August, on which date Roye was evacuated
by the enemy, and next day had been followed by a
general advance on the part of the French and British
forces between the Oise and the Somme. By the
night of the 29th August, allied infantry had reached
the left bank of the Somme on the whole front from
the neighbourhood of Nesle, occupied by the French
on the 28th August, northward to Peronne. Further
south the French held Noyon.

" During these days an increase in hostile artillery fire and the frequency and strength of the German counter-attacks indicated that our troops were approaching positions on which the enemy intended to stand, at any rate for a period.   In the face of this increased resistance, by a brilliant operation commenced on the night of the 30th/31st August, the 2nd Australian Division (Major-General C. Rosenthal) stormed Mont St. Quentin, a most important tactical feature commanding Peronne and the crossings of the Somme at that town.   Being prevented by floods and machine gun fire from crossing the river opposite Mont St. Quentin, the 5th Australian Infantry Brigade was passed across the Somme at Feuillieres, two miles farther west, by means of hastily constructed bridges.   By 10.15 p.m. on the 30th August the Brigade had captured the German trenches east of Clery, and was assembled in them ready for an assault which should turn the German positions from the north-west.   At 5 a.m. on the 31st August the assault was launched, and, despite determined opposition, was completely successful. . . . In this operation nearly 1,000 prisoners were taken and great numbers of the enemy were killed.   On the 1st September, as a direct consequence of it, Australian troops captured Peronne.

" In support of the operations against Mont St. Quentin, on the morning of the 31st August the left of the IVth Army (3rd Australian, 58th, 47th, and 18th Divisions) attacked towards Bouchavesnes, Rancourt, and Fregicourt, and by successful fighting on this and the following day captured these villages with several hundred prisoners. . . .

" In the obstinate fighting of the past few days the enemy had been pressed back to the line of the Somme River and the high ground about Rocquigny and Beugny, where he had shown an intention to stand for a time.   Thereafter, his probable plan was

to retire slowly, when forced to do so, from one intermediary position to another, until he could shelter
his battered divisions behind the Hindenburg defences.
The line of the Tortille River and the High Nurlu
Plateau offered opportunities for an ordered withdrawal of this nature which would allow him to secure
his artillery as well as much of the material in his
forward dumps."

The line taken over by the 229th Brigade was just
south-east of Buchavesnes, the recently captured
village.    The Divisional Artillery moved to the valleys
south of Maricourt.

The IIIrd Corps was waiting to attack, with the
74th Division on the right, the 47th in the centre, the
18th on the left ; the 2nd Australian Division, on the
right of the 74th, were to co-operate.    The objective
was the spurs mentioned by Sir Douglas Haig west
and south-west of Nurlu.

General Girdwood's orders provide for the attack
to be undertaken by the 229th Brigade at 5.30 a.m.
on the 2nd September.    The artillery barrage was
ordered to come down 200 yards east of the starting-
line and remain there for fifteen minutes ; it would
then advance at the rate of 100 yards per five minutes.
At Midinettes Trench the barrage would cease and
the infantry would be supported by the two mobile
brigades of the 74th artillery.    The feature of the plan
of attack was that the attacking brigade was to avoid
Moislains, but would be responsible for " mopping
it up."    The objective of the Australian Division was
Midinettes Trench, and of the 47th Division Monastir
Trench, and a flank south of Moislains.

The Somerset Light Infantry led the attack, with
the Black Watch in support, with orders to come into

line on the left of the Somersets as soon as Moislains had been passed.

Some difficulty was found in reaching the forming-up ground. There were a number of battered trenches in front of the British line—this ground had been fought over many times—and the Germans held a line west of Moislains and the canal. Scutari Trench had been selected as the jumping-off ground for the 229th Brigade, and during the night the enemy pushed forward a few machine guns into Brussa Trench. This was the first occasion when he had occupied this trench, and the enterprise was probably due to reinforcements from the crack Alpine Corps.

When the Somersets started to the assault, soon after 5.30, these German posts were inside the barrage, and had to be dealt with before any advance could be made. They did not cause much trouble, but necessitated a delay, with the result that the barrage went on right ahead and the Somersets never regained touch with it. The distance was further increased by another divergence from their line. Having cleared Brussa Trench, they pushed on, only to be enfiladed by heavy machine gun fire from Haut Allaines. The battalion swung round towards this opposition, cleared the village, captured about seventy prisoners, and then resumed the advance in a more northerly direction.

At this point the Black Watch came up on the left.

A possible attack from Moislains had been foreseen, and machine guns were posted at the small copse south-west of the village to deal with it. The Germans left their trenches and attempted to close on the left flank of the Black Watch, but were themselves caught in enfilade and forced to ground again.

They had still to be reckoned with. Soon a hail of machine gun fire was directed on to the flank of the Black Watch which caused many casualties. There seems to have been many machine guns in this place, as the "mopping up" companies of the Devons never succeeded in entering the village.

The bulk of the attacking troops did, however, cross the canal, and hand-to-hand fighting took place in the vicinity of the huts; the right of the Somersets also reached the neighbourhood of Aizecourt. At this stage of the attack the line was loose, and slightly disorganised : it was an opportunity for the Germans, who were not slow in taking advantage of it. Reinforcements of the Alpine Corps had been pushed forward, and they counter-attacked in considerable strength and forced the brigade back to the Canal du Nord : the presence of those troops was unexpected.

The position was not favourable. A battalion of the 47th Division had also passed on the right of Moislains, with the object of forming a flank to the attacking troops, and were now inextricably mixed up with the two assaulting battalions. It was decided to withdraw to the west of the village and reorganise. The casualties were heavy.

On the right the Sussex had advanced in rear of the attack, and found themselves in touch with the Australians about Haut Allaines, but not with the 229th Brigade. They were under the direct observation of the enemy artillery and subjected to heavy artillery fire ; after consultation with the Australian battalion commander, Major Sayer, who was in command, decided to remain where he was and not offer his troops as a target by a withdrawal.

The gap was filled, and the line remained in the

same position, about Anspach and Scutari Trenches, merely advancing a post here and there, until the early morning of the 4th, when it was pushed forward to the canal immediately east of Moislains, and so across the canal to a point about midway between Haut Allaines and Aizecourt, the flanks in touch with the Australians and the 47th Division.

Early the next morning the 47th Division reported that their patrols had reached the Quarries east of Monastir Trench. The Divisional front had been readjusted and extended during the night: the 230th relieved the 229th Brigade, and the 231st took over a portion of the line held by the Australian Division. On receipt of the news, General Girdwood ordered the 230th Brigade to move as advance guard, and the 231st, while coming into support, to form a defensive flank along the southern divisional boundary.

Opposition to the advance was not strong: Midinettes Trench and Aizecourt le Haut were occupied by the Suffolks and the Buffs by midday, and in the evening the 230th Brigade was close to Templeux Trench, in touch with the Australians at Bussu, but not with the 47th Division, who were some distance in rear on the left.

The next day the retreating enemy was followed to the east of Longavesnes, and the 231st Brigade was ordered to take up the advance in the morning of the 7th. The 3rd Australian Division relieved the 2nd on the right, and the 58th Division the 47th on the left.

The advance was carried forward by the 24th Welsh Regiment on the right and the Shropshire Light Infantry on the left, in face of considerable artillery and machine gun fire. Villers Faucon was occupied without much difficulty and the enemy pursued to the east of the railway.   The Division had gone ahead of the two flanking divisions, and the 25th Royal Welsh Fusiliers and Suffolks (attached to the Brigade) were called upon to assist in forming flanks.

On the 8th the Welsh Fusiliers made an attempt on the trenches north-east of Hargicourt, but the position of this battalion was distinctly bad.   Owing to the enemy opposition west of Epéhy, the 58th Division was still west of that village.   Consequently, when the Welshmen moved forward, they were enfiladed by heavy machine gun fire from Epéhy and the high ground south-east of it.   Considerable casualties were suffered.   Patrols pushed forward with great boldness, but encountered the enemy in strength in all directions.   Heavy bombardment throughout the day failed to shake the Germans, and when darkness fell the brigade was back in its original line.   The Australian Corps did not advance that day. The 231st Brigade was relieved during the night by the 229th.

The 58th Division attempted the capture of Epéhy on the 10th, and the 229th Brigade co-operated with an attack on the horse-shoe trench system on their front delivered by the Devons and Black Watch. All efforts to sneak forward during the night had been foiled by the enemy.   It was one of those co-operating attacks which are always unpleasant, the paragraph in Brigade Orders covering the main attack being headed : Exact time cannot be fixed, but will depend upon success at Epéhy, and will not take place before 6 a.m.

The 58th Division was unable to take Epéhy, but the 229th Brigade attack was made.   The two battalions seem to have entered the enemy trenches in many places, and to have become involved in bomb fighting. Casualties were heavy. They were compelled to withdraw to their original line.

It was clear that the Germans were making a stand, and that advance guard actions had not sufficient weight to move him from the strong positions he had occupied. A fully organised attack would have to be made.

# CHAPTER XVI

## THE BATTLE OF EPÉHY

Heavy gas casualties—Operation orders—The attack.

THE sequence of events since Marshal Foch had commenced his great attack, flinging armies at the Germans as though they were so many divisions, must be followed from the moment the IIIrd and Ist Armies were launched. The Canadian Corps, of the Ist Army, and the left of the IIIrd Army had made great progress between the Sensee and Scarpe Rivers, and on the 2nd September the right of the Hindenburg Line was broken by the Canadians. This was followed by a general withdrawal, a rapid falling back of the enemy on the whole of the IIIrd Army front, and on the right of the Ist Army astride the Scarpe, on the line of the Canal du Nord. And he commenced to withdraw south of Peronne.

From the neighbourhood of Havrincourt the Hindenburg Line left the Canal du Nord and ran south-east across the Beauchamp and la Vacquerie and Bonavis Ridges, to the Scheldt Canal at Bantouzelle, and along the canal to St. Quentin. In front of the Hindenburg Line there were formidable positions at Havrincourt and Epéhy, which had to be taken before a final attack on the main line could be launched. On the 12th September the IVth and VIth Corps, Third Army, on the left of the IVth Army and the front where the 74th Division was engaged, attacked and captured the villages of Trescault and Havrin-

court. This was the position from which the
Hindenburg Line had been broken in November 1917,
at the First Battle of Cambrai.

The 18th September was the date fixed for the
IVth and IIIrd Armies to attack on a front of seven-
teen miles, in conjunction with the Ist French Army
on their right. The British attack was from Holnon
to the southern edge of Havrincourt Wood. It was
a preliminary to the attack by the Ist and IIIrd
Armies on the Canal du Nord, which took place on the
27th September.

General Girdwood decided to attack on the 18th on
a two-brigade front—the 230th on the right, the 231st
on the left.

The Division was suffering from severe casualties,
and on the 16th no less than 350 gas casualties occurred
amongst the two attacking brigades. The Somersets
were notably weak, and a company of the Black Watch
was attached to them for the attack.

The following are extracts from the orders :

" The IIIrd Corps is continuing the attack in conjunction with Corps and Armies on either flank, with
a view to securing a position affording good observation of the Hindenburg Line.

" The 38th Division, with 96th, 95th, 94th Infantry
Regiments from right to left, is believed to be holding
the line from Templeux to Ronssoy.

" 230th Brigade will be the right attacking unit,
231st the left. To each brigade one battalion of the
229th Brigade will be attached—16th Devons to 231st,
12th Somersets to 230th. To each brigade will also
be attached :

" 1/2 Troop Northumberland Hussars for inter-
communication.
" 1/2 Section R.E.

" One Machine Gun Company (less two sections).
" Detachment of Tunnelling Company.

" Both brigades will attack the first objective with two battalions, and will leap-frog two battalions through for the attack upon the second objective.

"230th will, on Y/Z night, move its right battalion south of the Cologne River, and will be allotted ground by the 1st Australian Division. . . . 230th will attack Templeux and Quarries east of it, with the battalion south of the river, moving in a north-east direction in close co-operation with the left of the 1st Australian Division, which will attack Bolsover Switch . . . simultaneously with the 230th attack upon the Quarries.    The left battalion, 230th Brigade, will attack Templeux and the Quarries from the north-west.  Special parties will be detailed for mopping up Templeux and the Quarries.

" The barrage will come down at zero 200 yards in front of the infantry.

" The 230th Brigade will be covered by a group formed of the 44th and 104th F.A. Brigades, under Lt.-Colonel C. C. Robertson.  The 231st will be covered by a group formed of the 86th and 117th F.A. Brigades, under Lt.-Colonel Kinnear.

" The attack will be carried out under the protection of :

" (a) A creeping field artillery barrage ;
" (b) Heavy artillery barrage ;
" (c) Machine gun barrage.

" There will be no preliminary bombardment on Z day.  The lifts of the barrages, which will always be 100 yards, will be at the following times : 1st lift, $0 + 3$ ; 2nd lift, $0 + 5$ ; 3rd lift, $0 + 8$, and so on, in three-minute lifts, till the 11th lift at $0 + 32$.  The 12th and all subsequent lifts will be at the rate of 100 yards in four minutes.

" There will be a halt at the first objective (Green

Line) of over an hour, and the barrage will commence
to creep from the Green Line at Zero + 3 hours and
10 minutes, and continue at the rate of 100 yards in 4
minutes to the Red Line (2nd objective). The barrage will thicken up three minutes before the advance
to warn all troops of the lift.

" On lifting off the 2nd objective, the barrage will
remain as a protective barrage for fifteen minutes,
and will then die away.

" Machine Guns.—(a) Barrage to cover advance
from starting-line will be carried out by two companies 2nd Life Guards Machine Gun Battalion. On
completion one company will remain in, or about, the
old front line as a garrison. Remainder will withdraw to Divisional Reserve. (b) Barrage to cover
advance from 1st objective to 2nd objective will be
carried out by two sections A Company, D Company,
and two sections D Company, 74th Machine Gun
Battalion. On completion, two sections A and two
sections C Companies will undertake consolidation
west of and including 1st objective. D Company
will remain in, or about, 1st objective, but will be
disposed in depth. All these guns will be prepared to
put down an S.O.S. barrage in front of the 2nd objective. (c) Advance to last objective will be covered
by direct overhead fire of two sections of each of A
and C Companies, allotted to 230th and 231st Brigades
respectively. These sections, under orders of B.G.'s
C., will be responsible for the consolidation of ground
between 1st and 2nd objectives. (d) After stand to
on Z + 1 day, unless otherwise ordered, D Company
will revert to Divisional Reserve, and the whole of
A and C Companies to the 230th and 231st Brigades
respectively. (e) B Company will be in Divisional
Reserve ready to move forward at short notice. (f)
The machine gun barrage will move 250 yards in
front of the 18-pounder barrage, and will lift 250
yards at a time."

Three objectives were given to the Division known as the Green, Red, and Blue Lines.

On the 18th (the day before the opening of General Allenby's great attack in Syria) the infantry formed up in the gloom and chill of downpouring rain, and at 5.30 a.m. the attack was launched.

The enemy reply to the opening barrage was prompt and heavy, and, what with the rain and the smoke of bursting shells, the early stages of the attack were made in a dense fog, in which it was impossible to see more than a dozen yards ahead. It was extremely difficult to keep touch and direction, but, on the other hand, the storming troops were hidden from the enemy and behind a very effective barrage, so that they were upon him before he realised that the artillery had lifted.

The 230th Brigade attacked with the Suffolks, supported by the Buffs, on the right, and the Sussex, supported by the Somersets, on the left. The Suffolks, attacking from the Australian area, swept through Templeux and over the Quarries. This flank attack took the enemy completely by surprise. Captain Lascelles, with about fifteen men, got round the biggest mound, in the thick mist, and discovered there were about twenty of the enemy on top *looking the other way ;* they were all captured. This officer showed dashing and brilliant leadership throughout the day. The whole of the 1st objective on this brigade front was taken by 7.15 a.m.

There was then a pause, and the assault of the Red Line commenced. The Buffs went through the Suffolks, and, after patchy fighting, secured their objective. One company seems to have reached the Blue Line, which was the outpost of the Hindenburg

System, but was unable to maintain this position, and fell back to the 2nd objective, having suffered severely from machine gun fire.  On the left the Somersets, and the attached company of the Black Watch, went through the Sussex, carrying out the " leap-frog " form of attack, but were held up before reaching the 2nd objective by increasing enemy resistance towards the left.  The enemy shelling and machine gun fire was intense.  All telephone lines from battalion Headquarters were cut.  The Somersets showed the greatest tenacity, and by 2 p.m. the whole of the Red Line on the Brigade front was taken.  The 230th Brigade captured between 700 and 800 prisoners, two batteries of field guns, one 4·2 howitzer, many trench mortars, and at least fifty machine guns.

The 231st Brigade had met with fierce opposition. Attacking with the Devons on the right and the Welsh Regiment on the left, the 1st objective was taken without much trouble, the garrison surrendering freely ; but when the Shropshires and Welsh Fusiliers passed through to carry on the assault, they found the 2nd objective was strongly held and defended.  There was, on the extreme left of the Divisional front, a work known as the Quadrilateral, which should have been attacked by the Welsh Fusiliers and troops of the 18th Division simultaneously, but the 18th Division had met with resistance at the first stage of the battle which could not be overcome.  The result was that a mass of machine guns was concentrated on the Welsh Fusiliers and the Shropshires and the advance was held up.

A heavy bombardment of the Red Line was arranged, and at 3.50 p.m. the Shropshires, who had crept up close to the enemy trenches during the

16

bombardment, rushed the line on the right of the Brigade front. The Welsh Fusiliers, however, had the strongest and best defended position in front of them, and did not succeed in reaching the forward trenches. They therefore formed a defensive flank along the Bellicourt Road.

Throughout the day the 18th Division had been unable to make any appreciable advance beyond the 1st objective. On the right the Australians had taken the 2nd objective, and, in conjunction with the Buffs, sent patrols out towards the Blue Line. In spite of the weakness on the left flank of their attack the threat of the 74th Division was fully appreciated by the enemy. About 6 p.m. a fresh German division, the 121st, advanced through the 38th and counter-attacked, but were repulsed. The Red Line, except on the extreme left, was held.

On the whole, although the final objective had not been captured, it had been a profitable day for the 74th Division. Many of the prisoners taken by the 230th Brigade were passed through the Australian cages, but the Divisional cage registered 18 officers and 873 other ranks. There were also ten 77 mm. guns, three 4·2 howitzers, and about 80 machine guns. The prisoners were from the 2nd Guards Division, 96th, 95th, 94th Infantry Regiments.

Sir Douglas Haig's Despatch records that:

" In this operation our troops penetrated to a depth of three miles through the deep, continuous, and well-organised defensive belt formed by the old British and German lines. On practically the whole front our objectives were gained successfully ; the 1st, 17th, 21st, and 74th Divisions and the 1st and 4th Australian Divisions distinguished themselves by the vigour and success of their attack. On the extreme right, and in the left centre about Epéhy, the enemy's resistance was very determined, and in these sectors troops of the 6th, 12th, 18th, and 58th Divisions had severe fighting."

.    .    .    .    .

The further attack was not continued until the 21st, when the 18th Division was launched on the left, but only one battalion of the Australians on the right. Some very heavy fighting took place.

The attack started at 5.40 a.m. under a creeping barrage, and the action which ensued is one of confusion, in which much heroism was displayed and heavy casualties suffered. The object was to secure the Line of Exploitation, or the Blue Line of the 18th.

On the right the 230th Brigade attacked with the Buffs and Sussex. The enemy was very prompt in putting down his protective barrage on the front line as the storming troops left it, but the advance was, nevertheless, rapid until the wire in front of the Blue Line was reached : there were several belts, which proved to be a serious obstacle in places and split up the attacking battalions. This wire and the heavy artillery barrage forced the Buffs to seek the protection of shell-holes.

The Sussex pushed on to the neighbourhood of Quennet Copse, and captured about ninety prisoners of the 26th and 60th Infantry Regiments of the 121st Division. Unfortunately the Copse area seems to have been overlooked, as the battalion found, on advancing beyond the line of it, that they were being shot in the back. A desperate situation resulted. The leading companies of the Sussex and Buffs were extremely weak, and the German artillery fire, together with machine guns which had been passed and remained in action in rear of the assaulting troops, made it impossible for support companies to reinforce. The forward troops were isolated and kept under punishing fire. Three separate attempts were made by patrols from the supporting companies to try to find a way through the complicated enemy cross-fire, some of which came from the Quadrilateral on the left flank of the Division, but the patrols were killed to a man.

The advanced troops of this Brigade held on to their positions in shell-holes until 12.30 p.m., when a strong counter-attack was organised and launched by the enemy from Quennet Copse trenches, and part of the leading troops of the Sussex and the Buffs were surrounded. It is said that at least 100 German prisoners were released by this attack. There was nothing for it but to retire, which was done under cover of very gallant Lewis-gun teams, many of whom sacrificed themselves in saving their comrades. One company of the Sussex which returned twenty-eight strong, and was the strongest company in the battalion, claimed to have bayoneted over forty Germans. Briefly, survivors of both battalions dribbled in as best they could, and reformed on the Red Line, with the Suffolks, moved forward, holding the centre.

The Black Watch was attached to the Brigade as reserve.

The attack on the left, of the 231st Brigade, which had been holding a flank thrown back from the Red Line, had to provide for a change of direction in the middle of the assault—the Division had done this frequently in Palestine, but it was always a dangerous thing to attempt on the comparatively flat, but shell-smashed battlefields of France.

The plan was for the 25th Royal Welsh Fusiliers, with four tanks, to advance on, and to pass through, the Quadrilateral followed by the 24th Welsh Regiment. The barrage was to halt for fifteen minutes 200 yards east of this objective. Then the Welsh Regiment was to capture the position Gillimont Farm, and the Royal Welsh Fusiliers, moving east, would capture and consolidate the Blue Line. The Shropshires, advancing in rear, were to mop up the dugouts and shafts of the Quadrilateral.

The tanks were unable to give any assistance, as they failed to reach the starting-point, or were knocked out before reaching the 1st objective.

The actual movements appear to be that the Welsh Fusiliers passed over the Quadrilateral and swung eastwards through an intense barrage, and the Welsh Regiment, following in rear, lost direction in the smoke of the bursting shells, and kept in the tracks of the Fusiliers instead of carrying the attack forward to Gillimont Farm. At the same time the 18th Division was held up on the left. The whole attack had then swept forward with no one on the left flank.

The enemy grasped the situation with commendable quickness—no doubt many of them were still in their dugouts—and dribbled men into the Quadrilateral from the left, or 18th Division area, through the sunken road. And when the Shropshires came up to consolidate and " mop up," they were met by heavy machine gun and rifle fire, and found they were unable to advance. But having regained a foothold in the Quadrilateral, the enemy was able to fire into the rear of the Royal Welsh Fusiliers and the Welsh

Regiment, and also inflict heavy casualties on the
230th Brigade. Repeated attempts during the day
to bomb the Germans out were frustrated.

At nightfall the 231st Brigade was back in its
original line.

Very heavy casualties had been incurred, and it was
decided not to attack again with the 74th Division.
But the enemy was giving a lot of trouble from
the Quadrilateral, and it was obvious that he must
be ejected from that stronghold. An attack was
accordingly arranged, and took place in conjunction
with the 18th Division at 3 a.m. on the 22nd. It was
confined to the Shropshires.

After a quarter of an hour of intense bombardment
from the field gun batteries, the Shropshires rushed
the position, which yielded slightly over 200 prisoners
and 30 machine guns. A great number of dead were
found. Later in the day a further small attack was
made to assist the 18th Division, and touch was
secured with that unit.

After this operation the 230th and 231st Brigades
were relieved by the 229th. On the night 24th/25th
the Division was relieved by the 27th American
Division.

The casualties for the Division during the month
of September were 34 officers and 436 other ranks
killed, 143 officers and 2,712 other ranks wounded.
There were 8 officers and 188 other ranks returned as
missing, most of whom were killed.

# CHAPTER XVII

## THE ADVANCE OF THE Vth ARMY

### To Wavrin and Lattres—East of Ronchin—Crossing the Scheldt.

DURING the morning of the 25th September the Division entrained from Tincourt and Peronne, and left for Villers Bretonnieux. Divisional Headquarters opened at Fouilly Château. Two days later it entrained again for the Vth Army area, and arrived at Norrent Fontes on the 28th. On the 1st October the Division relieved the 19th Division in the line.

On the 27th September the Ist and IIIrd Armies attacked the Hindenburg System on the Canal du Nord and broke through those historic defences. On the 28th the King of the Belgians, having under him the Belgian Army, certain French divisions, and the IInd Army, with a record second to none, attacked in the north, and from Ypres to the sea drove deep into the enemy lines. These two attacks must be borne in mind. Between them lay the Vth Army.

These two attacks were pressed with vigour, and the enemy was forced to retire on the Vth Army front.

It was not part of the general scheme for the Vth Army to attack.

General Girdwood issued the following order :

"29th September 1918.—The successful offensives being conducted by the allied armies may cause the enemy opposite the front of the Vth Army to continue his withdrawal to the line of the Douai–Lille Canal and the Lille defences.

" In order to test the strength of the enemy forces opposite to the XIth Corps, minor operations are being carried out by three divisions to-morrow morning.

" On taking over the front of the 19th Division, it is of great importance that the Division should be prepared to act promptly as soon as indications are obtained that the enemy intends to withdraw, or is in process of retiring.

" It is not the intention of the Divisional Commander to force a withdrawal, but he intends to follow up a withdrawal should it commence, and to cut off isolated posts of the enemy should the opportunity occur. Troops in the front line must act with vigour, and be prepared to go on a pre-arranged plan without waiting orders.

" Each Brigade will have its own advance guard ready detailed, which will be directed on the most important tactical localities during the advance, and will not necessarily advance in lines or waves.

" In order to gain information of the intentions of the enemy, the following steps will be taken :

" (a) Patrols will maintain touch with the enemy's front line system of defences.

" (b) Raiding parties will kill or capture the garrison of small posts with the object of obtaining information as to the enemy's dispositions.

" (c) In those parts of the line where patrols and raiding parties cannot find any hostile posts, our line will be advanced and promptly held, and defences will be constructed so as to form a jumping-off place for further action of patrols and raiding parties.

" The road allotted to the Division for traffic and for signal communication is the Halpegarbe–Herles Road. Brigade and Divisional Headquarters will be located as near this road as is possible."

The Divisional front extended to about 5,000 yards

with Neuve Chapelle in the centre, and was taken over from the 59th Division by the Buffs and the Sussex.

At 11 o'clock on the morning of the 2nd battalions reported that the enemy had vacated his line and were ordered to push forward.   The German retreat was well done.   Cross roads were blown up and culverts destroyed ;  wire obstacles were frequent and booby traps plentiful.   The objective given to advancing battalions was the la Bassée–Aubers–Fromelles line of trenches :  darkness fell before it was attained.

The 231st Brigade then went into line, relieving the 56th Brigade, with the Shropshires on the right and the Welsh Regiment on the left.

The next day the line was carried forward without opposition to Basse Rue, Fourmes, Petite Hate Bourdin, le Marais, Hockon, Sainghin.   On the 4th opposition was encountered chiefly from artillery, and the Division rested finally on the line east of Wavrin and Lattres, along the railway to la Haie, with a definite enemy outpost line in front of them.   Patrols found the position held in force.   For some days the situation remained unchanged.

On the 8th October command of the sector held by the 55th and 74th Divisions passed from the XIth Corps to the IIIrd Corps.

On the 9th the enemy raided the Shropshires, under the support of a heavy barrage and in a thick fog. Twenty men were found to be missing ; one dead and two wounded Shropshires and four enemy dead were all that was discovered in the trench.   This successful enemy enterprise was not allowed to pass unavenged, for the Shropshires raided the Germans on the following night, the raiding party consisting of two officers

and two platoons, and killed twenty Germans ; one
live prisoner was brought back, and proved to be of
the 91st Reserve Infantry Regiment, 2nd Guard
Division.

After that, patrols kept in closest touch with the
enemy, but always found him in force until the 15th,
when the 230th Brigade discovered la Haie to be
unoccupied.  The Division then advanced.

The 230th Brigade, on the right, met with local
machine gun opposition, and did not succeed in
securing the line of the canal, the line resting east
of Mangre.  The 229th Brigade, on the left, reached
the line Santes–les Habourdin.  The Brigade on the
left of the Division having met with stronger opposition, no further advance was attempted.

A small advance of about a mile was registered on
the 16th, but still the line of the canal was not
secured.

On the 17th " the enemy vanished " !  He had
kept up an active machine gun fire from the canal
until 4.30 a.m., although his artillery did not fire
after midnight ; but in the morning patrols could find
no sign of him, and civilians reported that Lille had
been evacuated.

" Our advance on the north of the Lys," writes Sir
Douglas Haig, " had brought our troops far to the
east of the Lille defences on the northern side, while
our progress on the le Cateau front had turned the
Lille defences from the south.  The German forces
between the Sensee and the Lys were once more
compelled to withdraw, closely followed by our
troops, who constantly drove in their rear-guards and
took a number of prisoners.  The enemy was given
no opportunity to complete the removal of his stores

and the destruction of roads and bridges, or to evacuate the civil population.

" The movement began on the 15th October, when, in spite of considerable opposition, our troops crossed the Haute Deule Canal on a wide front north of Pont-a-Vendin. By the evening of the 17th October the 8th Division, of General Sir A. Hunter Weston's VIIIth Corps, had entered Douai, and the 57th and 59th Divisions, of Lt.-General Sir R. C. B. Haking's XIth Corps, were on the outskirts of Lille. At 5.50 a.m., on the 18th October, our troops had encircled Lille, which was clear of the enemy."

The 74th Division promptly took up the pursuit, and, with the Suffolks as advance guard to the 230th Brigade, crossed the canal and marched forward to the line Wattignies–l'Arbrisseau, when the Buffs took the advance guard and continued to the east of Faches, while on the left the Devons and Black Watch, advancing to the line of the canal, found that the bridges had been partially destroyed and could only be crossed by infantry in file; they crossed the canal and entered Habourdin, but a general advance was not made on the 229th Brigade front until 3 p.m., by which time a pontoon bridge had been thrown across the canal for the transport. The Devons then marched forward to the line of the railway, east of Ronchin, a distance of 12,000 yards.

The advance was slower on the 18th, being retarded by a fog. The 231st Brigade had taken over the right and found the enemy rear-guard, mostly machine guns covered by a battery of field guns, at Sainghin. The village was cleared without difficulty, and an outpost line taken up on the River la Marcq.

The 229th Brigade encountered the enemy on that day at Ascq, but he retired before the patrols, and was found to be holding the east bank of the river. An outpost line was established on the line of the railway, west of the river.

The advance was continued on the 19th, and the 231st Brigade reached Camphin, and the 229th Brigade Baisseur.   During the evening the Monmouth Company of Royal Engineers threw a bridge over the Austaign.

The next day a patrol of King Edward's Horse, reconnoitring ahead of the 229th Brigade, met the enemy in Marquain, and lost one man killed and one wounded.   The town was occupied by the infantry late in the day, and the outpost line ran east of it. Owing to the narrowing of the Divisional front, the 231st Brigade had been squeezed out in the morning, so that the 229th Brigade found the picquets in touch with the 55th Division on the right and the 57th on the left.

The Division was now only about a mile from Tournai.   The village of Orcq was strongly held by machine guns.   During the day the Somersets, edging ever closer, got astride of Orcq, and attacked behind a barrage at dusk.   Only a small gain, to the eastern outskirts of the village, was made ;   the enemy machine gun fire was very heavy.

The enemy was making a determined stand behind belts of wire.   A company of the Black Watch tested the strength of the position on the 23rd, and got to within fifty yards of their objective ; but the opposition was too great, and they retired to their original position, having lost six killed and twenty-eight wounded.

On the right and left armies were still pressing forward, making tremendous captures of men and material ; but on the 74th Division front the situation remained the same until the 8th November, when, early in the morning, patrols of the Welsh Fusiliers entered Tournai. Soon after their report a Belgian lady came into the outpost line, and stated that the enemy had left Tournai at 3 a.m. Incidentally this lady was entertained by the Brigadier, who was discussing the situation with Major Stable over two cups of cocoa, and politely offered her Major Stable's cocoa ! Patrols of the 231st Brigade then entered the town. Through the centre of Tournai runs the River l'Escaut, and the Germans lined the eastern bank with machine guns. All the bridges had been blown up.

By 9 a.m. the Engineers had thrown a footbridge across the river, and the Shropshires went over to the east bank. The 25th Royal Welsh Fusiliers passed through the Shropshires and moved forward as advance guard, with the 55th Division on the right and the 47th on the left. The enemy had once more completed the destruction of roads and railways, but the infantry was able to advance without opposition to the line Beclers–Thimougies. Thimougies was entered at 6.45 p.m., and the civilians stated that the Germans had left at 4 p.m.

On the 10th the advance was resumed to the railway line north of Grundmetz. No contact was obtained with the enemy. The roads to the east were all mined, but had not been fired.

At 8.30 a.m. on the 11th the 231st Brigade entered Ath, and at 8.45 a.m. General Girdwood sent the following message to Brigades : " Hostilities cease 11.00 to-day, after which hour no further easterly movement will take place. Outposts will be put out,

and all military precautions taken.  Contact with
the enemy will be avoided.  Troops at present in
movement will halt at 11.00 and occupy best available
billets, or return to last night's billets if no facilities
exist."

.        .        .        .        .

On reading through the mass of papers which
constitute the records of the 74th Division, one sums
up the character of the Division with the words,
tenacity, determination, willing sacrifice, cheerful
disposition—these are great qualities.  The difficulties overcome by the infantry, artillery, engineers,
service corps, and medical staff are of such a nature
as to strike amazement.  The patience, the ingenuity
and skill, the tireless energy, the indomitable spirit,
the courageous collective gallantry excite the pro-
foundest emotion.  Many people will no doubt conclude with a sense of sadness, maybe with horror of
the evils of war, and will determine, by every means
in their power, to combat a repetition of those horrors,
but—what else could we have done ?

The British Empire was not an aggressive Power,
trailing a sabre across the world.  If it is any consola-
tion, we must frankly admit that we were not prepared
for war, that we turned a deaf ear to all warnings of
future need for an army.  The militarists' view of
British preparation, and, indeed, of British attitude
and intention, is contained in the classic utterance of
the German Emperor, " their contemptible little
army " !  Whether it was wise to deserve such
complete exoneration from all warlike spirit depends
not on the facts as now established, but on the mental
strength of those who are called upon to express an
opinion.  Can one bear to face nature which embraces

the whole scheme of life ?   Are we to worship the Goddess of Reason, or the frail idol of Logic, which one man, armed with a stick, can shatter with a blow ?

Mr. Page, the American ambassador, has described an interview he had with His Majesty the King at the outbreak of war, and declares that the King put to him the question : " What else could we do ? "

What else, indeed, except submit to the yoke of an alien Power, and that is not the spirit of British yeomen.

Each man, each " unknown soldier " of the 74th Division, did his duty to his family, his country, and himself, in the heat of the desert, in the storms, the rain, the cold, the winds which swept across the barren bleak Judean hills, in the festering muddy trenches of France.   There can be no greater praise for the living, no more glorious epitaph for the dead.

# APPENDIXES

# APPENDIX I

## THE VICTORIA CROSS

*(In " London Gazette," 18th December 1917.)*

No. 355652, A/Corporal J. COLLINS (Merthyr Tydvil), 25th Bn., Royal Welsh Fusiliers.

For most conspicuous bravery, resource, and leadership when, after deployment, prior to an attack, his battalion was forced to lie out in the open under heavy shell and machine gun fire, which caused many casualties.

This gallant non-commissioned officer repeatedly went out under heavy fire and brought wounded back to cover, thus saving many lives. In subsequent operations throughout the day, Corporal Collins was conspicuous in rallying and leading his command. He led the final assault with the utmost skill, in spite of heavy fire at close range and uncut wire. He bayoneted fifteen of the enemy, and with a Lewis gun section pressed on beyond the objective and covered the reorganisation and consolidation most effectively, although isolated and under fire from snipers and guns.

He showed throughout a magnificent example of initiative and fearlessness.

(Beersheba, 31st October 1917.)

*(In " London Gazette," 8th May 1918.)*

No. 230199, Private Harold WHITFIELD (Oswestry, Salop), 10th Bn., Shropshire Light Infantry.

For most conspicuous bravery, initiative, and absolute disregard of personal safety.

During the first and heaviest of three counter-attacks made by the enemy on the position which had just been captured by his battalion, Private Whitfield, single-handed, charged and captured a Lewis gun which was harassing his company at short range. He bayoneted or shot the whole gun team, and, turning the gun on the enemy, drove them back with heavy casualties, thereby completely restoring the whole situation in his part of the line. Later, he organised and led a bombing attack on the enemy, who had established themselves in an advanced position close to our line, and from which they were enfilading his company. He drove the enemy back with great loss, and by establishing his party in their position, saved many lives and materially assisted in the defeat of the counter-attack.

(Burj el Lisaneh, 10th March 1918.)

(*In " London Gazette,*" 6th *January* 1919.)

No. 295536, Sergeant Thomas CALDWELL (Carluke), 12th Bn., Royal Scots Fusiliers.

For most conspicuous bravery and initiative in attack near Audenarde on the 31st October 1918, when in command of a Lewis gun section engaged in clearing a farmhouse. When his section came under intense fire at close range from another farm, Sergeant Caldwell rushed towards the farm, and, in spite of very heavy fire, reached the enemy position, which he captured single-handed, together with eighteen prisoners.

This gallant and determined exploit removed a serious obstacle from the line of advance, saved many casualties, and led to the capture by his section of about seventy prisoners, eight machine guns, and one trench mortar.

# APPENDIX II

## BEERSHEBA

### FORCE ORDERS

BY GENERAL SIR E. ALLENBY, K.C.B.

G.H.Q.,
*22nd October* 1917.

*(Extract covering movement of infantry.)*

It is the intention of the Commander-in-Chief to take the offensive against the enemy at Gaza and at Beersheba, and, when Beersheba is in our hands, to make an enveloping attack on the enemy's left flank in the direction of Sheria and Hareira.

On Z day the XXth Corps (with the 10th Division and the Imperial Camel Brigade attached) and the Desert Mounted Corps (less one mounted division and the Imperial Camel Brigade) will attack the enemy at Beersheba with the object of gaining possession of that place by nightfall.

As soon as Beersheba is in our hands and the necessary arrangements have been made for the restoration of the Beersheba water supply, the XXth Corps and the Desert Mounted Corps complete will move rapidly forward to attack the left of the enemy's main position, with the object of driving him out of Sheria and Hareira, and enveloping the left flank of his army. The XXth Corps will move against the enemy's defences south of Sheria, first of all against the Kauwukah line and then against the Sheria and Hareira defences. The Desert Mounted

249

Corps, calling up the division left in General Reserve
during the Beersheba operations, will move north of the
XXth Corps, and will be prepared to operate vigorously
against and round the enemy's left flank if he should
throw it back to oppose the advance of the XXth Corps.

On a date to be subsequently determined, and which
will probably be after the occupation of Beersheba, and
24 to 48 hours before the attack of the XXth Corps on
the Kauwukah line, the XXIst Corps will attack the
south-western defences of Gaza with the object of capturing
the enemy's front line system from Umbrella Hill to Sheikh
Hasan, both inclusive.

The Royal Navy will co-operate with the XXIst Corps
in the attack of Gaza and in the subsequent operations
which may be undertaken by the XXIst Corps.

On Z—4 day G.O.C. XXIst Corps will open a systematic
bombardment of the Gaza defences, increasing in volume
from Z—1 to Z—2 day and to be continued until Z—4
day at the least.

The Royal Navy will co-operate. . . .

The XXth Corps will move into position during the
night Z—1/Zero, so as to attack the enemy at Beersheba
on Zero day south of the Wadi Saba with two divisions,
while covering his flank and the construction of the railway east of Shellal with one division on the high ground
overlooking the wadis el Sufi and Hanafish.

The objective of the XXth Corps will be the enemy's
works west and south-west of Beersheba as far as the
Khalassa–Beersheba Road inclusive.

The Desert Mounted Corps will move on the night
Z—1/Zero from the area of concentration about Khalassa
and Asluj, so as to co-operate with the XXth Corps by
attacking Beersheba with two divisions and one mounted
brigade.

The objective of the Desert Mounted Corps will be the
enemy's defences from the south-east to the north-east of
Beersheba, and the town of Beersheba itself.

The G.O.C. Desert Mounted Corps will endeavour to turn the enemy's left with a view to breaking down his resistance at Beersheba as quickly as possible. With this in view the main weight of his force will be directed against Beersheba from the east and north-east. As soon as the enemy's resistance shows signs of weakening, the G.O.C. Mounted Corps will be prepared to act with the utmost vigour against his retreating troops, so as to prevent their escape, or at least to drive them well beyond the high ground immediately overlooking the town from the north. He will also be prepared to push troops rapidly into Beersheba in order to protect from damage any wells and plant connected with the water supply not damaged by the enemy before Beersheba is entered.

Special instructions will be issued to G.O.C. Desert Mounted Corps. . . .

The Yeomanry Mounted Division will pass from the command of G.O.C. XXth Corps at 05.00 on Zero day, and will come directly under General Headquarters as part of the general Reserve. . . .

When the situation as regards the water at Beersheba has become clear, so that the movement of the XXth Corps and Desert Mounted Corps against the left flank of the enemy's main position can be arranged, G.O.C. XXIth Corps will be ordered to attack the enemy's defences south-west of Gaza, in time for this operation to be carried out prior to the attack of the XXth Corps on the Kauwukah line of works.

*Artillery.*—. . . The general average for one day's firing has been calculated on the following basis :

| | |
|---|---|
| Field and mountain guns<br>Mountain howitzers | } 150 rounds per gun. |
| 4·5 howitzers | 120 ,, ,, |
| 60-pounders<br>6-inch howitzers | } 90 ,, ,, |
| 8-inch howitzers | 60 ,, ,, |
| 6-inch VII | 60 ,, ,, |

This average expenditure will only be possible in the XXIst Corps up to Z—16, and for the Desert Mounted Corps and XXth Corps to Z—13. After these dates (if the average has been expended) the daily average will have to drop to the basis of 100 rounds per 18-pounder per day, and other natures in proportion. . . .

# APPENDIX III

## BATTLE OF SHERIA

### 53RD DIVISION OPERATION ORDER

*3rd November* 1917.

*(Extract.)*

The Turks were holding the vicinity of Khuweilfeh yesterday and Dhaheriyeh, and our cavalry were unable to dislodge them.

The 53rd Division will advance on Khuweilfeh to-day in two columns:

Left Column: Brigadier-General N. Money, Commanding. Route, road facing Brigade Headquarters, leading north-east towards cross-roads at Kehleh.

Right Column: Brigadier-General V. Pearson, Commanding. Route, by guide to Towal Abu Jerwal, thence on Tel Khuweilfeh.

The 229th Infantry Brigade Group, if required to move, will do so under the orders of G.O.C. 74th Division. . . .

### XXTH CORPS ORDER

H.Q., XXTH CORPS,
*5th November* 1917.

The G.O.C. XXth Corps intends to resume the attack on 6th November with the object of securing the Sheria water supply and capturing the Kauwukah trench system as far as and inclusive of the long communication trench . . . 1¾ miles south-east of Hareira. The attack must be pressed with the utmost rapidity and determination, as the enemy must be given no respite until his resistance is broken down, and it is essential to secure the water at Sheria before nightfall.

The Desert Mounted Corps, to which the 53rd Division will be attached temporarily from 06.00 on 6th November, is allotted the following tasks :

(a) To protect the right flank of the XXth Corps.

(b) To take advantage of any retirement of the enemy to press forward and seize the Nejileh and Jennana water supplies.

The 53rd Division is about Ain Kohleh, and will extend its left so as to occupy the general line Kuweilfeh–Rijm el Dhib. The Yeomanry Mounted Division of the Desert Mounted Corps is to be concentrated south-west of Ain Kohleh by 07.00 on November 6th, ready to close the gap between the 53rd and 74th Division, which attacks on the right of the XXth Corps, and to take advantage of any enemy retirement to push forward to the line Kh. Abu Rasheid–el Zubala, and thence to the right of the 74th Division.

The artillery of the Yeomanry Mounted Division will march at the head of its division to the position of concentration, and will be placed, in the first instance, at the disposal of the G.O.C. 53rd Division under special instructions to be given by the G.O.C. Desert Mounted Corps.

Divisions will move as follows to positions of assembly to be reached before dawn on 6th November.

*74th Division.*—Leading Brigade to be in position west of the Wadi Union as near as possible to the flank of the enemy works running eastward from the railway, the remaining brigade of the Division being echeloned on its right flank in readiness to meet any counter-attack by enemy troops from a north-westerly direction.

*60th Division.*—Leading brigades in position on the enemy's outpost position in W3 and W4 (north-west of Kuweilfeh).

During the night 5th/6th November the 10th Division will concentrate between the left of the 60th Division and the Gaza–Beersheba Road at Point 570, one infantry brigade to be in position by 4 a.m. on 6th November to attack on the left of the 60th Division, remaining infantry of the division in covered positions near Culvert in R12d.

74th, 60th, and 10th Divisions of the XXth Corps will attack on 6th November in the order named from right to left, tasks and objectives as below, 74th Division being the leading and directing division.

*74th Division.*—1st objectives : The line of enemy's works east of the railway at Point P21b55. After reaching the railway, the task of the 74th Division will be :

(a) To protect the right of the 60th Division and drive the enemy out of Sheria.

(b) To seize the high ground north of Sheria to protect the water supply.

(c) To assist as far as possible the attack of the 60th Division on the enemy works west of the railway by such artillery fire as can be spared.

*60th Division.*—1st objectives : Works of the Kauwukah system west of the railway and north of a line through P27 central and O24 central as far as the communication trench S78–S56 inclusive.

After attaining the 1st objective, the task of the 60th Division will be to assist if necessary the 74th Division to secure the high ground north of Sheria and covering the water supply of that place.

*10th Division.*—The 10th Division will employ one infantry brigade, supported by all the artillery of the division, to attack the works of the Kauwukah system south of the boundary allotted to the 60th Division. The remaining two brigades of the 10th Division will be concentrated behind the brigade allotted to the attack, will be in Corps reserve, and will not be employed without the sanction of Corps Headquarters.

The attack of the 74th Division will be made as early as possible on the 6th November, the infantry of the 60th and 10th Divisions moving forward during the initial stages sufficiently to cover suitable positions from which their artillery can begin the preliminary bombardment of the Kauwukah system.

G.O.'s C. 10th and 60th Divisions will report to Corps Headquarters when they consider the artillery preparation to be complete.

The heavy artillery group, less one 60-pounder battery attached to 53rd Division, will move into position north of the Gaza–Beersheba Road to support the attack under the orders of the G.O.C., R.A., XXth Corps, who will allot objectives to the group commander. . . .

# APPENDIX IV

## SHERIA

*(The following extracts from a paper issued prior to the Battle of Beersheba, and outlining the general intention of subsequent operations, is not without interest.)*

The general intention in the 2nd phase is to strike with two divisions (60th on the right, 74th on the left), right leading, from a south-easterly direction against the enemy's lines . . . and the 53rd Division attacking the Kauwukah Group. . . . Final objective—the general line Kh. Zuheilika–Kh. Um Adrah.

This line would probably be the extreme limit of the available supply services for the Corps as a whole, but, in the event of a general retirement of the enemy, at least one division, and if possible more, will be directed on Huj, or even Akra, to co-operate with the cavalry which throughout the battle will be operating on the right flank of the XXth Corps with the object of reaching the Ludd-Beersheba railway about Nejilah. The immediate right of the XXth Corps during the advance will be protected by the Corps Cavalry Regiment, while the Imperial Camel Brigade acts as a link with the Cavalry Corps.

The 10th Division will be moved to the neighbourhood of Bir Imleigh or Abu Irgeig some time before the attack on the enemy's main position, and will be in general reserve.

It will be remembered that by the evening of Z day it is hoped that the troops of the XXth Corps will be distributed as follows :

*I.C.C. Brigade.*—North of Beersheba, covering a line

between Khasim el Buteiyir and the Beersheba–Ain Kohleh track, sufficiently far forward to deny the enemy positions from which Beersheba can be shelled.

*60th Division.*—On the conquered position, with possibly some troops in Beersheba to commence water development as soon as possible.

*74th Division.*—Between the Fara–Beersheba Road and Kh. el Sufi, with an infantry brigade and a brigade of artillery ready to move to the support of the I.C.C.

*53rd Division.*—(With one infantry brigade and one artillery brigade 10th Division attached.) On the line Kh. el Sufi–Bir Imleigh–el Girheir, with outposts covering the left of the 74th Division and holding the approaches from Wadi Sufi and Wadi Imleigh.

*10th Division.*—(Less one infantry brigade and one artillery brigade.) About Shellal.

*XXth Corps Cavalry Regiment.*—Withdrawn to water in the Mirtaba Valley.

It is hoped that at least one cavalry division will be in the water area about Bir Salim, Abu Irgeig (near Tel el Saba), and Tel el Saba holding the approaches to Beersheba from the east and watching the Hebron Road.

Our first objective after the capture of Beersheba will be the enemy's outpost position. . . . As a preliminary to the attack, the 74th Division will move as early as possible on Z—1 day to the high ground south-east of Irgeig, and the 60th Division will be brought up on the right, so that we can move to the attack of the outpost position, with the heads of the 60th, 74th, and 53rd Divisions in line.

The task of the I.C.C. Brigade on Z—1 day remains as on Z day, but the brigade will move forward to hold the high ground between Towal Abu Jerwal and Kh. el Nuweileh, if not already occupied on the evening of Z day, and may have to be supported by infantry.

The 10th Division will be brought up from Shellal to the neighbourhood of Khasif, on the night before the attack on the enemy's outpost position in front of the Kauwukah line. . . .

Beyond this point it is not at present possible to make any forecast of the date of movement, but it must be our object to seize the enemy's outpost position as early as possible.

As regards the attack, there would seem to be no doubt that if we can do so we should make its axis south-east and north-west. I have drawn parallel lines (on the map) . . . which show that should we be able to attack in this manner, we shall take the whole of the enemy works as far west as the railway obliquely and partly in enfilade. The attack on the south-eastern face of the Kauwukah system—which looks very strong—will be a frontal one, but once we have gained this line, we shall be able, by pushing forward our right centre, to take the Kauwukah Group and Rushdi system in reverse, while our left will take the centre of the Kauwukah system and the whole of the Rushdi system directly in enfilade, though, of course, the long perpendicular communication trenches will probably be available for fire trenches, but I doubt if they will be wired. At a later stage the lines on the map show that the left of our attack will take Hareira Tepe and Mustapha and Labbi trenches almost in reverse.

. . . It is obvious that a large number of the troops will have to make a considerable change of front as they move off for the attack, and that the left of our attack, directed against the Kauwukah system, will have to remain in position until the right and right centre have reached the approximate line which I have drawn in green. The movement, or wheel, of the troops . . . will not be simple, as during the wheel they may be exposed to flanking fire, and it will have to be very carefully synchronised with the movement of our right and centre.

We must try to conduct a very considerable amount of wire-cutting on the day previous to the assault. . . . The ideal would be, after having cut the wire in the Kauwukah system, to keep a few guns of the 53rd Division on that part of the line during the first stages, turning the remainder on to the assistance of the right and centre. . . . It will also be necessary to move forward the guns of the 60th Division and some from the 74th . . . so as to assist the 53rd Division in their attack on the Kauwukah system. . . . This move of the 60th Division and the 74th Division guns to the assistance of the left will, of course, be contingent on the cavalry having so occupied the enemy's reserves as to prevent our right and centre being counter-attacked from Sheria and the north.

. . . The principle which should underlie the whole operation should be the continual pressing forward of the right and a constant endeavour to bring cross-fire to bear from the centre across the front of our left attack to assist its progress.

Until the effect of our cavalry on the position of the enemy reserves is known, the right and right centre (60th and 74th Divisions) must retain as large a reserve as possible in hand, and continue the advance after they have captured the enemy's system east of the railway in as close formation as possible, covered by strong advance guards, so as to retain control of their troops and to be ready to meet unforeseen enemy irruptions from the north against our centre and right flank. It will be essential for the 60th and part at least of the 74th to gain possession of the high ground north of Sheria by nightfall to give us the use of the water in that place.

There must be the greatest flexibility on the part of all the artillery, and the closest touch must be maintained between them and the infantry, and I am inclined to think that after the opening phases of the action, there should be a large amount of divisional control exercised with regard to artillery. Throughout the action it is obvious that the artillery along the whole front will have to be continually changing position, not only the field artillery, but also the heavy artillery, for the latter will have to

endeavour to get within effective range of the enemy's
artillery north of Hareira at the earliest possible moment.
General Officers commanding Divisional Artillery will
have to be extremely active in personal reconnaissance,
and exercise personal command over their brigades.

So far as I can see, therefore, the attack will be carried
out roughly in the following stages :

(a) Occupation of the outpost line.

(b) Occupation of a line further forward, if possible to
place the artillery in suitable wire-cutting position.

(c) The advance of the right and centre . . . followed
by a pause and readjustment of artillery.

(d) The attack of the Kauwukah system and the
advance . . . followed by another readjustment of the
artillery, and if possible, in conjunction with the cavalry,
an encircling movement by our right with the object of
bringing reverse artillery fire on the Hareira–Mustapha
trenches.  At this stage there will also have to be a
considerable readjustment of heavy artillery.

(e) If it is possible during one day to advance further,
we should try to reach . . . at least the red dotted line
which includes the Hareira Tepe Redoubt.

. . . General Officers Commanding will clearly understand that the above is only a rough outline of what I
hope may happen. . . . It is in no way a definite plan,
which cannot possibly be made till after we have taken
the enemy's outpost position.

The only thing that will not alter, is my determination
to find the enemy's flank if manœuvre or fighting can
give it me, and to attack generally from south-east to
north-east.

18

# APPENDIX V

# THE ATTACK ON JERUSALEM

ADVANCED HEADQUARTERS, XXTH CORPS,
*5th December* 1917.

The XXth Corps, pivoting on the Neby Samwil and Beit Izza defences, will attack the enemy south and west of Jerusalem, and the Corps Commander intends :

(*a*) To secure the general line Pt. 2670 Kh. Ras el Tawil– Neby Samwil.

(*b*) To block the approaches to Jerusalem from Jericho.

The 53rd Division (less one brigade group), with the Corps Cavalry Regiment attached, will advance on December 6th from the Dilbeh area to the Bethlehem– Beit Jala area, which must be reached on 7th December.

The attack of the XXth Corps will be carried out on 8th December by the 53rd Division (less one brigade group), 60th Division and 74th Division (less one brigade group), in the order named from right to left.

The 53rd Division will protect the right flank of the Corps operating under special instructions attached to this order.

The dividing line between the 60th and 74th Divisions will be the Enab–Jerusalem Road as far as Lifta (village and road inclusive to the 60th Division), and thence the Wadi Beit Hannina as far as Y15d66.

The attack will be divided into four stages, and the tasks and objectives of the 60th and 74th Divisions in each stage are as follows :

*1st Stage.*—The 60th Division will capture the enemy works between the railway in B36 and the Enab–Jerusalem Road in Y25.

The 74th Division will capture the enemy works covering Beit Iksa between the Enab–Jerusalem Road in Y25 and the Wadi el Abeideh.

The commencement of the advance of the 74th Division will be timed by that of the 60th Division, G.O.C. 60th Division to report to Corps Headquarters by 08.00 on 6th December, the hour at which his advance will begin.

*2nd Stage.*—The 60th Division will advance to the line of the Jerusalem–Lifta Road on the approximate front H11c45–Lifta (inclusive).

*3rd Stage.*—The 60th Division will advance to the general line of the track which leaves the Jerusalem–Nablus Road at H5d96 to Kh. Mekikarh.

The 74th Division will advance to the spur which runs south-east from Neby Samwil, and on which is marked the word "Tombs," and Kh. Ras el Bad.

*4th Stage.*—The 60th Division will advance to a line astride the Jerusalem–Nablus Road about Shafat, and push forward thence to secure the high ground about Kh. Ras el Tawil.

The 74th Division will link up with the 60th Division occupying Beit Hannina if the ground is suitable for this purpose.

The G.O.C. 53rd Division and 60th Division will arrange to send out patrols to establish communication and will arrange for co-operation between the 53rd Division Group east of Jerusalem (*vide* instructions to G.O.C. 53rd Division) and the right flank of the 60th Division north of Jerusalem.

The 96th Heavy Artillery Group (less one 6-inch battery at Beit Likia) will be placed from 09.00 on December 7th under the command of the G.O.C. 60th Division, who will be responsible for its employment in consultation with the G.O.C. Royal Artillery XXth Corps, who will be at 60th Division Headquarters.

Orders for movement of trains and convoys will be issued by D.A. and Q.M.G., XXth Corps.

Reports to Advanced Headquarters, XXth Corps, at Latrun.

# APPENDIX VI

## CASUALTIES

### PALESTINE

|  |  | Officers. | Other ranks. |
|---|---|---|---|
| 30th Oct./5th Nov. 1917 . | Beersheba | 38 | 794 |
| 6th/16th Nov. 1917 . | Sheria . | 47 | 1,007 |
| 30th Nov./7th Dec. 1917 . | Foka . | 32 | 537 |
| 8th/26th Dec. 1917 . . | Jerusalem . | 18 | 293 |
| 27th Dec./9th Jan. 1918 . | Zeitun . | 27 | 395 |
| 10th Jan./3rd April 1918 . | Tel Asur . | 22 | 355 |

### FRANCE

| July 1918 . . . . . | 11 | 171 |
|---|---|---|
| August 1918 . . . . . | 31 | 686 |
| September 1918 . . . . | 185 | 3,333 |
| October 1918 . . . . . | 33 | 444 |
| November 1918 . . . . | 9 | 186 |

# APPENDIX VII

## COMMANDING OFFICERS

### 229TH BRIGADE

#### 16TH BN. DEVONSHIRE REGIMENT

Jan./April 1917 . . R. A. Sanders, T.D.
April/Nov. 1917 . . A. C. Thynne.
Nov. 1917/Nov. 1918 . A. C. Mardon, D.S.O.

#### ROYAL SCOTS FUSILIERS [1]

Jan./June 1917. . . J. D. Boswell.
June/June 1918 . . W. T. R. Houldsworth.

#### SOMERSET LIGHT INFANTRY

March/Oct. 1917 . . F. N. Q. Shouldham.
Oct. 1917/Nov. 1918 . . G. S. Poole.

#### BLACK WATCH

Jan./Nov. 1917. . . Sir John Gilmour,
                         Bart., M.P., D.S.O.
Nov. 1917/Sept. 1918 . J. Younger.
Sept./Nov. 1918 . . J. M. McKenzie.

### 230TH BRIGADE

#### 10TH BN. THE BUFFS (EAST KENT)

March/Dec. 1917 . . Arthur O'B. ffrench
                         Blake.
Dec. 1917/May 1918 . . Lord Sackville, T.D.
May/Nov. 1918 . . . C. M. Balston.

[1] Left the Division June 1918.

### NORFOLK REGIMENT [1]

| | |
|---|---|
| March/Aug. 1917 | A. F. Morse. |
| Aug. 1917/June 1918 | J. F. Barclay. |

### SUFFOLK REGIMENT

| | |
|---|---|
| Jan. 1917/Sept. 1918. | F. W. Jarvis, D.S.O. |
| Sept. 1918/end. | T. de la G. Grissell, M.C. |

### SUSSEX REGIMENT

| | |
|---|---|
| March/June 1917 | G. S. Whitfield. |
| June 1917/Oct. 1918. | H. I. Powell Edwards, D.S.O. |
| Oct./Nov. 1918 | J. B. Dodge, D.S.O. |

## 231ST BRIGADE

### 24TH BN. ROYAL WELSH FUSILIERS [1]

| | |
|---|---|
| Jan. 1917/June 1918 | H. N. M. Clegg. |

### 25TH BN. ROYAL WELSH FUSILIERS.

| | |
|---|---|
| Jan./Aug. 1918 | Lord Kensington, C.M.G., D.S.O. |
| Aug./Nov. 1918 | J. G. Rees, D.S.O. |

### 24TH BN. WELSH REGIMENT

| | |
|---|---|
| Jan. 1917/Nov. 1918 | C. Spence-Jones,[2] C.M.G., D.S.O. |

### SHROPSHIRE LIGHT INFANTRY

| | |
|---|---|
| March 1917/June 1918 | H. H. Heywood-Lonsdale, D.S.O. |
| June/Nov. 1918 | H. J. Howell Evans, D.S.O. |

[1] Left the Division June 1918.

[2] Assumed the name of Colby, but we retain the above to avoid confusion.

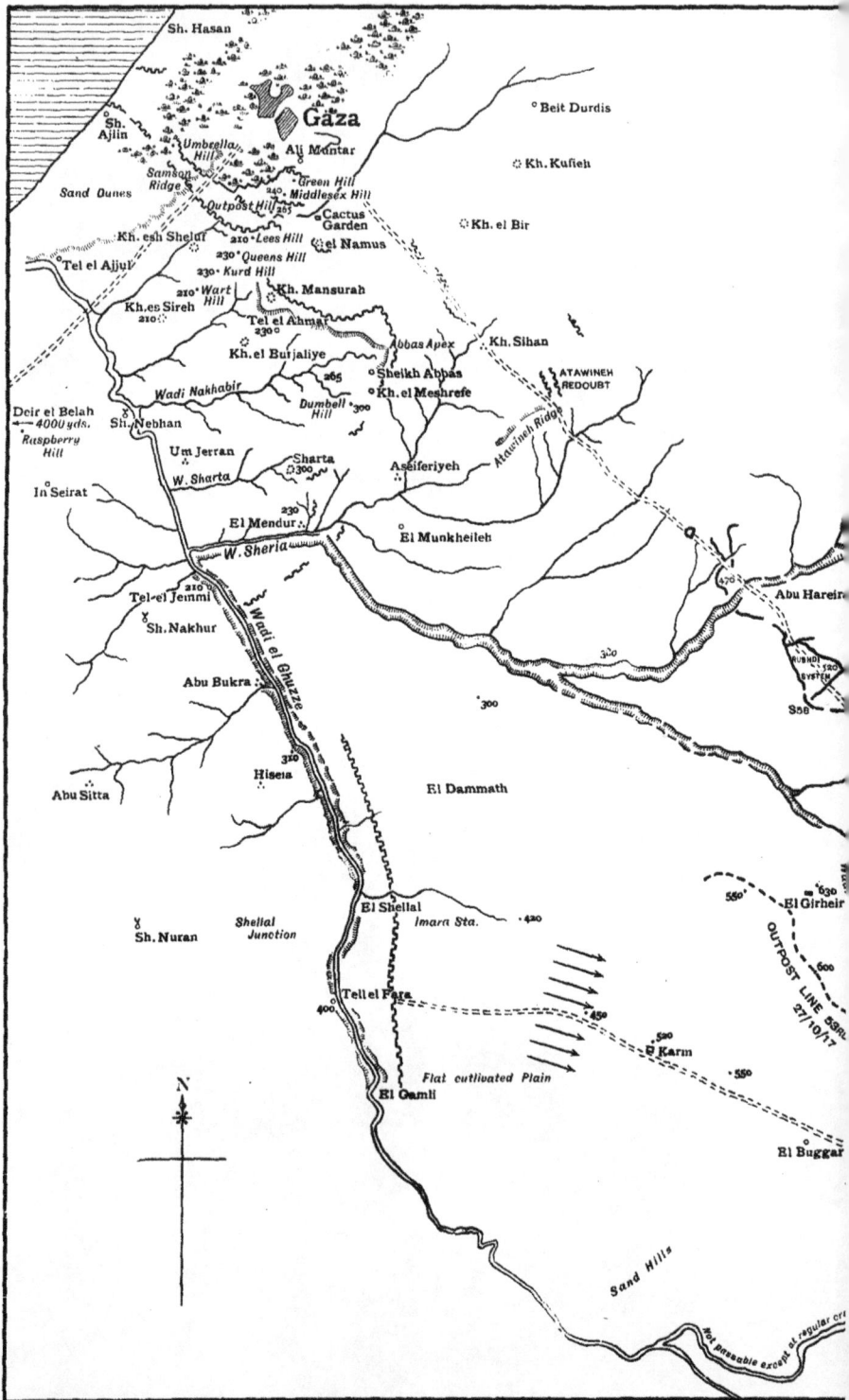

# GAZA - BEERSHEBA

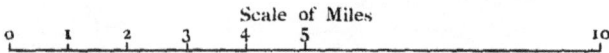

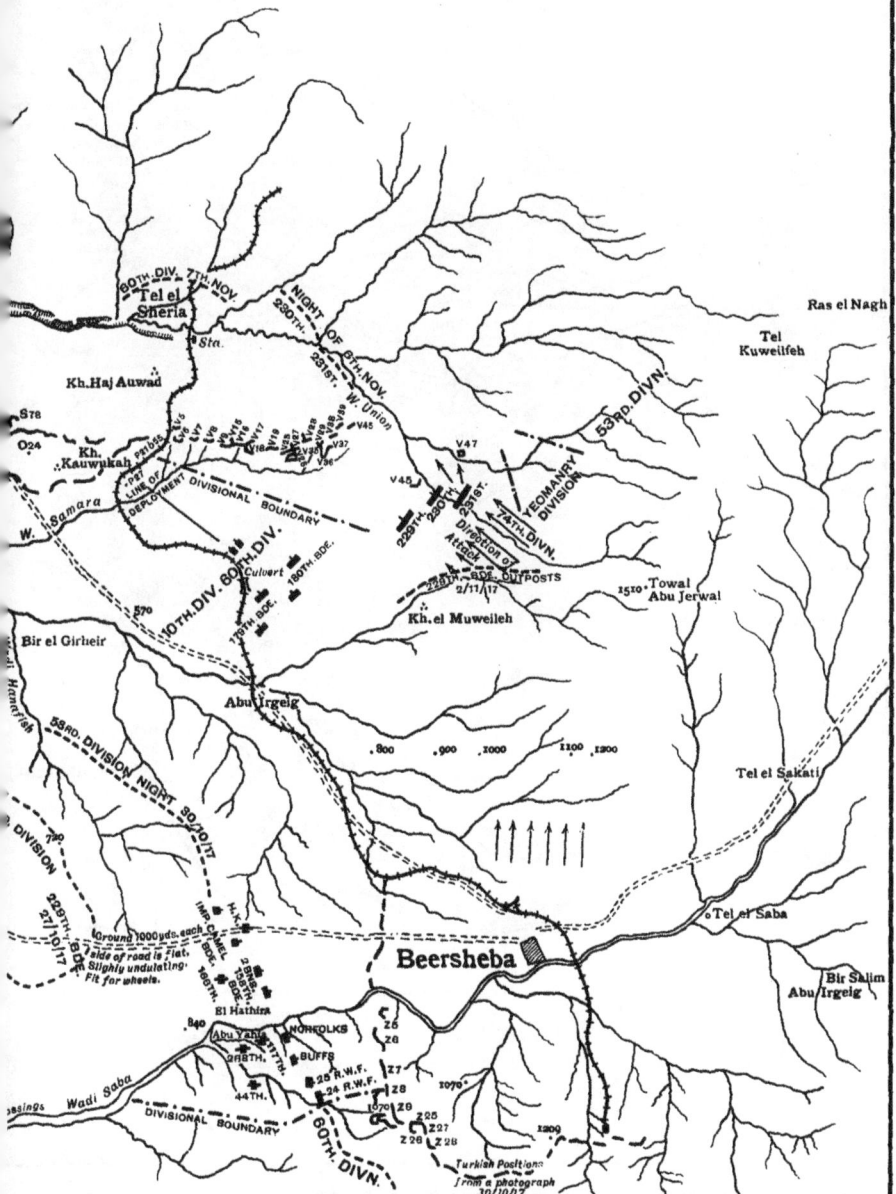

Scale of Miles

0   1   2   3   4   5                    10

Ras el Nagh

Tel Kuweilfeh

60TH. DIV. 7TH. NOV.

Tel el Sheria

Sta.

NIGHT OF 8TH. NOV.

Kh. Haj Auwad

S78

O24

Kh. Kauwukah

V47

V45

53RD. DIVN.

W. Hamara

LINE OF DEPLOYMENT

DIVISIONAL BOUNDARY

Direction of Attack

OUTPOSTS

YEOMANRY DIVISION

74TH. DIVN.

60TH. DIV.

Culvert

180TH. BDE.

179TH. BDE.

570

2/11/17

Kh. el Muweileh

1510 Towai Abu Jerwai

Bir el Girheir

Abu Irgeig

.800    .900    .1000    .1100    .1200

Tel el Sakati

53RD. DIVISION NIGHT 30/10/17

DIVISION

27/10/17

Ground 1000 yds. each side of road is flat, slightly undulating. Fit for wheels.

Tel el Saba

Beersheba

Bir Salim Abu Irgeig

840

El Hathira

NORFOLKS

Z5

Z6

Abu Yang

BUFFS

Z7

1070

25 R.W.F.

24 R.W.F.

Z8

Z9   Z25

Z27

Z28

1070

Z26

DIVISIONAL BOUNDARY

60TH. DIVN.

Wadi Saba

1200

Turkish Positions from a photograph 30/10/17

Emery Walker Ltd. sc.

el Kefr

Beit Rima

Deir es Sadan
2638

Arura

Abwein

Jiljilia

Sinjil
3000

Kh. Aliuta

et Tell

BUFFS

Kh. es Sahl

Neby Saleh

Kir Abu el Tyur

SUSSEX

NORFOLKS

Attara

Sh. Kairawany

Kh. Abu el Muhr

NORFOLKS

Ain Sinia

Burj Bardawil

SUFF

Kh. Kefr Aas

DIVISION BOUNDARY

Bir ez Zeit

Bir ez Zeit
3065

Jufna
2730

NORFOLKS

LINE 7/3/18

Durah

Abu Yehud

Ain Jebrum

Jarnutieh

Sh. Abdallah

Abu Kush

Surdah

Kh. Wadi
es Serab

Kh. Maratah
3020

Kh. Deir Sbeh

Kh.
Bir ez Zeit

Kh.
el Burj

Kh.
Tireh

60TH. DIV.
el Balua

60TH. DEC.

Beitin

Shilta

10TH. DIVISION

Abu Ainein

Kh. el Hafy

Kh. 20TH. DEC.

60TH.

Bireh

Ram Allah

Burkah

Suffa
1010

10TH. DIVISION

Beit ur et Tahta

W. Sunt

el Muntar
2685

Peitania
2435

74TH. 20TH. DEC.

Rafat

Beit Sira
840
2740

Beit ur
el Foka
2451

Sh. Abu Zeitun
2418

74TH. 20TH. DEC.

Kh. Shata

60TH. DEC.

60TH.

er Ram

Jeba

W. Imaish

1750

et Tireh
1910

Kh. Dreihemeh
2450

Kulundia

Beit Likia

Kh. Jufna
1720

2343

Kh. Jufier

Beit Nuba

Beit Anan
2075

Beit Dukka

el Jib

Amwas

Valo

Kubeibeh
2440

Beit Izza

W. Reqt

Nebala

Biddu

24TH. R.W.F.

Neby Samwil
2935

Beit Hannina
2462

Tel el Ful
2754

Katanneh

Beit Surik

Wadi Meideh

Kh. el Burj

DAWN 10TH.

NORFOLKS
SUFFOLKS
BUFFS
S.L.I.
R.S.F.

SUSSEX

Beit
Iksa
2525

74TH.

Kh. Ras el Bad

Shafat

60TH. NIGHT 8/9

Kuryet el Enab

Kh. Mekikarb

H5d

Kulonieh

Lifta

Kh. Khamis

H11.045

Jerusalem

Soba

Deir Yesin

60TH. NIGHT 8/9

Ain Karim

Station

Abu

10TH. AUSTRALIAN
LIGHT HORSE

B36

Sheralat

Beit
Sufafa

Sur Bahir
2418

el Kabu

Kulat el Ghuleh

Beit Jala

Ain el Hand

53RD. DIVISION NIGHT 8/9

Ras el Balua

Bethlehem

181 BDE.

180 BDE.

179 BDE.

W. es Surar

W. es Sikkeh

The line from Suffa to Beit Dukka is marked for the Neby Samwil Battle. For the affair at Foka and the Battle on the 27th Dec.
the disposition of troops must be taken from the text.

# JUDEA AND THE JORDAN

Scale of Miles

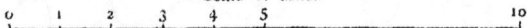

0   1   2   3   4   5                                    10

rmus Aya

Kh. Amurieh

el Mugheir
2246

Sh. Selim          Kh. Abu Malul
Sh.                Kh. Abu Felah
amil
arah esh Sherkiyeh

Tall Asur

Kefr Malik

et Talyibeh
2850

en Neimeh
2302

Kh. Beiyudat

Abu Tellul

W. Aujah

205

Rummon
1950

205

B'MS.

Diwan

Tel es Siwan
mas

W. el Makuk

ed Dawarah          Ras et Tawil
1964

Tel es Sultan

Jericho

W. el Kult

W. Farah

Arak Ibrahim

Talat ed Damm

Jebel Ehteif
840

Neby Musa
318

W. Makelik

Jebel el Kahmun
286

Tubk Kaneiterah  306

W. Kumran

el Muntar
1725

N

D E A D

S E A

1292

350

1900

R. Jordan

Emery Walker Ltd. sc.

Jericho is 820 ft. below sea-level.   As a general guide the line of the escarpment marks the drop below sea-level, but it is carried
further east where the descent is more gradual.

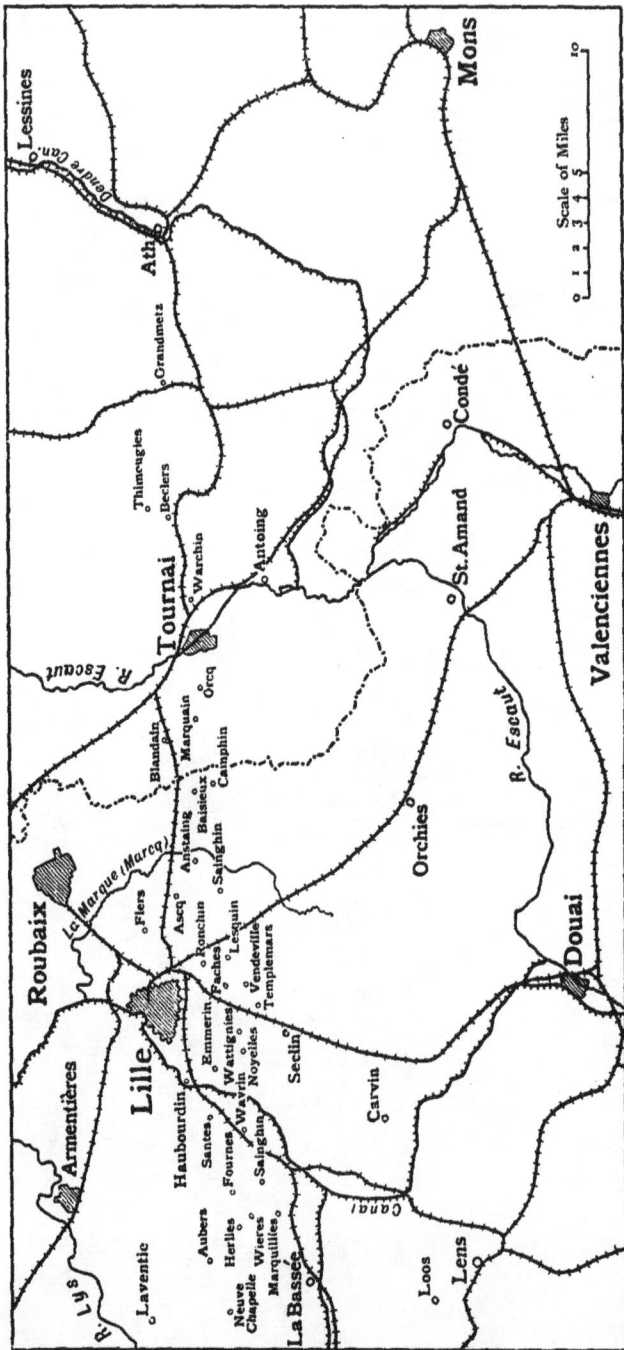

THE ADVANCE INTO BELGIUM.

Emery Walker Ltd. sc.

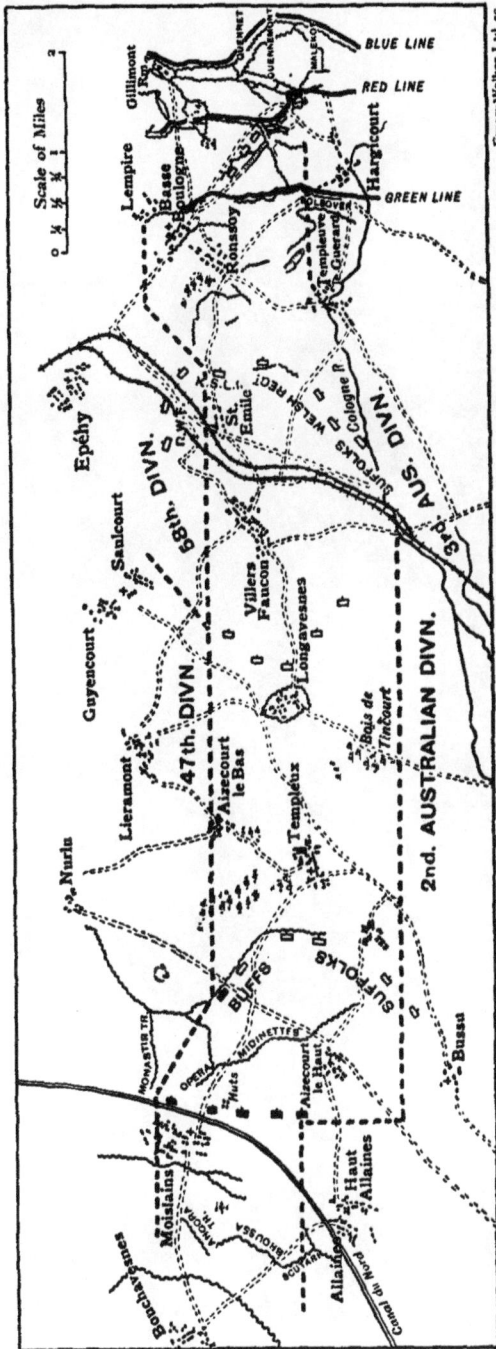

THE ADVANCE FROM BOUCHAVESNES.

Scale of Miles

BLUE LINE
RED LINE
GREEN LINE

Guillemont Fm.
Lempire
Basse Boulogne
Ronssoy
Hargicourt
Templeuve
Guérard
Epéhy
Saulcourt
Guyencourt
Lieramont
Nurlu
Villers Faucon
Longavesnes
Aizecourt le Bas
Templeux
Bois de Tincourt
58th. DIVN.
47th. DIVN.
3rd AUS. DIVN.
2nd. AUSTRALIAN DIVN.
BUFFS
SUFFOLKS
Aizecourt le Haut
Bussu
Moislains
Haut Allaines
Allaines
Bouchavesnes
Canal du Nord

Emery Walker Ltd. sc.

# INDEX

Descriptive terms and abbreviations :

Abu = Father
Ain = Spring
Beit = House
Birket = Pool
Bir = Well
Deir = Monastery
Ed, el, er, es, ez = The

Jebel or Gebel = Mountain
Jish = Bridge
Kefr = Village
Khan = Inn
Khurbet, abbreviation
Kh. = Ruin

Makhadet = Ford
Nahr = River
Neby = Prophet
Ras = Head, top.
Sheikh, abbreviation
Sh. = Chief, saint
Tel = Mound
Wadi = Watercourse